THE
NO-SALT,
LOWEST-SODIUM,
LIGHT MEALS
BOOK

ALSO BY DONALD A. GAZZANIGA

The No-Salt, Lowest-Sodium Baking Book
The No-Salt, Lowest-Sodium Cookbook

THE
NO-SALT,
LOWEST-SODIUM,
LIGHT MEALS
BOOK

❖❖❖ ❖❖❖ ❖❖❖ ❖❖❖ ❖❖❖ ❖❖❖

DONALD A. GAZZANIGA
and
MAUREEN A. GAZZANIGA

FOREWORD BY
DR. MICHAEL FOWLER, F.R.C.P.

THOMAS DUNNE BOOKS
ST. MARTIN'S PRESS   ❦   NEW YORK

THOMAS DUNNE BOOKS.
An imprint of St. Martin's Press.

THE NO-SALT, LOWEST-SODIUM LIGHT MEALS BOOK. Copyright © 2005 by Donald A. Gazzaniga.
Foreword © 2005 by Dr. Michael B. Fowler. Salt Skip Program © 2005 by Dr. Trevor C.
Beard. All rights reserved. Printed in the United States of America. For information, address
St. Martin's Press, 175 Fifth Avenue, New York, N.Y. 10010.

www.thomasdunnebooks.com

www.stmartins.com

Library of Congress Cataloging-in-Publication Data

Gazzaniga, Donald A.
    The no-salt, lowest sodium light meals book / Donald A. Gazzaniga and Maureen A.
Gazzaniga.
        p. cm.
    ISBN-13: 978-0-312-33502-1
    ISBN-10: 0-312-33502-4
    1. Salt-free diet —Recipes. I. Title.

RM237.8 .G393 2004
641.5'6323—dc22

                                                                    2004052780

D 10 9 8 7 6 5 4 3 2

Dedicated to

Sarah, Justin, Gabriella, David,

Joshua, Liam, Aidan, Alexander, Olivia,

Gianna, Seamus, and Augustus.

These are the twelve grandchildren who help keep us going.

CONTENTS

ACKNOWLEDGMENTS

I want to thank my wife, Maureen, for devoting so much of her valuable time to helping the thousands of people who will use this book over the ensuing years. When Maureen was diagnosed with breast cancer right after I was diagnosed with heart failure, she went through much the same thing I did, only worse. Breast cancer is a very scary and emotionally draining event for any woman. First, there's the denial, then acceptance, then the fight to survive.

After her chemotherapy she immediately dove into helping others who had recently had the same dreaded diagnosis, working directly with the American Cancer Society to help them through trying times. Maureen is a survivor and a fighter, and she recognizes the need for others to be the same.

That's why she has lent us so much of her time and her expertise in the kitchen. The soups and salads you'll find in this book are her creations. Her instinct for what's good with soups and salads—and what isn't—surpasses mine by a lifetime. She understands ingredients where the rest of us might only recognize them for what they are called. She knows when a spice should be used and what makes a sauce or soup good, and what makes it "dull." She can match and combine different foods to produce a flavor that you'll want to have again long after you have finished one of her soups.

Every soup and salad in this book is a gourmet dish with a gourmet flavor, and not one of them uses anything other than the best fresh, natural ingredients.

As this book is published, I have known Maureen for forty-five years. We have been married for forty-four of those years. Now I share a bit of her with you, and I think you'll find her as enjoyable and loving as I do.

We both would like to thank our family for their patience with the two erascible "old folks" who have spent more time in the kitchen than with them.

And we thank each and every visitor to Megaheart.com. We have been encouraged by your candid words, your thank-yous, and your help. Without you, this effort would not have been.

And there are more to thank.

We owe huge thank-yous to the editor of this book, who worked very hard to make it as perfect as possible. It wasn't easy to work with our material. The patience, the guidance, and the expertise are shown here with the best results yet for this series of *No-Salt, Lowest-Sodium* cookbooks. We are both delighted and extremely happy with your help.

And to the doctors and nurses and registered dietitians who have supported our efforts by recommending these books to their patients, not the least of whom is Dr. Michael Fowler, Director of the Stanford Heart Transplant Program. Dr. Fowler is the one who encouraged me in 1997 to cut my salt down to "unheard of" levels. I did, and I avoided the heart transplant because of it.

The great pleasures we've had meeting doctors, nurses, dietitians, and other medical practitioners from the book efforts through www.megaheart.com, have also helped to keep us going. For that, we thank each of you and hope that in turn you are able to continue helping your patients with the no-salt challenges they face.

FOREWORD

SALT OF LIFE . . .

By Dr. Michael Fowler, F.R.C.P.,
Director of Stanford Heart Transplant Program

. . . Not if you have salt-sensitive hypertension, heart failure, or any other condition where sodium retention contributes to disease. Heart failure is the most important condition where regulation of sodium, or salt balance, plays a fundamental role in symptoms an individual may experience. Appropriate and consistent reductions in sodium intake—by restricting or avoiding completely the salts added to food during preparation or processing, and of course not adding further salt "at the table"—enable the drugs used to remove sodium to be optimized at minimally effective doses, reducing the risk of hospitalization and death from heart failure.

Heart failure is the result of injury to the heart. High blood pressure (or hypertension) is related to a high salt intake, especially in salt-sensitive individuals, and is by far the most common initiating factor in the development of heart failure. Not only does a high salt intake contribute to the development of hypertension, a very common condition that almost 90 percent of individuals may develop during their lifetime, but salt may also play an important role in the abnormal composition of the arteries and hearts of individuals who do develop hypertension. The alterations in the structural composition of the arteries and hearts of individuals with hypertension in turn contributes to the high risk of strokes, heart attacks, and sudden death which accompany hypertension and heart failure.

Heart failure develops in one in five individuals. The symptoms and clinical manifestations of heart failure are almost entirely due to the consequences of sodium retention, which in time causes fluid retention. Sodium is the major mechanism by which the body retains normal body water content. When the heart begins to fail, the kidneys are "signaled" by hormones and nerves to adjust the kidneys to retain sodium, and consequently water. The subsequent retention of salt and water takes place because the kidney and hormonal systems have incorrectly assumed that the changes detected around the body and especially by the kidneys are the result of the individual being dehydrated. The body does not recognize that the problem has been caused by an injured, weakened heart and makes the "error" of causing more salt to be retained to correct a "dehydration" that has not taken place. This excess salt and water retention cause the "congestion" of congested heart failure (CHF) and result in the waterlogged lungs that cause patients with heart failure to become short of breath with exertion, unable to breathe at night lying flat, causes a "gurgling," waterlogged sensation in the lungs, wheezing, coughing, or a sensation of drowning. When extreme, some patients with the symptoms of salt (and water) retention may have to be placed on mechanical ventilation ("breathing machine").

Similar features of salt and water retention may cause weight gain, abdominal swelling, congestion, swelling of the legs and ankles, and may interfere with the liver, as well. An experienced physician can determine the amount of salt being retained by the symptoms a patient may describe, and from the evidence of fluid buildup in the lungs and other sites. Most important, he can often find evidence of the salt and water buildup by examining veins in the neck and estimating the elevated pressure in the large central veins. An echo-Doppler examination of the heart can add accurate estimations of the elevation of pressures in the arteries and veins of the lungs. Moreover, a blood test has recently been developed, the BNP test, which measures a hormone provided by the failure of the heart that reflects the elevation of pressure caused by salt and secondary fluid retention. All the assessments of fluid retention can be linked to the risk of dying or being hospitalized for heart failure and therapies for heart failure and principally aimed at reducing the tendency away to retain salt and water by inhibiting the hormones and nervous systemic activity which acts to promote salt (and subsequently water retention) as well as reduce the structural changes in the heart and blood vessel which accompany this activation.

Physicians and nurses who manage heart failure recognize the pivoted role that sodium intake from the diet can have on the clinical manifestation of heart failure and the ability to use the drugs at optimal doses that improve or reverse the structural changes; referred to as "remodeling," that would otherwise progress after an initial injury to the heart has resulted in heart failure. Most patients have been told about restricting sodium but have little practical idea about how to make the appropriate changes in the diet.

"Watching sodium," usually watching salt enter your mouth, is not an approach that is effective in reducing the dire consequences of sodium retention to patients with heart failure and to only a somewhat lesser extent to the patient with salt-sensitive hypertension (a majority of hypertension patients). Other patients with conditions such as renal failure, patients with Meniere's disease, and other conditions where diuretics are used will benefit immensely from a diet that dramatically reduces sodium intake, while providing an enjoyable and highly nutritious varied diet.

Patients who complain they will have nothing to eat if they adopt a serious approach to salt restriction cannot appreciate that an appropriate sodium-restricted diet is simply a diet in which the processed (or salt-added) foods or ingredients have to be omitted. It is much easier not to count milligrams of sodium, but to simply avoid adding salt during food preparation, only employing ingredients which do not include additional salt. Hidden sodium sources include many canned foods, prepared sauces, most ketchups, some mustard, most but not all bottled mayonnaise, most but not all prepared salad dressings, almost all breads and cheeses. Following the recipes in Donald Gazzaniga's book will enable individuals to enjoy tasteful, nutritious food without adding excess sodium to the diet.

The benefits to an individual with heart failure of adopting a low-sodium diet are frequently striking. In some patients a substantial improvement in symptoms will result from diuretics, the drugs used in patients with heart failure to remove the excess salt (and water). Frequently the dose of diuretics can be reduced (this depends on the level of sodium in the diet prior to adopting a low-salt diet).

Patients characteristically lose their sensation of driving at night and can sleep with less or no additional pillows. Patients are unlikely to be short of breath at rest. Patients can walk and exercise further. Patients experience no or less ankle swelling, a liver tenderness (pain under the ribs or right side). Patients do not run the risks of alteration in potassium and kidney function when additional diuretics have to be prescribed to counter salt (and fluid) buildup. Daily weights tend to fluctuate less.

Higher doses of b-adrenergic blocking drugs or ACE inhibitors, which improve survival in heart failure, can be given without side effects from excessive lowering of blood pressure, or worsening kidney function in patients with high doses of diuretics chosen to be effective when the sodium intake was high.

Patients switching from a high conventional American diet, which consists of about 10 grams of sodium per day, should be cautioned to have their fluid status carefully checked by a physician. Frequently the dose of diuretics (which act by increasing salt retention) will need to be reduced to prevent excess dehydration when the low-sodium diet is first started.

In my experience, the patients who consistently followed a low sodium diet—not adding sodium and avoiding processed food, including restricting foods high in sodium—are much more likely to respond to the current therapies that have fundamentally changed the outcomes for patients with this potentially devastating condition. Patients who adopt the low-sodium lifestyle, combined with the appropriate use of the drugs and devices that are effective in heart failure, not only live much longer with heart failure, but they also live better, avoiding the hospitalizations and symptoms that principally occur when salt intake and doses of diuretic therapy can never be balanced due to an excessive and varying sodium intake.

INTRODUCTION

Soups are my favorite winter meals. They are generally healthy, re-freshing, and usually easy to prepare. When I decided to put this book together, however, I invited my wife Maureen, an excellent chef, to author the soups and the salad sections. She jumped at the chance. Her soup-making talent is the best I've ever known. She not only understands how to make a pot of soup, but what should go with what and how it should taste afterward. As for salads, well, wait until you try our assortment, including the homemade dress-ings. No commercial salad dressings are used. Instead we provide you with some very delicious-tasting recipes, all of them using sup-plies you probably have on hand or will find easy to obtain.

The short introductions for most recipes were written by me. But it was Maureen who took the information I may have brought back and translated them into great soups and salads. Of course, Mau-reen has also ventured around the world and brought back many of her own memories and recipes, many of which are enjoyed in our monthly Megaheart.com newsletters.

What helped us make these no-salt wonders is that Maureen is free to use salt if she wants to. This made it easy for her to taste and compare and come up with salt-free dishes as tasty, if not more so, than their salted versions. She spent two years working on the soups and salads in this book, until she got each one to a point where it tasted so good that it passed muster among salt lovers.

Although there are some broth substitutes on the market today including Herb-ox, Redi-Base, Bernardo's, and Home Again to name the most recognizable, she tried to create each soup without using any of the above. Our reasons for this varied, but our feeling is that most of them use either too much potassium chloride or too many trans fatty ingredients.

From putting many recipes online at www.megaheart.com, I learned how varied soups are around the world. We could have written an encyclopedia of world recipes since those of other countries and cultures can be so very different from one another. Instead we chose thirty-five of Maureen's very best recipes for this book.

Before our no-salt lifestyle, we used to pick up a can of soup at the grocery store, pop off the top, pour it into a pan, and bring it to a "boil." Serve, and that was it. Low budget, easy-to-make, and full of preservatives, salt, and overcooked vegetables and meat.

Our new lifestyle demands we make soups from fresh high-quality vegetables, fresh or dried spices and herbs, and occasionally lean meat. Your homemade soup will be healthier than canned, more appealing, and much, much tastier than the canned variety (many of which seem to taste of salt rather than anything else). So when making it, why not make a few meals to be enjoyed during the week? Most of the soups in this book will store for three to five days in your refrigerator, in a covered airtight container or a covered stockpot. They'll also freeze well for up to three months.

Maureen is also a salad maker extraordinaire. She doesn't just throw a pile of lettuce on a plate and smother it in olive oil and vinegar (that's my trick). No, she builds a salad that can often serve as an entrée or can be broken up into side-dish servings. You'll find dressings without salt or high-sodium ingredients, "fixings" with loads of flavor and presentations that would compete with the best restaurants—and above all, they are easy to make. We have kept the fats very low (blue cheese, feta cheese, and other such toppings are often high in calories, fats, and sodium, and, of course, are not in this book).

We hope you enjoy Maureen's soup and salad recipes. They were created just for you.

The sandwiches in this book are my creations, so you'll have to blame me for the results. I love sandwiches and could have added many, many more. At times I will do that on our recipe page at megaheart.com. I have also included some new bread recipes in here tailored to use with many of the sandwiches, soups, and salads. Of course, any of the sandwich breads in *The No-Salt, Lowest-Sodium Baking Book* would also work for you.

THE SALT SKIP PROGRAM

❖ ❖ ❖ ❖ ❖ ❖ ❖ ❖

By Dr. Trevor C. Beard

AUTHOR'S NOTE

Dr. Trevor C. Beard, who heads up The Salt Skip Program in Australia, wrote the following article to include in this book for his readers in Australia. The Australian "program" for controlling hypertension is somewhat different than that in the United States but has the same goals. Lower sodium intake; get healthier. Salt Skip reaches out to Australians who are healthy and those with hypertension. The program is under the aegis of the Menzies Centre for Population Health Research, University of Tasmania. When reading it, you should understand that it was designed to address challenges within Australia.
—Donald A. Gazzaniga

BACKGROUND

I am a medical graduate of Cambridge and London Universities and a public health graduate of the University of California at Berkeley. The Salt Skip Program has its roots in public health and is now my retirement hobby at the Menzies Centre for Population Health Research, University of Tasmania.

The name came from a low-salt cookery class at the pilot stage of a high blood pressure trial. (1) Our teacher said we were *skipping* salt. *Skipping*—positive, happy, and healthy—said it all.

The references at the end of these notes are for readers who want to follow these ideas further, or check where they came from.

The Salt Skip Program

About 90 percent of the sodium added to processed food and that served at your dinner table is common salt (sodium chloride), (2) so the public health position worldwide is that *everybody*, including the healthy, *should skip salt*. The Salt Skip Program tries to make it easy:

1. It *takes you off a diet* (the high-salt diet of industrial societies) and gives you better food.
2. It uses calories and milligrams of sodium only to identify better food.
3. It offers the whole family better food. If salt makes you sick, those who carry your genes need better food even more than the general public does, and it's easier to cook if you all get better food.
4. It tells serious salt skippers how their doctors can help them to check progress and measure their sodium intake by twenty-four-hour urine collections.

1. Salt Skippers Are Not on a Diet

When salt skippers find better foods they eat as much or as little as they like, within the limits of appetite and common sense, also of course within the need for a trim waistline.

The Salt Skip Program follows all the international dietary guidelines for better health, skipping fat (especially saturated fat and trans fats), and for many, sugar. Instead we suggest increasing dietary fiber, fruit, and vegetables (guidelines familiar to readers of Don's books). Salt Skip focuses on salt because that's where people need special attention and usually get very little help. (Don's books have provided exceptional help for those who use them, by breaking down sodium levels in all foods, so readers can adjust recipes and their lifestyle as close to what they want to consume as they can.)

2. Choosing Better Food

The Australian salt guideline is simple—*choose foods low in salt/ sodium*—and the 100-gm column on our labels lets us use the European definition of low-salt/sodium foods (sodium up to 120 mg/100 g).

We know in Australia from twenty-four-hour urine collections that strict adherence to this advice leads to sodium intakes around 500 to 1,000 mg/day, which we find is all that patients usually need to abolish the vertigo of Ménière's syndrome, a fact that has been known since 1934. (3)

3. Better Food for the Whole Family

Often whole families might benefit from a lowered sodium daily lifestyle. We have an opportunity to give our families a better start in life for instance when feeding youngsters right from the cradle onward. Young babies are easier to wean with unsalted foods even though in many parts of the world baby formula contains a high sodium level and high trans fat level. Manufacturers always add these fats and sodium levels. Again, mother's milk is the often the best start for a baby. Older children miss salt at first, but are happy to change slowly.

A dietitian told me her family refused to eat porridge the first time she made it without salt, so she gradually reduced salt in other foods the rest of that winter and all the next summer. The following winter she made porridge without salt and no one noticed.

There was a sequel. Next time they stayed with their grandmother the children discovered they couldn't eat Grandma's porridge anymore—they didn't know why, but it tasted awful.

In 2002 the American Public Health Association and the American National Institutes for Health called for a 50-percent reduction in the sodium content of all processed foods; they wanted the whole population educated to choose lower-sodium foods. There remains opposition from the Salt Institute, from many chefs but not all, and from some sections of the food industry that depend on salt as a preservative. (Salt in bread is a preservative, offering more shelf life for the marketers. It is not necessary in the making of bread. Just check out some of the bread recipes in this book and in

No-Salt, Lower-Sodium Baking Book and you'll learn how to make great bread without salt.)

Many chefs argue that salt is a condiment and one of the four flavor sensations (salty/sweet/sour/bitter) and essential to good cuisine, but they have a problem. Each diner's "need" depends on habitual intake, which is becoming patchy and unpredictable. Heavy users want more, light users want less, and nonusers want little if any. The palate alters in a month. (4, 5) (Americans who have stuck to Don Gazzaniga's 28-day Meal-Planning Guide in his *The No-Salt, Lowest-Sodium Cookbook* have written an endless string of testimonials concerning not only this fact but they say that their chronic illnesses have vastly improved.

It's a problem for food writers, too. An article about an up-market Australian restaurant contained these gems: "The salmon was heavily seasoned with salt, which doesn't suit my taste," and "the food was well executed as well as presented, although I am not used to the strong use of salt in almost all the dishes we tried." (6)

The Seventh Report of the U.S. Joint National Committee on Prevention, Detection, Evaluation, and Treatment of High Blood Pressure says people with "normal blood pressure" (below 140/90) are sick if their blood pressure is 120/80 or more. (7)

People with prehypertension don't need a doctor; they only need books. The reader already has Don Gazzaniga's books. The Australian edition of my book *Salt Matters* was published by Lothian in February 2004 and is available through any Australian bookstore and Amazon.com.

4. DIURETICS MAKE YOUR KIDNEYS EXCRETE SODIUM FASTER THAN NORMAL.

That is why diuretics are the standard treatment for sodium related illnesses. Add a low-sodium diet to your lifestyle (generally between 1,500 mg and 2,000 mg per day is considered a low sodium diet), and you can possibly become ill from too much excretion. You have to monitor your diuretics along with your new no-salt, low-sodium lifestyle. Don Gazzaniga, for instance, worked himself off diuretics after just a few years on his 500 mg a day lifestyle.

In some situations—especially the intolerable vertigo of Ménière's syndrome—patients are tempted to drop to 1,000 or 500 mg/day. If you are in that category, let your doctor know so that the two of you can monitor your health as you go along.

Note: It is true that patients in heart failure can be very strict with sodium, dropping easily to 500 mg a day, and still take a diuretic, but people with failing hearts are under closer medical supervision with frequent blood tests to check that their blood sodium is not getting too low.

The Salt Skip literature and MegaHeart.com each recommend to all patients who must adopt a low-sodium lifestyle to do what their doctor recommends. That doesn't mean you can't discuss your willingness to stop eating salt and to lower your sodium even below the doctor's initial recommendation. Many times your doctor will be happy to proceed—and will discover its benefits right along with you when you succeed.

References

1. Beard, T.C., H.M. Cooke, W.R., Gray, and R. Barge. "Randomized controlled trial of a no-added-sodium diet for mild hypertension." *Lancet* 1982;2:455–58.

2. Select Committee on GRAS Substances. "GRAS evaluation of the health aspects of sodium chloride and potassium chloride as food ingredients." Bethesda, Md.: Life Sciences Research Office; 1979:4.

3. Furstenberg, A.C., F.H. Lashmet, and F. Lathrop. "Ménière's symptom complex: Medical treatment." *Ann Otol Rhinol Laryngol* 1934;43:1035–46.

4. Bertino M, Beauchamp, G.K., and K. Engelman. "Long-term reduction in dietary sodium alters the taste of salt." *Am J Clin Nutr* 1982;36:1134–44.

5. ———. "Increasing Dietary Salt Alters Salt Taste Preference." *Physiology & Behavior* 1986;38:203–13.

6. Brewer C. "Axis restaurant at the National Museum." *Canberra Times* 2001; Friday (April 6): 6.

7. U.S. Joint National Committee. "The seventh report of the Joint National Committee on Prevention, Detection, Evaluation, and Treatment of High Blood Pressure." *JAMA* 2003;289:2560–72.

ALSO REFERRED TO:

Sacks, F.M., L.P. Svetkey, W.M. Vollmer, L.J. Appel, G.A. Bray, D. Harsha, et al. "Effects on blood pressure of reduced dietary sodium and the Dietary Approaches to Stop Hypertension (DASH) diet." *N Engl J Med* 2001; 344:3–10.

www.nhlbi.nih.gov/new/press/may17-00.htm.

National Health & Medical Research Council. *Dietary Guidelines for Australian Adults*. Canberra: Australian Government Publishing Service; 2003.

SOURCES

The sodium values in this cookbook are based on the most recent data supplied by the Food and Drug Administration (FDA), and the United States Department of Agriculture (USDA), and by manufacturers of many of the food products we use. We used a USDA-based software program called Foodworks 5, from the Nutrition Company, to list calories and all other nutrients.

Please see *The No Salt, Lowest-Sodium Cookbook* for more explanations concerning FDA and USDA listings and FDA food labels.

Nutrient Values in this book are based upon USDA figures from the years between 2002 and 2004. Figures may vary at times from one list to another, but usually in a range not more than a milligram or two.

What Is MegaHeart.com?

MegaHeart.com is operated by Donald A. Gazzaniga and a small staff of volunteer helpers. The Web site is committed to enhancing the quality of life for members who have been ordered by their medical practitioner to "cut the salt out." These include heart patients, hypertension patients, those with liver and kidney diseases and Ménières syndrome, and others wishing to reduce their risk of suffering heart failure—by delivering no-salt/lowered-sodium recipes. MegaHeart also provides links to reliable resources for information relating to heart failure and other maladies demanding a low-sodium lifestyle.

The Web site has a monthly newsletter with fresh new recipes that are not found in our cookbooks. Information also abounds at the site concerning sodium, locations to purchase no-salt-added ingredients, and other helpful information.

You can visit the author at www.megaheart.com and if you have any questions he's always there to help you.

A NOTE ABOUT NAMED PRODUCTS

We often name food products so that you might find the low-sodium versions more easily. The challenge here is that sometimes the manufacturers or processors of these ingredients take the products off the market. We have in just the past few years lost Hain Very Low Sodium Mayonnaise, Alpine Lace Swiss Low Sodium Swiss Cheese, Heluvagood Low Sodium Cheddar Cheese, Tillamook Low Sodium Cheddar Cheese, in addition to named brands of low-sodium pickles, low-sodium relish, and so on. At Megaheart .com we asked our members to write to these producers. We were able to successfully urge Heluvagood Cheese back on the market with their very excellent low-sodium cheddar, but have run up against some pretty hard walls with most of the others. Fortunately we do have a great selection of other products that seem to remain stable as far as staying with us. Canned low-sodium tomatoes, tomato sauces, tomato paste, and ketchup come from top national brands. Low-sodium beans from Eden Organic, and other products, are available in many local stores, but always at www.healthyheart market.com if you can't find them locally. You can also get low-sodium cheddar and some other cheeses from Rumiano and Heluvagood. The online addresses for these can be found at www.megaheart.com/kit_pantry.html.

We also list a few appliances by brand name or model because they are simply an excellent tool to work with when putting together our recipes. We have designed recipes so that you don't have to do too much laborious work, a challenge for heart patients and others whose strength wanes due to a heart that isn't beating quite correctly.

We recommend Braun Handheld (500 series) tools as a food processor or blender, simply because they are convenient. We have learned that the Braun (at this writing, Model #550) competes with countertop food processors and at a much lower cost. Of course, these are recommendations only; you may use your own blender or food processor.

We like Breadman bread machines for their stability, efficiency, and longer life span, as well as good factory support if one breaks down. We have tested and worn out many bread machines, but our Breadman still stands, still makes the best loaf out of the bunch. We now use the TR2200 Breadman, although the TR850 is a great machine as well. (These model numbers may change in the future, but the machines pretty much remain the same.) Both the Braun and Breadman can be found by visiting http://www.megaheart.com/kit_cabitnet.html and visiting the "Pantry." We receive no money for these sales, but have located the best prices for them for you.

SOUPS

❖ ❖ ❖ ❖ ❖ ❖ ❖ ❖

THE HISTORY OF SOUP

My favorite explorer is Captain Cook, who, in the mid-to-later 1770s, drew maps of the world that even satellite imaging haven't changed much. He was a genius at sailing, navigation, and using a sextant. I would like to attribute the first soups to him, but in fact his contribution was the "stock cubes" he took on his voyages to make soup. His sailors referred to that soup as a portable soup. It was made by evaporating clarified broth until it reached the consistency of glue. It could be stored for a very long time. Cook was also knowledgeable enough to take along citrus fruit to help prevent scurvy, something no other sailor had done before him.

What most likely happened was that primitive humans, given much more credit for intelligence today after years of research, invented soup. What they probably did was drop a heated stone into a bladder of liquid containing whatever their diet held back then and then added nuts and bugs to flowers and wild roots.

The containers for primitive humans were crude at best, most likely animal bladders.

Thus, when the "bronze age" arrived, soup makers probably blossomed. A bronze kettle or pot was made available to them and cooking over an open flame did become popular. (There were iron kettles, too.) It is known that migrants from northern France arrived in Great Britain in the fourth millennium B.C. with farming skills and apparently soup-making skills. Historians and archaeologists tell us that these same migrants brought cultivated wheat and barley as well as sheep and goats. They also brought along their knowledge of making pottery bowls, which some declare, put an end to the dropping of stones into containers of gruel. Instead, the new pots and bowls made cooking possible and provided starch from farmed cereals, which gave them their new "soup" texture.

Archaeologists have found pottery and old pots as well as old stomachs (hope you have the stomach for that), with signs of berries, wheat, nuts, and fish in them. These from Switzerland and Denmark. Two TV on camera types in a 1954 documentary tried the soup recipes that were estimated by archaeologists. They very nearly did a dive in front of the cameras, representing the soup after swallowing a few bites. Our ancestors must have been "tough old birds."

It was a long haul between those first "soups" and recording newer, probably more flavorful versions. We know for instance that the Romans brought across the seas—when they visited their neighbors in England—a variety of new ingredients, from leeks, onions, carrots, herbs, and spices such as coriander, parsley, thyme, and fennel. The Romans weren't using *The Joy of Cooking*, however. Their recipes were very complicated.

I found this old Roman recipe on a Web site, one of those listed in the References at the end of this section. I thought it interesting because it shows signs of linkage to Southeast Asia. The recipe is from the writings of Apicus's fourth-century A.D. cookbook. The recipe was created three centuries earlier.

First prepare a wheat gruel by boiling up some presoaked wheat with water and a little olive oil, and stir vigorously to thicken. Then pound up half a pound of minced meat in a mortar, with two brains, some pepper, lovage and fennel seed, and add wine and liquamen [fermented fish sauce, a little like modern Southeast Asian versions]. Cook the mixture in a metal vessel, add some stock, and add the result to the wheat gruel. [*Voilà!*]

As early as the 1500s we have a record of that era's soup from Andrew Boorde, whose first book (1542) was titled: *The Fyrste Boke of the Introduction of Knowledge*. Boorde was a physician and a traveler who was concerned about human health during the mid- and later-1500s. In his last treatise he wrote about a soup that began to take the form that we may recognize today in some older recipes: "A new, thinner type of pottage becomes fashionable. The French call it "soupe" from the practice of placing a "sop" of bread at the bottom of pottage bowls to soak up the juices." Tell me you haven't done that!

During the 1700s, a Frenchman named Monsieur Boulanger opened a soup shop, in Paris in 1765. His small shop was the world's first restaurant, and it sold only soup. (There are many

Boulanger restaurants today, most likely named after this man. There are also restaurants named Boulangerie that sell soups and other luncheon meals.) The name derived from a sign hanging above the door, which read, *Boulanger vends les restaurants magiques* or BOULANGER SELLS MAGIC RESTORATIVES.

Soup history began to move along much more quickly at the beginning of the 1800s. Peter Durand invented the "tin canister" for food storage and preservation. Twenty years later the first canned goods went public, available for sale to anyone.

Opening those cans was not an easy task however. One had to use a hammer and chisel and all without available bandages, which were often needed.

So in 1858, a (most likely frustrated man named Ezra Warner) patented his new can opener. Things were moving along for soups and other canned goods rather quickly.

Fourteen years later a woman named Amanda Theodosia Jones invented the vacuum-packing procedure, which changed the world of processed and preserved foods and soups. The manufacturing of canned foods took off.

Twenty-five years after that momentous event, Joseph Campbell Soup Company developed a formula for condensed soups. Five new soups hit the market with a "bang." Tomato, Consommé, Vegetable, Chicken, and Oxtail.

It wasn't until 1928 that we saw the first wheel can openers advertised in a Sears Roebuck catalog.

From 1934 until now, we've seen a stream of new soups, new recipes, and new marketing approaches. Dried soups, wet soups, condensed soups, low-fat soups, low-sodium soups, and then, of course, the famous Seinfeld show titled: "The Soup Nazi." Think that's nuts. Well, immediately after that show, soup cafés began opening in cities all over the United States. That was when soup became known as a hearty, satisfying full meal.

And now, in 2004 we have no-salt and lowest-sodium soups. No chemicals, no additives, no crutches. And particularly, no salt. They taste absolutely wonderful and were created by Maureen Gazzaniga. Read on, you'll want to make every one of them.

References

A few of the resources used to write this history of soup:

http:/shwww.bartleby.com/213/0517.html
www.encarta.com
http://my.execpc.com/~milanow/other_stuff.htm
www.campbellssoup.com
www.MegaHeart.com

 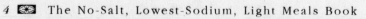

Apple and Cauliflower Soup

❧ with Curry ❧

DIABETIC ACCEPTABLE

SERVES 6 SODIUM PER RECIPE: 127.8 MG
SODIUM PER SERVING: 21.3 MG

2 **Granny Smith apples (trace)**
2 **cups no-sodium bottled water (trace)**
2 **onions, chopped (4.5 mg)**
4 **cloves garlic, minced (2.04 mg)**
1 **teaspoon extra virgin olive oil (trace)**
1 **teaspoon curry powder (1.081 mg)**
4 **cups cauliflower florets (120 mg)**
White pepper to taste (trace)

Rinse, peel, and core the apples. Chop the apple coarsely and set aside in a bowl with ½ cup of the no-sodium bottled water (to keep the apples from browning).

Over low to medium heat, in a medium-size (4-quart) saucepan, sauté the onions and garlic in the olive oil until translucent, then add the curry powder, stir for another minute.

Add the cauliflower, the remaining bottled water, and the chopped apples with their soaking water to the pan and simmer, covered, until the cauliflower is soft or tender. This will take between 15 and 20 minutes.

Using a handheld mixer, puree the mixture in the pan. (You can also use a blender or a food processor.) Cook the pureed mixture over medium heat until hot.

Serve hot. Stir in the white pepper before serving.

Nutrient Values per Serving:
Calories: 64. Protein: 1.868 g. Carbohydrate: 13.5g. Dietary Fiber: 3.516 g.
Total Sugars: 0 g. Total Fat: 1.146 g. Saturated Fat: .164 g. Monounsaturated Fat: .589 g.
Polyunsaturated Fat: .206 g. Cholesterol: 0 mg. Calcium: 28.2 mg. Iron: .57 mg.
Potassium: 307.5 mg. Sodium: 21.3 mg. Vitamin K: 4.197 mcg. Folate: 44.7 mcg.

❧ Beefy Mushroom and Rice Soup ❧

While stationed in the Far East I ate a great deal of rice. Rice with fish heads, rice soup, fried rice, steamed rice. Rice in any shape or form you could imagine. What I missed was my "steak and potato" diet, although I think I may have been a bit healthier eating rice and raw vegeta-

bles. *Beef was missing, always. Back then the Japanese just didn't have it in their diet. So, as soon I returned to the States, I pulled my hot plate out of my duffel bag and after returning from the commissary, whipped up my own rice and mushroom and beef soup. I hope you like it.*

SERVES 4   SODIUM PER RECIPE: 181 MG
SODIUM PER SERVING: 45.2 MG

1   tablespoon extra virgin olive oil (trace)
1   pound beef stew meat or round steak cut into bite size pieces
     (124.8 mg)
1   cup chopped onion (4.8 mg)
4   small to medium cloves garlic, minced (2.04 mg)
1½ teaspoons Don's Herbes de Provence Spice Mix (page 175)
     (1.866 mg)
3   cups no-sodium bottled water (trace)
½   cup uncooked rice (.975 mg)
1   medium carrot, thinly sliced (21.4 mg)
1   medium stalk celery, thinly sliced (17.4 mg)
¾   pound fresh cremini mushrooms, thinly sliced (7.68 mg)

Heat the olive oil and brown the meat over medium heat in a large non-stick saucepan, or in a heavy stainless steel pan. When browned, add the onion and garlic; cook until softened. Add Don's Herbes de Provence Spice Mix, then the bottled water, and bring to a boil. Add the rice, reduce the heat to a simmer, and cook for about an hour or until the meat is tender.

Add the thinly sliced carrot, celery, and mushrooms to the soup. Simmer, covered, for another 15 to 20 minutes. If, after cooking, the rice absorbs too much liquid, add more water, ½ cup at a time, until the texture is the way you like it.

Nutrient Values per Serving
Calories: 257.7. Protein: 15.2 g. Carbohydrate: 28.2 g. Dietary Fiber: 2.731 g. Total Sugars: 0 g. Total Fat: 9.324 g. Saturated Fat: .445 g. Monounsaturated Fat: .065 g. Polyunsaturated Fat: .164 g. Cholesterol: 4.08 mg. Calcium: 50.1 mg. Iron: 3.839 mg. Potassium: 536.7 mg. Sodium: 45.2 mg. Vitamin K: 2.172 mcg. Folate: 80.4 mcg.

❖ BEEFY VEGETABLE WITH BARLEY ❖

Maureen's mushroom barley soup is hearty, tasty, and wholesome, so why add anything to it? Flavors, even the slightest change with an herb or spice, or in this case some meat, give even the best of soups a chance for yet another

*life. So, she added some extra lean stew meat to her Mush-
room Barley and came up with another terrific success
and one I believe you'll really enjoy.*

SERVES 8   SODIUM PER RECIPE: 313.6 MG
SODIUM PER SERVING: 39.2 MG

½ **pound extra lean beef stew meat (133.8 mg)**
1 **quart no-sodium bottled water (trace)**
1 **pound mushrooms (15.4 mg)**
3 **medium carrots, sliced (64.1 mg)**
½ **cup chopped celery (52.2 mg)**
½ **cup chopped onion (2.4 mg)**
5 **small tomatoes, peeled and seeded (41 mg)**
¼ **cup barley (4.5 mg)**
¼ **cup fresh chopped basil (.424 mg) or ½ teaspoon dried basil,
     Oregano, marjoram, or other favorite spices to taste
     (use dried)**
¼ **teaspoon white pepper (.03 mg)**

Brown the meat lightly at a medium heat. Cut the meat into smaller pieces
if you like after browning. Remove any visible fat. After cooking, add 2
cups bottled water; simmer until the water is gone. Add another 2 cups of
bottled water along with the mushrooms, scraping up any meat droppings
that are stuck to the pan. Let simmer 30 minutes before adding the
chopped vegetables and tomatoes.

Cook the barley according to direction on the package.

After an hour, add the barley and any remaining water to the mush-
room/veggie/meat mixture. Add the chopped or dried basil. Add oregano, marjoram, or other favorite spices. Add ¼ teaspoon white pepper.
Serve hot.

Nutrient Values per Serving:
*Calories: 106.4. Protein: 9.144 g. Carbohydrate: 13 g. Dietary Fiber: 3.242 g. Total
Sugars: 0 g. Total Fat: 2.568 g. Saturated Fat: .816 g. Monounsaturated Fat: 1.032 g.
Polyunsaturated Fat: .295 g. Cholesterol: 16.7 mg. Calcium: 21.6 mg. Iron: 1.805 mg.
Potassium: 543.8 mg. Sodium: 39.2 mg. Vitamin K: 5.666 mcg. Folate: 26.6 mcg.*

❖ BORSCHT ❖

DIABETIC ADAPTABLE

I once had the great treat of "slipping" into the Soviet Union, along the Finnish border right at the Gulf of Finland, to enjoy, if you could call it that, a real Russian restaurant. The place was bleak. Dark. Depressing. We were served blinis, a spread of caviar and vegetables, and a deeply red soup called borscht. If memory serves well, their borscht had everything in the kitchen in it. You can shorten the list to your own taste, if you desire. I enjoyed that evening and will always remember it as an exciting "adventure." My hosts were two Communist agents who had been assigned to keep an eye on me while I filmed just a few miles away. But then, that's another story. I hope you enjoy the soup. We make it often.

MAKES 8 CUPS   SODIUM PER RECIPE: 157.6 MG
SODIUM PER CUP: 19.7 MG

1   **tablespoon olive oil (trace)**
1   **cup chopped onion (4.8 mg)**
1   **cup chopped green bell pepper (2.98 mg)**
5   **cloves garlic, crushed (2.55 mg)**
4   **cups thinly shredded Napa cabbage (50.4 mg)**
½   **cup shredded carrot (19.2 mg)**
1   **large beet, coarsely shredded (64 mg)**
2   **large red potatoes, cut into quarters (12.9 mg)**
6   **cups no-sodium bottled water (trace)**
2   **bay leaves (.092 mg)**
1   **teaspoon paprika (.714 mg)**
1   **teaspoon granulated sugar (.042 mg) or Splenda* (0 mg)**
½   **teaspoon dried dill seed (.21 mg)**
1½   **tablespoons red wine vinegar (.225 mg)**
   Pepper to taste (trace)

Use a large stockpot. Heat the oil over medium heat and then add next three ingredients, stirring frequently. Cook for about 5 minutes. Add the remaining ingredients except the vinegar. Bring to a boil, stirring occasionally. Reduce the heat to low, cover, and simmer for about 25 to 35 minutes, or until the veggies are tender. Add the vinegar (more to taste if you like). Chill overnight in refrigerator. Remove the bay leaves, purée and serve cold or reheat and serve with a dollop of sour cream (6 mg) on each bowl.

*Diabetics may substitute Splenda for the sugar.

CAULIFLOWER SOUP
❈ WITH CURRY ❈

DIABETIC ADAPTABLE

SERVES 4   SODIUM PER RECIPE: 88.4 MG
SODIUM PER SERVING: 22.1 MG

½ tablespoon extra virgin olive oil (trace)
 1 large onion, chopped (4.5 mg)
 1 teaspoon curry powder (1.04 mg)
1¾ tablespoons granulated sugar or Splenda* (.223 mg)
½ teaspoon turmeric (.418 mg)
¼ teaspoon cumin (.882 mg)
 2 cups chopped cauliflower florets from a large head (60 mg)
 2 medium potatoes, peeled and chopped (17.1 mg)
 2 cups Maureen's Chicken Broth (page 48) 41.6 mg
 8 dollops sour cream (50.9 mg)
    White pepper to taste (trace)

In a large stockpot heat the oil over medium-high heat. Sauté the onion until translucent. Stir often for about 5 minutes. Add the curry powder, sugar, turmeric, and cumin, stirring for another minute. Add the cauliflower and potatoes and stir another minute. Add the broth and bring to a boil.

Reduce the heat, cover, and simmer until the vegetables are tender. This can take between 20 and 30 minutes. Using a handheld mixer, puree the soup in the stockpot. You may also use a blender or food processer, but do so in small quantities. Return to the pot and heat through before serving.

Serve in soup bowls. Garnish each serving with a dollop of light sour cream.

*Diabetics may substitute Splenda for the sugar.

❖ CHICKEN NOODLE SOUP ❖

MAKE IN CROCK-POT

I love plunking a whole chicken into a Crock-Pot and then going away for the day to work or play. In six to eight hours the soup is ready with very little work to do once I get home.

MAKES 10 CUPS   SODIUM PER RECIPE: 617 MG
SODIUM PER CUP: 61.7 MG

  2 **medium onions, chopped (6.6 mg)**
  2 **medium carrots, sliced (42.7 mg)**
  2 **medium stalks celery, sliced (69.6 mg)**
  ¼ **teaspoon white pepper (0.3 mg)**
  ½ **teaspoon dried basil (1.238 mg)**
  ¼ **teaspoon dried thyme (.192)**
  1 **pound fresh mushrooms (5.6 mg)**
  1 **3- to 4-pound whole fryer (439.3 mg)**
  4 **cups no-sodium or distilled bottled water (trace)**
1½ **cups small noodles (12 mg)**
     Pepper to taste

Place all the ingredients into a Crock-Pot in listed order except for the dry noodles. Cover the Crock-Pot and cook on high for 5 to 6 hours.

While the soup is cooking, cook the noodles per package instructions (except for any recommended salt), drain, and set aside.

Remove the chicken, cool for about 15 minutes. Skim any fat that has accumulated on the top of the soup. A defatter works well.

Add noodles.

While the noodles reheat in the soup, remove the meat from the bones and return two cups of the meat (bite-sized) to the Crock-Pot. You may choose to reserve some of the chicken for another meal, possibly our Enchilada Soup (page 19) or your favorite casserole.

If you wish you may freeze in plastic containers. Store in refrigerator in sealed container for up to 3 days. Serve hot with toasted French Baguettes (page 113).

Nutrient Values per Cup:
Calories: 174.3. Protein: 13.2 g. Carbohydrate: 8.257 g. Dietary Fiber: 1.282 g. Total Sugars: 0 g. Total Fat: 9.671 g. Saturated Fat: 2.732 g. Monounsaturated Fat: 3.896 g. Polyunsaturated Fat: 2.12 g. Cholesterol: 61.9 mg. Calcium: 22.6 mg. Iron: 1.453 mg. Potassium: 284.9 mg. Sodium: 57.6 mg. Vitamin K: 2.013 mcg. Folate: 42.1 mcg.

❖ CHILI CORN CHOWDER ❖

Maureen has always loved true Mexican food. Being from southern California that wasn't a hard meal to find or cook. When she traveled to Spain with our youngest daughter, who was enrolled in Salamanca University, she tasted Spanish food and brought home an idea for a chowder that proves to be a combination of both Spanish and Mexican dishes. You'll like this one a lot.

SERVES 4 TO 6   SODIUM PER RECIPE: 356.4 MG
SODIUM PER SERVING (4): 89.1 MG
SODIUM PER SERVING (6): 59.4 MG

1 medium onion (3.3 mg)
4 cloves garlic (2.04 mg)
1 medium red bell pepper (2.38 mg)
2 tablespoons unsalted butter* (3.124 mg) or 2 tablespoons
   extra virgin olive oil
1 fresh chopped serrano or jalapeño chili† (.61 mg)
1½ 15¼-ounce cans no salt-added corn‡ (86.8 mg)
1 cup low-fat milk (124.4 mg)
1 cup no-sodium bottled water (trace)
½ cup half and half (99.2 mg)
½ cup fresh cilantro, chopped (12.4 mg)
2 fresh tomatoes (22.1 mg)

Chop the onion, garlic and red pepper.

In a stockpot melt the unsalted butter (or use the extra virgin olive oil) and sauté the onion, garlic, and red pepper until soft.

While sautéing, blend the chilies, 1 can of the corn, and ½ cup of the milk with a blender or food processor to cream the corn. Add to the onion mixture.

Add the bottled water, bring to a boil, and simmer for 5 minutes.

Add the remaining can of corn, the remaining ½ milk, and the ½ cup half and half.

---

*To cut saturated fats and cholesterol, use extra virgin olive instead of the butter.
†Caution: When preparing hot peppers such as jalapeños, make sure to wear rubber gloves and wash your hands thoroughly afterward. If you cut a jalapeño and then touch your eyes, you will appreciate this word of caution.
‡Many producers now make this product. Can sizes are generally 15¼ ounces (453 grams). Some brands we have used include Jolly Green Giant, Del Monte, and Safeway Stores house brand. Frozen corn may be substituted. Use 1½ pounds. Divide in two: Use half for making cream corn, the other half leave as whole kernels.

Boil the tomatoes until the skin loosens, peel, seed, and chop. Add the tomatoes to the soup. heat, before serving. Garnish with the cilantro.

Nutrient Values per Serving (4):
Calories: 308.6. Protein: 8.823 g. Carbohydrate: 41.8 g. Dietary Fiber: 3.313 g. Total Sugars: 0 g. Total Fat: 14.6 g. Saturated Fat: 8.504 g. Monounsaturated Fat: 4.174 g. Polyunsaturated Fat: 1.06 g. Cholesterol: 40.4 g Calcium: 168.2 mg. Iron: 1.46 mg. Potassium: 750.5 mg. Sodium: 89.1 mg. Vitamin K: 4.271 mcg. Folate: 98.8 mcg.

Nutrient Values per Serving (6):
Calories: 205.7. Protein: 5.882 g. Carbohydrate: 27.9 g. Dietary Fiber: 2.208 g. Total Sugars: 0 g. Total Fat: 9.746 g. Saturated Fat: 5.67 g. Monounsaturated Fat: 2.783 g. Polyunsaturated Fat: .707 g. Cholesterol: 26.9 mg. Calcium: 112.1 mg. Iron: .973 mg. Potassium: 500.3 mg. Sodium: 59.4 mg. Vitamin K: 2.847 mcg. Folate: 65.8 mcg.

❖ CREAM OF ASPARAGUS SOUP ❖

DIABETIC ADAPTABLE*

While visiting my very good friend Walter Forbes, Jr., in Tennessee, we spent some time on his large pecan farm/ranch. At the time it seemed that Walter had more land than my hometown did. Walter was a gifted banjo picker as well as guitar player and a wonderful bluegrass singer. He often played with Lester Flatt and Earl Scruggs and was at one time a regular guest on the Grand Ole Opry. *He played with all the "big boys" back then. He also recorded for RCA. While we were there, we toured his farm on dirt bikes. Suddenly after rounding a corner I came upon a vast open area of tilled land with tiny little spears sticking up in perfect order all the way down each row. My boyhood experience on my father's ranch was with alfalfa and cattle. This looked to me like someone did a lousy job tilling the ground leaving a perfect row of thistle stems behind. Walter pulled up, spotted my look of consternation, and laughed. "Gus," he said to me, "those are asparagus spears." They were the spears indeed, all by themselves, no leaves, no branches, nothing but spears sticking straight up out of the ground. It was my first experience seeing how these excellent, tasty vegetables grow. I had always enjoyed asparagus, but never wondered how they grew or how they were picked. When I got home and told my wife about it she thought it would be great to make something out of them other than just spears on a plate. Thusly, she created this soup. Add more spices or herbs if you like, but do use a dollop of sour cream for each serving and enjoy it as we do.*

MAKES 4 CUPS   SODIUM PER RECIPE: 234.8 MG
SODIUM PER CUP: 58.7 MG

1½ pounds asparagus spears (12 mg)
2 small red or white potatoes, peeled and cubed (9.923 mg)
2 cups Maureen's Chicken Broth (page 48) or Vegetable Stock
   (41.6 mg) (page 49)
1 tablespoon sugar granulated or Splenda* (.126 mg)
1 cup whole milk (119.6 mg)
⅛ teaspoon white pepper (trace)
1 cup no-sodium bottled water (trace) plus 2 tablespoons cold
   no-sodium bottled water
2 cups chopped raw spinach (47.4 mg)
1 tablespoon cornstarch
3 tablespoons no-sodium bottled water
2 to 3 tablespoons fresh lemon juice (.45 mg) or to taste
4 dollops sour cream (25.4 mg)

Boil potatoes until tender. Drain.

Wash the asparagus, cut off the tips about one inch from the top; reserve. (You should have 1 cup of asparagus tips.)

Break off and discard the tough white part of each stalk. Peel the stalk from the lower end. Slice in small pieces to equal 2 cups.

Place the broth, sugar, milk, potatoes and white pepper in a soup pan or stockpot. Bring to a gentle boil. Add the asparagus (not the tips) and cook for 10 minutes.

Meanwhile, in small pan, bring 1 cup of no-sodium bottled water to a boil, add the asparagus tips, and cook for 3 minutes or until bright green and tender. Add the spinach to the asparagus for about 1 to 2 minutes or until the spinach begins to wilt. Then add the spinach and the asparagus tips to the broth mixture.

In two different batches using separate bowls, puree with a handheld mixer or a blender. Return the soup to the pot.

Blend the cornstarch with 3 tablespoons no-sodium bottled water, add to the soup, and reheat.

Add lemon juice to taste. Garnish each serving with a dollop of sour cream. Serve hot.

Nutrient Values per Cup:
Calories: 283.8. Protein: 7.495 g. Carbohydrate: 18.2 g. Dietary Fiber: 4.098 g. Total Sugars: 3.118 g. Total Fat: 21.6 g. Saturated Fat: 6.721 g. Monounsaturated Fat: 11.4 g. Polyunsaturated Fat: 2.389 g. Cholesterol: 27.1 mg. Calcium: 135.2 mg. Iron: 2.05 mg. Potassium: 667.8 mg. Sodium: 58.7 mg. Vitamin K: 124.5 mcg. Folate: 232.1 mcg.

*May replace sugar with equal amount of Splenda.

❊ CREAM OF BROCCOLI ❊

I wanted Maureen to call this "instinct" soup. She has a great instinct for putting soups together and this one proves my point. Even "broccoli haters" will love this. Easy to make, it's a true winner.

SERVES 4   SODIUM PER RECIPE: 305.6 MG
SODIUM PER SERVING: 76.4 MG

2   **cups chopped onions (9.6 mg)**
2   **teaspoons extra virgin olive oil (trace)**
2   **teaspoons curry powder (2.8 mg)**
4   **cups Maureen's Chicken Broth (page 48) (38.8 mg)**
5   **cups chopped fresh broccoli (use peeled stems, too) (100.5 mg)**
4   **tablespoons fresh lemon juice (.6 mg)**
⅛ **teaspoon white pepper (trace)**
¾ **cup light sour cream plus 4 dollops for garnish (optional)**
    Chopped parsley for garnish (4.25 mg) (optional)

Sauté the onions in the oil until translucent. Add the curry and cook an additional 2 minutes.

Add the broth and broccoli, bring to a boil, turn down the heat and simmer for 10 to 12 minutes or until the broccoli is tender.

In a blender or food processor puree in small batches (no more than half the recipe per batch). Return the soup to the pot; add the lemon juice and pepper. Stir in the sour cream.

Gently reheat. Serve each bowl with a garnish of parsley and an optional dollop (9 mg per dollop) of light sour cream.

Nutrient Values per Serving:
Calories: 195.5. Protein: 8.747 g. Carbohydrate: 20.1 g. Dietary Fiber: 4.865 g. Total Sugars: 2.976 g. Total Fat: 10.4 g. Saturated Fat: 4.478 g. Monounsaturated Fat: 2.521 g. Polyunsaturated Fat: .855 g. Cholesterol: 34.5 mg. Calcium: 155.4 mg. Iron: 1.712 mg. Potassium: 676.2 mg. Sodium: 76.4 mg. Vitamin K: 150.1 mcg. Folate: 95.7 mcg.

Quick and Creamy Garbanzo Soup
Using Eden Organic
✦ No-Salt-Added Beans ✦

Diabetic Adaptable*

I'm always looking for an easy dinner to make and this one is right up there with the best. You can use any herb or spice you want in this soup, but make sure it is compatible with garbanzo beans.

Serves 4   Sodium per Recipe: 205.6 mg
Sodium per Serving: 51.4 mg

1   large onion, thickly sliced (about ¼ inch) (4.5 mg)
1   tablespoon extra virgin olive oil (trace)
4   cloves garlic, minced (2.04 mg)
¾   teaspoon ground cumin (2.646 mg)
2   15-ounce cans Eden Organic No-Salt Added Garbanzo Beans, drained (70 mg)
1   14-ounce can no-salt-added stewed tomatoes with juice (105 mg)
1   teaspoon sugar or Splenda* (.042 mg)
1   cup Maureen's Chicken Broth (page 48) (20.8 mg) or 1 cup no-sodium bottled water (trace)
1   tablespoon fresh lemon juice or grated lemon zest (.36 mg)
½   teaspoon dried thyme (.385 mg)
    White pepper to taste (trace)

Over medium heat sauté the onion in a nonstick saucepan with the olive oil until translucent or wilted. This will take about 10 minutes. Add the garlic and stir for another 2 minutes. Stir in the cumin and thyme and stir quickly.

Add the drained garbanzo beans and the tomatoes with their juice. Stir in the sugar, homemade broth, and lemon juice or zest and simmer, uncovered, until heated through.

Puree in small batches and return to the pot to heat through. Stir in the pepper. Serve immediately over rice or pasta or by itself.

Nutrient Values per Serving:
Calories: 297.5 Protein: 14.5 g. Carbohydrate: 43.4 g. Dietary Fiber: 10.8 g. Total Sugars: 3.664 g. Total Fat: 6.669 g. Saturated Fat: .617 g. Monounsaturated Fat: 2.748 g. Polyunsaturated Fat: .44 g. Cholesterol: 2.824 mg. Calcium: 25.4 mg. Iron: .729 mg. Potassium: 250.9 mg. Sodium: 51.4 mg. Vitamin K: 2.871 mcg. Folate: 10.7 mcg.

*Diabetics may substitute Splenda for the sugar.

❈ CREAMY ONION-GARLIC SOUP ❈

When I flew from Travis Air Force Base in Fairfield, California, headed to the Far East with the Marines, all I could smell back then were onions. It was 0500, and after a short trip from the crisp ocean air of San Francisco on a Navy bus, the scent of onions in the air seemed a radical change. That was in 1957. No houses, no buildings, no shopping centers, and just a two-lane highway. Today it's a jungle of concrete, asphalt, red-topped shopping centers, houses, and an airfield no longer visible from the highway. But still, we get some pretty good onions from near there and they help make a great soup when worked together with garlic from yet another nearby town, Gilroy, California. Maureen has been accused of knowing where every restaurant in California is, and in these two areas she has found a few great soup recipes. Here's one I swear by. It's absolutely the soup we should have put on the cover of this book.

SERVES 4   SODIUM PER RECIPE: 165.6 MG
SODIUM PER SERVING: 41.4 MG

1   **tablespoon extra virgin olive oil (trace)**
1   **cup peeled garlic cloves* (23.1 mg)**
2   **medium onions, thinly sliced (9 mg)**
1   **large shallot, sliced (2.4 mg)**
¼   **teaspoon white pepper to taste (.03 mg)**
2   **tablespoons red wine vinegar (.3 mg)**
2   **red potatoes, peeled and sliced (8.55 mg)**
1   **teaspoon dried rosemary (.6 mg)**
3   **cups Maureen's Chicken Broth (page 48) (62.2 mg)**
¼   **cup half and half (24.6 mg)**
¼   **cup low-fat (1 percent) milk (31.1 mg)**

In a large pot over medium-low heat, heat the olive oil. Add the garlic, onions, shallot, and white pepper and sauté, stirring off and on for about 10 minutes or until golden brown or caramelized.

Stir in the vinegar, red potatoes, and the rosemary. Bring the heat to high and sauté, stirring for another 2 minutes.

---

*About two large heads.

Add the broth and bring to a boil. Simmer, uncovered, for about 20 minutes or until all vegetables are tender.

Puree with a handheld mixer or in a food processor or blender in about two or three small batches. This is hot, so be careful. Puree until smooth. Stir in the half and half and low-fat milk.

Serve hot or store in the refrigerator in a tightly covered container for up to 2 days. Reheat to serve.

Nutrient Values per Serving:
Calories: 172.1. Protein: 7.151 g. Carbohydrate: 31.1 g. Dietary Fiber: 3.709 g. Total Sugars: .5 g. Total Fat: 7.077 g. Saturated Fat: 2.128 g. Monounsaturated Fat: 3.652 g. Polyunsaturated Fat: .825 g. Cholesterol: 14.6 mg. Calcium: 133 mg. Iron: 1.631 mg. Potassium: 639.5 mg. Sodium: 41.4 mg. Vitamin K: 6.006 mcg. Folate: 36.4 mcg.

❖ BEEF STEW ❖

MAKE IN CROCK-POT
DIABETIC ACCEPTABLE*

Every summer Don takes off for the coast to paint, write, and just duck out of our extreme heat. While there he takes a break from cooking sometimes, so he wants his C rations— now known as MREs (meals ready to eat)—when he gets back to the house. He became a Crock-Pot fan years ago for just this reason. And this stew is what he calls "heaven-sent" when he gets back from a long, rough day at the easel. (Yeah, right!)

—Maureen

SERVES 6   SODIUM PER RECIPE: 684.6 MG
SODIUM PER SERVING: 114.1 MG

3 cloves garlic, minced (1.53 mg)
4 medium carrots, thinly sliced (85.4 mg)
3 medium red potatoes, diced (19.3 mg)
1 medium to large onion, chopped (4.5 mg)
1 medium stalk celery, thinly sliced (34.8 mg)
2 pounds beef stew meat or your favorite beef cut,
     cut into bite-size cubes (535.2 mg)
¼ cup all-purpose white unbleached flour (.625 mg)
½ teaspoon white pepper (.06 mg)
1½ teaspoons low-sodium Worcestershire sauce (2 mg)
1½ cups no-sodium bottled water (trace)

*Sugars are in the potatoes. Most of the carbohydrates are in the flour and potatoes.

1 bay leaf (.046 mg)
¼ teaspoon ground cloves (1.276 mg)
4 dollops sour cream for garnish (25.2 mg)

Place the vegetables on the bottom of the Crock-Pot. Dredge the meat in the flour and pepper and place over the vegetables. Mix the low-sodium Worcestershire with the water and pour over the contents of the pot. Add the rest of the spices. Cover and cook on low for 8 to 10 hours or on high for 6 hours. Remove bay leaf and stir before serving. Serve hot. The stew may be stored in the refrigerator in a sealed container for up to 4 days. Reheat to serve.

Nutrient Values per Serving:
Calories: 280.7. Protein: 35.4 g. Carbohydrate: 13.8 g. Dietary Fiber: 3.15 g. Total Sugars: .391 g. Total Fat: 8.677 g. Saturated Fat: 2.925 g. Monounsaturated Fat: 3.859 g. Polyunsaturated Fat: .417 g. Cholesterol: 89.2 mg. Calcium: 35.5 mg. Iron: 4.657 mg. Potassium: 964.6 mg. Sodium: 114.1 mg. Vitamin K: 3.701 mcg. Folate: 48.5 mcg.

❖ CURRIED WINTER SQUASH SOUP ❖

Squash is obtainable year-round, but winter squash is our favorite. It's easy to grow by the way. If you can plant some for next winter, you'll be pleased with the freshness and the flavor from your own backyard. Try this soup; it may spur you to become the world's next backyard farmer. By the way, this soup will work well with any yellow winter squash except spaghetti squash.

MAKES 7 CUPS   SODIUM PER RECIPE: 89.6 MG
SODIUM PER CUP: 12.8 MG

2 tablespoons unsalted butter (3.124 mg)
2 cups chopped onions (9.6 mg)
2 teaspoons curry powder (2.08 mg)
2 cups cut-up winter squash (cut into 1-inch cubes) (9.28 mg)
3 tart apples, peeled, seeded, and chopped (trace)
3 cups Maureen's Chicken Broth (page 48) (62.2 mg)
½ cup apple juice (3.499 mg)

Melt the butter in a soup pot. Sauté the onions until translucent, about 10 minutes. Add the curry and mix with the onions until completely covered. Add the squash, apples, and broth. Bring to a boil, reduce the heat, and simmer until the squash is tender, approximately 25 minutes.

Puree in small batches of about 2 to 3 cups and reserve in another container until all has been processed. Return the pureed mixture to the pot. Add the apple juice. Reheat and serve.

Garnish each serving with a dollop of light sour cream. Serve hot.

Nutrient Values per Cup:
Calories: 118.6 Protein: 2.387 g. Carbohydrate: 19.1 g. Dietary Fiber: 2.915 g. Total Sugars: 2.143 g. Total Fat: 4.532 g. Saturated Fat: 2.353 g. Monounsaturated Fat: 1.341 g. Polyunsaturated Fat: .435 g. Cholesterol: 13.7 mg. Calcium: 31.8 mg. Iron: .684 mg. Potassium: 315 mg. Sodium: 12.8 mg. Vitamin K: 1.935 mcg. Folate: 21.7 mcg.

❧ MAUREEN'S SPECIAL ENCHILADA SOUP ❧

DIABETIC ACCEPTABLE*

If you like Mexican food or Southwestern food, you'll love this soup. Prepare the broth and Red Chili Sauce beforehand and store the remaining amount in pint-size containers in your freezer for future use. Maureen has been making soup and her special enchiladas for many years. They are always a big hit.

SERVES 4   SODIUM PER RECIPE: 360.8 MG
SODIUM PER SERVING: 90.2 MG

2 **cups chopped onions (approximately 1 large or 2 small) (9.6 mg)**

4 **cloves garlic, minced (2.04 mg)**

2 **teaspoons extra virgin olive oil (trace)**

4 **cups Maureen's Chicken Broth (page 48) (83.3 mg)**

½ **teaspoon cumin (1.764 mg)**

2 **boneless, skinless chicken half breasts, cut into bite-size pieces (153.4 mg)**

3 **low-sodium corn tortillas,† cut into ¼-inch strips (stack for easy slicing) (8.25 mg)**

½ **cup Red Chili Sauce (page 29) (1.988 mg)**

¼ **cup no-salt-added tomato sauce (20 mg)**

2 **ounces low-sodium Cheddar cheese, grated‡ (40 mg) plus 2 ounces for garnish**

*The carbohydrates come mostly from the tortillas and chicken broth.

†Labels will not state "low sodium." Most corn tortillas average between 2.5 mg to 16.5 mg per tortilla. Some however, may have salt added and will be higher although the package may state 0 mg per tortilla. Check the FDA Nutrient labels of the package you want to buy.

‡For the soup, use 2 ounces and use ½ ounce as a garnish for each serving. Nutrient values are based on USDA figures for the average of all brands.

1 tablespoon white wine vinegar (.15 mg)
   A few no-salt-added tortilla chips for garnish (3 mg per bowl)
      (optional)
4 dollops light sour cream for topping
   Chopped green onions for topping (36.6 mg) (4 mg per
      recipe) (optional)

Using a 2- to 3-quart saucepan, sauté the onion and garlic in olive oil until
translucent. Add the chicken broth and bring to a boil. Stir in the cumin.
Add the chicken, turn down the heat, and simmer for approximately 3 minutes or until the chicken is cooked through.

   Add the tortilla strips to the mix; stir and simmer an additional 2 to 3
minutes or until the tortillas disintegrate and the broth thickens. Stir in the
Red Chili Sauce, tomato sauce, and 2 ounces of the grated cheese; heat
through. Mix in the vinegar and it's ready to serve; pass the additional
grated cheese as a garnish.

Nutrient Values per Serving:
*Calories: 348.4. Protein: 26.6 g. Carbohydrate: 23.6 g. Dietary Fiber: 3.706 g. Total
Sugars: .992 g. Total Fat: 16.5 g. Saturated Fat: 2.319 g. Monounsaturated Fat: 2.783 g.
Polyunsaturated Fat: 1.083 g. Cholesterol: 78.3 mg. Calcium: 308.8 mg. Iron: 1.628 mg.
Potassium: 508.2 mg. Sodium: 90.2 mg. Vitamin K: 4.686 mcg. Folate: 55.4 mcg.*

❖ GARDEN FULL OF SOUP ❖

LOW FAT, LOW-SODIUM, LOW SUGARS
DIABETIC ADAPTABLE*

*Soups are great for winter, but this one works year round.
Fresh vegetables are the key to this delicious recipe. If you
are in need of a quick soup, this can be made with water
instead of broth.*

MAKES 6 CUPS SODIUM PER RECIPE: 416.4 MG
SODIUM PER CUP: 69.4

1   cup diced carrots (42.7 mg)
1   cup diced onion (4.8 mg)
4   cloves garlic, minced (2.04 mg)
3   cups Maureen's Chicken Broth (page 48) (62.5 mg)
1   14½-ounce can no-salt-added diced tomatoes (105 mg)
1   15-ounce can Eden Organic Pinto Beans 52.5 mg
½   teaspoon dried basil (.24 mg)

*Most of the sugars are in the canned tomatoes.

1 **cup diced celery (104.4 mg)**
1 **cup sliced zucchini (3.39 mg)**
2 **cups thinly sliced Napa cabbage (or other) (39.2 mg)**

Spray an 8-quart pan with olive oil (PAM). Sauté the carrots and onion, add the garlic and sauté at medium heat, 5 minutes longer, until softened. Add the broth and canned ingredients, basil, and celery.

Simmer for 15 minutes over medium heat, stirring frequently.

Add the zucchini and Napa cabbage for the last 5 minutes of cooking. Enjoy.

Nutrient Values per Serving:
Calories: 127.9. Protein: 6.963 g. Carbohydrate: 22.3 g. Dietary Fiber: 6.97 g. Total Sugars: 1.75 g. Total Fat: 1.152 g. Saturated Fat: .306 g. Monounsaturated Fat: .409 g. Polyunsaturated Fat: .295 g. Cholesterol: 5.649 mg. Calcium: 42.8 mg. Iron: .681 mg. Potassium: 633.2 mg. Sodium: 69.4 mg. Vitamin K: 4.885 mcg. Folate: 42.2 mcg.

❖ LEEK POTATO SOUP ❖

DIABETIC ADAPTABLE*

Ever eat leeks? Well, if you haven't, you're in for a tasty treat. Try this soup first, then expand other soups and dishes with your new find: the Leek. Found in most grocery store produce sections.

SERVES 6 SODIUM PER RECIPE: 365.4 MG
SODIUM PER SERVING: 60.9 MG

4 **large leeks, white part only[†] (71.2 mg)**
½ **yellow onion, diced (.42 mg)**
2 **tablespoons unsalted butter (3.124 mg)**
¼ **teaspoon ground coriander (.157 mg) plus more for**
   sprinkling (trace)
2 **cups no-sodium or low-sodium bottled water (trace)**
4 **white rose potatoes, skinned and diced (34.2 mg)**
2 **cups nonfat milk, vitamin A fortified (254.8 mg)**

Use only the white parts of the leeks. Clean the leeks thoroughly; dirt tends to hide in the layers.

Sauté the leeks and onion in the butter. After they soften, sprinkle with the coriander and stir, add the bottled water and potatoes, and simmer, covered, for about 30 minutes.

---

*Sugars are in the potatoes. Carbohydrates are mostly in the potatoes and nonfat milk.
[†]The greener parts of the leek become tough.

With a handheld mixer, puree the ingredients; add the milk and reheat on low, stirring occasionally.

Top each serving with a sprinkle of coriander.

Nutrient Value per Serving:
Calories: 137.9. Protein: 5.398 g. Carbohydrate: 16.8 g. Dietary Fiber: 3.093 g. Total Sugars: .691 g. Total Fat: 6.101 g. Saturated Fat: 3.705 g. Monounsaturated Fat: 1.715 g. Polyunsaturated Fat: .321 g. Cholesterol: 17.2 mg. Calcium: 148.7 mg. Iron: 2.113 mg. Potassium: 604.3 mg. Sodium: 60.9 mg. Vitamin K: 9.02 mcg. Folate: 65.5 mcg.

❖ CARROT AND CHICKPEA SOUP ❖

DIABETIC ADAPTABLE*

Maureen found this soup in southern France when she visited last year. The restaurant billed it as a Moroccan version of soup. The cumin, turmeric, and cayenne pepper make this one of the tastiest in our library of soups. We think you'll enjoy it.

SERVES 4 TO 6   SODIUM PER RECIPE: 288.7 MG
SODIUM PER SERVING (4): 72.2 MG
SODIUM PER SERVING (6): 48.1 MG

2 **15-ounce cans Eden Organic Garbanzo Beans, drained, or 4 cups fully cooked garbanzos (chickpeas) (70 mg)**
2 **teaspoons extra virgin olive oil (trace)**
1 **cup chopped onion (about 1 large onion) (4.8 mg)**
4 **cloves garlic, chopped (2.04 mg)**
1½ **teaspoons cumin (5.292 mg)**
½ **teaspoon turmeric (.418 mg)**
   Pinch of cayenne pepper (.032 mg)
5 **cups Maureen's Chicken Broth (page 48) (103.7 mg)**
2 **cups sliced carrots (85.4 mg)**
3 **tablespoons fresh lemon juice (about 1 lemon) (.45 mg)**
2 **tablespoons unsalted peanut butter (5.44 mg)**
1 **medium tomato, seeded and chopped, for garnish (11.1 mg)**

If you're not using Eden Organic Garbanzo Beans, prepare fresh garbanzos according to package directions.

Heat the olive oil in a large pan. Sauté the onion and garlic until translucent and soft. Add the spices and cook an additional minute. Add the

*Most of the carbohydrates are in the chicken broth and Eden Organic Garbanzo Beans. Neither contains sugar.

broth and carrots and cook until tender, about 15 minutes. Add the chick-peas.

Puree the mixture in 3-cup batches with your handheld mixer, food processor, or blender. Reserve each pureed batch in another pan or bowl until the entire recipe is pureed. Pour the puree back into the original pan; reheat. Add lemon juice and peanut butter.

Garnish each serving with some of the chopped tomato and serve hot.

Nutrient Values per Serving (4):
Calories: 388.1 Protein: 19.5 g. Carbohydrate: 52.5 g. Dietary Fiber: 13.4 g. Total Sugars: 0 g. Total Fat: 11.9 g. Saturated Fat: 1.881 g. Monounsaturated Fat: 4.707 g. Polyunsaturated Fat: 1.992 g. Cholesterol: 14.1 mg. Calcium: 60.5 mg. Iron: 1.843 mg. Potassium: 574.9 mg. Sodium: 72.2 mg. Vitamin K: 9.124 mcg. Folate: 42.2 mcg.

Nutrient Values per Serving (6):
Calories: 258.7 Protein: 13 g. Carbohydrate: 35 g. Dietary Fiber: 8.941 g. Total Sugars: 0 g. Total Fat: 7.922 g. Saturated Fat: 1.254 g. Monounsaturated Fat: 3.138 g. Polyunsaturated Fat: 1.328 g. Cholesterol: 9.414 mg. Calcium: 40.3 mg. Iron: 1.228 mg. Potassium: 383.3 mg. Sodium: 48.1 mg. Vitamin K: 6.083 mcg. Folate: 28.1 mcg.

❧ MUSHROOM AND BARLEY SOUP ❧

DIABETIC ACCEPTABLE*

Combine pearl barley with a wonderful variety of mushrooms, and the flavor is succulent and satisfying.

SERVES 6   SODIUM PER RECIPE: 282
SODIUM PER SERVING: 47 MG

2 **tablespoons extra virgin olive oil (trace)**
2 **cups chopped onions (9.6 mg)**
3 **cloves garlic, minced (1.53 mg)**
¾ **cup uncooked barley, rinsed (13.5 mg)**
6 **cups Vegetable Stock (page 49) or Maureen's Chicken Broth (page 48) (124.9 mg)**
6 **cups sliced mushrooms (about 1 pound)—use a combination of portobello, shiitake, button, and cremini mushrooms (23 mg)**
1 **cup chopped celery (104.4 mg)**
½ **teaspoon ground thyme (.385 mg)**
   Pepper to taste (trace)
2 **tablespoons chopped parsley for garnish (4.256 mg)**

*The bulk of the carbohydrates are found in the barley and the mushrooms. Neither contains sugars.

Heat 1 tablespoon of the olive oil in a large saucepan and sauté the onions and garlic at a medium heat. When the onions soften, add the rinsed barley and the stock/broth to the pan. Cook over medium heat until the barley softens (about 45 minutes). While this is cooking, heat the remaining oil in a smaller saucepan, and cook the mushrooms and celery at medium heat until slightly tender and the juice is released. Add all to the broth-barley mixture when the barley is cooked. Season with the thyme and pepper. Serve hot, sprinkling some of the chopped parsley on each serving.

Nutrient Values per Serving:
Calories: 222. Protein: 9.02 g. Carbohydrate: 33.2 g. Dietary Fiber: 7.626 g. Total Sugars: 0 g. Total Fat: 7.279 g. Saturated Fat: 1.309 g. Monounsaturated Fat: 4.169 g. Polyunsaturated Fat: 1.182 g. Cholesterol: 11.3 mg. Calcium: 63.1 mg. Iron: 2.786 mg. Potassium: 709.5 mg. Sodium: 47 mg. Vitamin K: 14.4 mcg. Folate: 48.3 mcg.

❈ MUSHROOM AND WILD RICE SOUP ❈

Maureen thinks she made this recipe up, but I keep reminding her of our trip through the northwest, then eastward to the Dakotas and a visit with our friend, Bob Crisman, at Mount Rushmore. He has been responsible for filling the cracks on the Rushmore monument for the past forty years. We ran into this soup in a restaurant that got its mushrooms from a town we had driven through in Oregon earlier.* We fell in love with the soup, and I think it had a lot to do with the great mushrooms they used. We tested many soups and dishes on that trip and brought home some wonderful ideas. You'll find this one easy to make. It's also great for serving when guests arrive. They won't even suspect it has no salt.

SERVES 4   SODIUM PER RECIPE: 118.4 MG
SODIUM PER SERVING: 29.6 MG

½ ounce dried portobello or cremini mushrooms (9.49 mg)†
1 cup hot no-sodium bottled water (trace)
1½ cups chopped onions (7.2 mg)
1 tablespoon unsalted butter (1.562 mg)
4 cups Maureen's Chicken Broth (page 48) or Vegetable Stock (page 49) (83.2 mg)
4 cups sliced mushrooms (about 1½ pounds) (11.2 mg)
½ cup uncooked wild rice (5.6 mg)
2 to 3 tablespoons fresh lemon juice or to taste (.3 mg)

*We used the same mushrooms for this recipe that we found on the road.
†For the best in dried mushrooms, visit www.pistolrivermushrooms.com/.

Cover the dried mushrooms with 1 cup hot (not boiling) water and soak for 10 minutes.

Sauté the onions in butter in a soup pot until translucent. Add the broth/stock, fresh mushrooms, and wild rice. Bring to a boil, turn the heat down, and simmer for 45 minutes.

While the soup is simmering, remove the dried mushrooms from the hot water, reserving the soaking liquid. Chop the mushrooms and add them to the soup. Pour the mushroom liquid through a fine sieve into the pot.

Add the lemon juice just before serving.

This is especially good when served with a dollop of light sour cream (4 mg).

Nutrient Values per Serving:
Calories: 234.5 Protein: 10.2 g. Carbohydrate: 40.8 g. Dietary Fiber: 6.125 g. Total Sugars: 0 g. Total Fat: 5.559 g. Saturated Fat: 2.466 g. Monounsaturated Fat: 1.72 g. Polyunsaturated Fat: .839 g. Cholesterol: 19.1 mg. Calcium: 37 mg. Iron: 1.944 mg. Potassium: 845.4 mg. Sodium: 29.6 mg. Vitamin K: 3.084 mcg. Folate: 80.7 mcg.

QUICK CHILI SOUP

❖ GREAT FOR TRAVELERS ❖

DIABETIC ACCEPTABLE

While traveling across the country in May of 2004, I tried to think of quick and convenient meals for Don's no-salt and low-sodium diet; meals that might be prepared in our motel room if we were lucky enough to have a microwave. This one worked quite well, and as it is only for two, one could easily double the amounts to serve four. It's quite good and oh so easy.

—Maureen

SERVES 2   SODIUM PER RECIPE: 180.8 MG
SODIUM PER SERVING: 90.4 MG

1 **can Eden Organic no-salt-added kidney or pinto beans (52.5 mg)**
1 **can diced, no-salt-added tomatoes in own juice (105 mg)**
½ **medium onion finely chopped (3.3 mg)**
2 **teaspoons Grandma's or other no-salt added chili powder (or more if desired) (trace)**
2 **ounces low-sodium Cheddar cheese, grated (20 mg)**

Combine all ingredients except cheese into two microwave approved bowls and cover with vented microwave approved lid. Cook on high for approximately 10 minutes. Mixture will be hot, so be careful while removing bowls when done. Keep in mind that cooking times vary with microwaves, so check and stir ingredients very 3 minutes.

It could also be made at home on a conventional stove top, in which case, I would sauté the onion in PAM before adding beans, tomatoes, and chili powder.

Add low-sodium Cheddar for topping in serving bowls or dishes.

Nutrient Values per Serving:
Calories: 244.6. Protein: 19.9 g. Carbohydrate: 44.2 g. Dietary Fiber: 13.2 g. Total Sugars: 5.25 g. Total Fat: 9.338 g. Saturated Fat: 6.014 g. Monounsaturated Fat: .013 g. Polyunsaturated Fat: .034 g. Cholesterol: 0 mg. Calcium: 11 mg. Iron: .121 mg. Potassium: 1119 mg. Sodium: 90.4 mg. Vitamin K: 1.1 mcg. Folate: 10.4 mcg.

PARSNIPS AND APPLESAUCE

❈ WITH CARROTS ❈

DIABETIC ADAPTABLE*

When we visited our daughter Kathleen's home for Thanksgiving this year, she surprised us with a great soup dish. And she made it without salt or a heavy sodium broth. It turned out great and here it is for you to enjoy also.

MAKES 6 CUPS   SODIUM PER RECIPE: 219.6 MG
SODIUM PER CUP: 36.6 MG

1⅓ cups onions, chopped (6.398 mg)
 4 cloves garlic, minced (2.04 mg)
 1 tablespoon grated fresh gingerroot (.78 mg)
 2 teaspoons olive oil (trace)
 1 teaspoon ground coriander (.63 mg)
 1 teaspoon ground cumin (3.528 mg)
   Pinch of dried red pepper flakes (trace)
 ½ teaspoon ground cinnamon (.299 mg)
 1 cup homemade applesauce* (.379 mg)
 5 cups Maureen's Chicken Broth (page 48) (104.1 mg)
1¾ cups sliced carrots (74.7 mg)
 2 cups sliced parsnips (26.6 mg)

*All the sugar in Nutrient Values per Serving comes from the applesauce. You can make your applesauce with Splenda instead and sugars would then be zero. This would also cut the carbohydrate nearly in half. Much of the carbohydrate after that will come from the chicken broth, which has no sugar in it.

1 **tablespoon fresh lemon juice (.15 mg)**
  White or black pepper to taste (trace)
6 **dollops light sour cream (15 mg) for garnish**
  Chopped cilantro for garnish (trace)

Sauté the first three ingredients in the olive oil on medium heat until the onions are translucent.

Sprinkle the onions and garlic with next four ingredients (spices); stir and sauté for about 2 minutes:

Transfer to a stockpot or soup pan and add the next four ingredients. Cook until the vegetables soften or for about 20 to 30 minutes.

Puree the mixture in small batches and stir in the lemon juice and pepper. Reheat and serve hot. Garnish each bowl with a dollop of sour cream (15 mg) and some of the chopped cilantro.

Nutrient Values per Serving (1 cup):
Calories: 149.4. Protein: 3.979 g. Carbohydrate: 27.3 g. Dietary Fiber: 6.067 g. Total Sugars: 2.357 g. Total Fat: 3.705 g. Saturated Fat: .745 g. Monounsaturated Fat: 1.921 g. Polyunsaturated Fat: .633 g. Cholesterol: 9.414 mg. Calcium: 62.4 mg. Iron: 1.747 mg. Potassium: 506.4 mg. Sodium: 36.6 mg. Vitamin K: 5.226 mcg. Folate: 52.9 mcg.

❖ PORK-SQUASH STEW ❖

MAKE IN CROCK-POT
NOT ADAPTABLE FOR DIABETICS

*Easy to make, this Crock-Pot dish is high in nutrients
and low in labor.*

SERVES 8   SODIUM PER RECIPE: 896.8 MG
SODIUM PER SERVING: 112.1 MG

One 6-ounce can Contadina or other no-salt-added tomato paste
    (149.6 mg)
  1 **8-ounce can no-salt-added tomato sauce (70 mg)**
  ¼ **cup unpacked brown sugar (42.4 mg)**
  3 **tablespoons olive oil (trace)**
  ¾ **cup no-sodium or low-sodium or distilled bottled water**
    (trace)
  1 **teaspoon Oregon Flavor Rack's Garlic Lover's Garlic (trace)**
  ½ **teaspoon Don's Special Provence Spices (trace)**
  3 **pounds lean boneless top loin pork roast (585.1 mg)**
  1 **tablespoon queen (acorn) squash, peeled and cubed* (12.9 mg)**

*Parboil the squash to peel and cube.

Mix the tomato paste, sauce, brown sugar, oil, water, and spices.

Put all the ingredients into a Crock-Pot, crank up to high, and enjoy hot after 6 hours.

Nutrient Values per Serving:
Calories: 473.1 Protein: 35.8 g. Carbohydrate: 25.8 g. Dietary Fiber: 1.908 g. Total Sugars: 13.2 g. Total Fat: 25 g. Saturated Fat: 7.552 g. Monounsaturated Fat: 12.6 g. Polyunsaturated Fat: 2.615 g. Cholesterol: 100.4 mg. Calcium: 71.2 mg. Iron: 2.393 mg. Potassium: 1153 mg. Sodium: 112.1 mg. Vitamin K: 2.481 mcg. Folate: 24.2 mcg.

◧ QUICK MEAT AND VEGGIE STEW ◧

DIABETIC ADAPTABLE*

Here's another of Don's favorite stews. You can use round steak or chuck, although butchers claim that chuck is the best for stew meat. Just buy one boned, and trim off as much fat as you can. Use Don's Flavor Enhancer for kick when serving.

—Maureen

SERVES 6   SODIUM PER RECIPE: 607.2 MG
SODIUM PER SERVING: 101.2 MG

1   **pound lean stew meat† (see Headnote above) (303.9 mg)**
5   **cups no-sodium bottled water (trace)**
½   **cup chopped onion (2.4 mg)**
3   **cloves garlic, sliced (1.53 mg)**
1   **cup sliced mushrooms (2.8 mg)**
1   **potato, skinned, chopped (7 mg)**
1   **cup chopped celery tops with leaves (104.4 mg)**
1   **cup sliced carrots (42.7 mg)**
1   **cup chopped cauliflower (30 mg)**
1   **tablespoon Don's Herbes de Provence Spice Mix (page 175) (3.733 mg)**
1   **14-ounce can no-salt-added tomatoes (105 mg)**
½   **cup frozen unsalted peas (3.625 mg)**
     Don's Flavor Enhancer (page 177) to taste (trace) (optional)

Lightly brown the meat at a medium-high heat, using PAM, in a 3-quart pan. Add 1 cup of water, and reduce the liquid on medium to high heat, uncovered. Repeat this step and add the onion and garlic. Repeat again

*Sugars in this recipe are in the canned tomatoes. Most of the carbohydrates are in the fresh vegetables and the canned tomatoes.
†Nutrient Values per Serving totals are based on boneless lean chuck.

and add the mushrooms and potato. When the mixture begins to thicken, add two more cups of water, and the celery, carrots, cauliflower, Herbes de Provence Spice Mix, and no-salt tomatoes. Continue to cook, uncovered, on medium heat until the meat is tender. The total cooking time is 1 to 1½ hours, depending on the tenderness of the meat. Right before you're ready to serve the stew, add the frozen peas and Don's Flavor Enhances. Continue to cook for 5 to 10 minutes before serving.

Nutrient Values Per Serving:
Calories: 162.7. Protein: 19.1 g. Carbohydrate: 14.2 g. Dietary Fiber: 3.928 g. Total Sugars: 1.75 g. Total Fat: 3.068 g. Saturated Fat: 1.085 g. Monounsaturated Fat: 1.054 g. Polyunsaturated Fat: .249 g. Cholesterol: 45.4 mg. Calcium: 61.5 mg. Iron: 3.58 mg. Potassium: 666.6 mg. Sodium: 101.2 mg. Vitamin K: 8.869 mcg. Folate: 38.4 mcg.

RED CHILI SAUCE

DIABETIC ACCEPTABLE

Like the movie title Some Like It Hot! *This one is* hot! *Yet, it's for everyone when Red Chili Sauce is used in other recipes to accent them, such as Maureen's Special Enchilada Soup (page 19). Try this with the soup and you'll find yourself using it in other recipes in addition to our enchilada soup. These chilies are the large dried chilies (often packaged and found in most produce sections of markets).*

MAKES ABOUT 3 CUPS   SODIUM PER RECIPE: 11.9 MG
SODIUM PER TABLESPOON: .248 MG

1 **dozen dried New Mexico or California chilies* (5.897 mg)**
1 **large onion, quartered (4.5 mg)**
3 **cloves garlic (1.53 mg)**
6 **cups no-sodium bottled water (trace)**

Place the chilies and the other ingredients in a 2- to 3-quart saucepan and simmer for 30 minutes.

Transfer half the cooked chilies, using tongs, and ¾ cup of the cooking liquid to blender or bowl and purée. When the mixture is puréed, pour it into a sieve and stir the mixture with a spoon so all the sauce, except the very coarse parts, seep through the sieve into another bowl. Repeat this procedure with the other half.

Red chili sauce is easy to make and excellent to use in Mexican dishes such as enchiladas. It's featured in this book as Maureen's Special Enchi-

---

*Caution: Remove the stems and seeds of the chilies (you must wear rubber gloves because the oils are irritating to the skin if you don't).

lada Soup. If you want to make enchilada sauce, simply add no-salt-added tomato sauce to equal amounts of red chili sauce. If it's too spicy, add more tomato sauce.

Both red chili sauce and enchilada sauce may be stored in the refrigerator for 3 to 5 days in a sealed container, or frozen for up to 3 months.

Nutrient Values per Tablespoon:
Calories: 1.904. Protein: .062 g. Carbohydrate: .426 g. Dietary Fiber: .099 g. Total Sugars: 0 g. Total Fat: .014 g. Saturated Fat: .002 g. Monounsaturated Fat: .001 g. Polyunsaturated Fat: .007 g. Cholesterol: 0 mg. Calcium: 1.025 mg. Iron: .018 mg. Potassium: 8.183 mg. Sodium: .248 mg. Vitamin K: .062 mcg. Folate: .668 mcg.

❖ RED PEPPER WITH CARROT SOUP ❖

DIABETIC ACCEPTABLE*

Carrots are one of the best vegetables we can eat. Even though relatively high in sodium for a fresh vegetable, they aren't so high that we can't enjoy them as snacks, on salads, or in soups. Try this one. It makes a terrific cold winter night supper.

SERVES 4   SODIUM PER RECIPE: 179.6 MG
SODIUM PER SERVING: 44.9 MG

8 **medium-size carrots, peeled, sliced (170.8 mg)**
3 **cups no-sodium bottled water (21.3 mg)**
2 **teaspoons olive oil (trace)**
1 **medium yellow onion, chopped (3.3 mg)**
1 **medium red pepper, chopped (2.38 mg)**
1 **teaspoon ground coriander (.63 mg)**
½ **teaspoon turmeric (.418 mg)**
½ **teaspoon cinnamon (.299 mg)**
½ **teaspoon cumin (1.764 mg)**
   Pepper to taste (trace)

Boil the carrots in the water; simmer for 20 minutes until tender. While the carrots are simmering, in another pan, sauté the chopped onion, red pepper, and spices in the olive oil; cook for about 5 to 10 minutes at a medium heat or until softened. When everything is done, put the carrots and their cooking water, the onion, and the red pepper into a deep bowl and puree with a handheld mixer, blender, or food processor. Return to pan and reheat before serving.

*Most of the carbohydrates are in the fresh vegetables.

Nutrient Values per Serving:
Calories: 94.7. Protein: 1.976 g. Carbohydrate: 17.4 g. Dietary Fiber: 5.18 g.
Total Sugars: 0 g. Total Fat: 2.735 g. Saturated Fat: .372 g. Monounsaturated Fat: 1.766 g.
Polyunsaturated Fat: .352 g. Cholesterol: 0 mg. Calcium: 50.8 mg. Iron: 1.287 mg.
Potassium: 508.7 mg. Sodium: 44.9 mg. Vitamin K: 7.741 mcg. Folate: 29.1 mcg.

❧ MOCK PORK SAUSAGE ❧

SERVES 6   SODIUM PER RECIPE: 372.7 MG
SODIUM PER SERVING: 62.1 MG

12 ounces ground lean turkey (319.8 mg)
 3 ounces ground pork (40.8 mg)
 1 teaspoon dried sage (trace)
 ¼ teaspoon dried tarragon (.249 mg)
 ¼ teaspoon dried oregano (trace)
 ¼ teaspoon red pepper flakes (.135 mg)
 ½ teaspoon cumin seed, lightly toasted in a skillet (1.762 mg)
 ½ teaspoon garlic powder (.369 mg)
 ½ teaspoon onion powder (.369 mg)
 ½ teaspoon freshly ground black pepper (.462 mg)
    Nonstick olive oil pan spray (trace)

Combine all the ingredients except the olive oil spray. Form the mixture into 3- to-4-inch diameter patties. Lightly coat a nonstick skillet with pan spray and put the pan over medium heat. Brown the patties on both sides, about 3 to 4 minutes per side, or until cooked through. Serve hot.

Nutrient Values per Serving:
Calories: 125.5 Protein: 12.5 g. Carbohydrate: .648 g. Dietary Fiber: .17 g.
Total Sugars: 0 g. Total Fat: 7.793 g. Saturated Fat: 2.415 g. Monounsaturated
Fat: 3.136 g. Polyunsaturated Fat: 1.431 g. Cholesterol: 55.2 mg. Calcium: 15.4 mg.
Iron: 1.075 mg. Potassium: 187.8 mg. Sodium: 62.1 mg. Vitamin K: 0 mcg.
Folate: 5.611 mcg.

HOMEMADE SAUSAGE SOUP
❖ WITH PASTA ❖

A COMPLETE MEAL
DIABETIC ADAPTABLE*

The Italians love sausage but of course it's high in sodium—it has a lot of salt. Most Italian recipes for soups, sausages, vegetable pies, and other entrées call for as much salt as 2 or 3 teaspoons. After eating this delicious soup years ago in southern Italy, my wife came home with a plan in her mind. We could use my homemade sausage, zip in a few more spices, and change the high level of Parmesan cheese in the soup she had to a low-sodium cheese. We also added Eden Organic Kidney Beans. If you like sausage, you'll be applauding with loud bravos and more! More!

SERVES 8 SODIUM PER RECIPE: 1,059.2 MG
SODIUM PER SERVING: 132.4 MG

1 pound Don's Homemade Mock Sausage (page 31) (256.5 mg)
3 medium carrots, peeled and chopped (64.1 mg)
1 medium to large onion, chopped (4.8 mg)
5 cloves garlic, minced (2.55 mg)
4 cups Beef Broth (page 51) (74.3 mg)
1 14.5-ounce can no-salt-added diced tomatoes with juice
     (105 mg)
1 15-ounce can Eden Organic Kidney Beans, drained and rinsed
     (52.5 mg)
1½ teaspoons dried basil (.714 mg)
1 cup large egg noodles (7.98 mg)
6 ounces fresh, washed spinach leaves (the small salad variety)†
     (268.6 mg)
   Pepper to taste
   Don's Herbes de Provence Spice Mix to taste (page 177)
     (trace) (optional)
   About 4 ounces low-sodium Cheddar (40 mg) or 2 ounces
     low-sodium Swiss (18 mg)

---

*Most of the sugars come from the canned tomatoes. All ingredients have some carbohydrates.
†Want to cut the sodium down lower? Just leave out the spinach.

In a medium to large saucepan or sauté pan, prepare the sausage per the recipe instructions.

When cooked, drain off any fat. Add the carrots, onion, and garlic. Stir often or until onion is limp or translucent (about 5 minutes). Add the Beef Broth, canned tomatoes, Eden Organic Kidney Beans, and basil. Bring to a boil, stirring frequently.

Add the noodles, reduce the heat, and simmer, covered, stirring occasionally or until the noodles are just tender to your bite—about 10 to 11 minutes.

Stir in the spinach and cook only until the spinach is wilted, which should take no more than 20 to 30 seconds.

Serve hot. Add white pepper to taste. If desired, add Don's spice mix and the low-sodium Swiss cheese, laying strips of cheese (or grated cheese) across the top of the soup bowl.

Will store covered in the refrigerator for about 3 days. Excellent reheated.

Nutrient Values per Serving (all Ingredients Included):
Calories: 254.1. Protein: 19.5 g. Carbohydrate: 21.4 g. Dietary Fiber: 5.658 g. Total Sugars: 1.812 g. Total Fat: 9.734 g. Saturated Fat: 4.183 g. Monounsaturated Fat: 3.235 g. Polyunsaturated Fat: 1.394 g. Cholesterol: 57.3 mg. Calcium: 217.5 mg. Iron: 2.573 mg. Potassium: 769.2 mg. Sodium: 132.4 mg. Vitamin K: 171.5 mcg. Folate: 106.4 mcg.

❖ SPICY THAI SOUP ❖

DIABETIC ADAPTABLE

If you thought you were never going to have Thai food again, think again. Here's a great Thai-flavored soup, created by Maureen, who happens to love Thai food.

SERVES 6   SODIUM PER RECIPE: 561.6 MG
SODIUM PER SERVING: 93.6 MG

2 **tablespoons extra virgin olive oil (trace)**
½ **cup chopped onion (2.4 mg)**
4 **cloves garlic, minced (2.04 mg)**
½ **cup chopped celery (52.2 mg)**
1 **pound raw chicken half breasts (about 4 medium-size),
    cut into small bite-size pieces* (184.6 mg)**
2 **teaspoons chili oil† (trace)**
¼ **teaspoon white pepper (trace)**

---

*If you use cooked chicken (like chicken off the bones when making stock) or leftovers from another chicken dinner, then use 2 to 3 cups diced chicken and add after the mushrooms.
†Add another teaspoon of chili oil if you like your soup spicier.

1 cup sliced or chopped mushrooms (2.8 mg)
2 cups Vegetable Stock (page 49) or Maureen's Chicken Broth
   (page 48) (39.6 mg)
2 cups 2 percent milk (244 mg)
3 medium fresh tomatoes, seeded and chopped (33.2 mg)
1 tablespoon grated lemon zest (.36 mg)
1 cup cooked rice (.244 mg)

Heat the olive oil at medium level in a stockpot and sauté the onion and garlic and celery until translucent. Add the chicken and continue cooking until the chicken is cooked through but not browned. Add the chili oil and pepper, stir to coat the chicken pieces. Add the mushrooms, sauté until they begin to lose their juices. Add the stock/broth and milk. Add the tomatoes. Heat the mixture but don't boil. Add the zest and cooked rice. Heat and serve.

Nutrient Values per Serving:
Calories: 181.3. Protein: 16.6 g. Carbohydrate: 17.2 g. Dietary Fiber: 1.668 g. Total Sugars: 0 g. Total Fat: 5.173 g. Saturated Fat: 1.746 g. Monounsaturated Fat: 2.308 g. Polyunsaturated Fat: .631 g. Cholesterol: 41.8 mg. Calcium: 134.5 mg. Iron: 2.801 mg. Potassium: 530.6 mg. Sodium: 93.6 mg. Vitamin K: 11.8 mcg. Folate: 27.7 mcg.

❂ SWEET POTATO SOUP ❂

SOMEWHAT ADAPTABLE FOR DIABETICS*

My friend Nancy Vanberg and I traveled to the East Coast in the spring of 2003 to watch her daughter-in-law, Debbie, run in the Boston Marathon. Afterward, we ventured south to visit historical sights. We had heard about the superb mac-and-cheese and candied sweet potatoes at Delilah's in Philadelphia. We soon found ourselves at the Amtrak station where Delilah's has a take-out stand. We concurred that both dishes were truly delicious. When we returned home, I kept thinking about those sweet potatoes and felt that I could get that same wonderful flavor into a sweet potato soup. Here it is and it's delicious, nutritious, and low in fat and calories. By the way, Debbie finished the race in a respectable time and said it was one of the most difficult that she has run.

—Maureen

**SERVES 4 SODIUM PER RECIPE: 210 MG
SODIUM PER SERVING: 52.5 MG**

3 cups cubed sweet potatoes† (33.8 mg)
½ onion, chopped (1.65 mg)
1 clove garlic, minced (.51 mg)
2 teaspoons olive oil
¼ large fresh red bell pepper, chopped (.82 mg)
¼ teaspoon white pepper (trace)
¼ teaspoon nutmeg (trace)
¼ teaspoon ground cloves (1.276 mg)
¾ teaspoon cinnamon (.448 mg)
1 teaspoon grated gingerroot (.26 mg) or ¼ teaspoon ground
    ginger (.144 mg)
1 cup nonfat milk‡
2 cups Maureen's Chicken Broth (page 48) or Vegetable Stock
    (page 49) (41.6 mg)
1 tablespoon natural maple syrup* (1.8 mg)
    fresh sliced red peppers (1.19 mg) or parsley (6.348 mg) for
    garnish (optional)

In a medium soup pot or stockpot, boil the sweet potatoes in their jackets about 35 minutes or until tender. Drain and remove jackets. Return potatoes to stockpot.

Meanwhile, sauté the onion, garlic, and red bell pepper on medium heat in 2 teaspoons of olive oil until translucent. Sprinkle with the white pepper and cook an additional minute. Add onion mixture to the sweet potatoes.

Add the spices and stir thoroughly.

Using a handheld mixer or a blender or a food processor, blend the mixture until smooth while adding the milk. Add the broth/stock and the maple syrup.

Heat gently until the soup is warm. Stir frequently and do not allow to boil.

Serve hot. Garnish each serving with sliced red peppers or parsley.

Nutrient Values per Serving:
Calories: 155.8. Protein: 4.909 g. Carbohydrate: 26.6 g. Dietary Fiber: 3.208 g. Total Sugars: 3.185 g. Total Fat: 3.669 g. Saturated Fat: .747 g. Monounsaturated Fat: 2.088 g. Polyunsaturated Fat: .537 g. Cholesterol: 6.874 mg. Calcium: 112 mg. Iron: .968 mg. Potassium: 353.3 mg. Sodium: 52.5 mg. Vitamin K: 2.314 mcg. Folate: 23 mcg.

*Most of the sugars come from the maple syrup. You can replace the maple syrup with 1 teaspoon Splenda unless the sugar levels are okay for you.
†The sweet potatoes may exchange with yams. Yams, however, have three times the potassium.
‡May exchange with 2 percent milk for a creamier soup, but fat rises to 2.6 g and calories to 219. Sodium remains the same.

SWEET AND SOUR CHICKEN SOUP
❂ WITH LEMONGRASS ❂

DIABETIC ADAPTABLE*

A complete meal! With this soup serve some of Don's French Baguettes (page 113), toasted and spread with some minced garlic and olive oil. Hmmmm, delicious!

Lemongrass (*Cymbopogon citratus*) is a native of India; however, it is more widely used in Thai and Vietnamese cooking. Lemongrass is easy to grow and hard to get rid of. Once it begins growing, this perennial relentlessly returns each new year. Considered an aromatic herb, it is also used in Caribbean and other Asian cooking. For the past few decades it has become popular with U.S. chefs and households. Locally we have a restaurant called Lemongrass Restaurant. Generally, you can find it in your produce section. Lemongrass usually comes in stalks of about 12 to 18 inches and is dry. Always remove after cooking. Most of the commercial crops for the United States are grown in California and Florida. I think you'll like the flavor a whole lot. This soup uses lemongrass to enhance it although Thai and Vietnamese chefs might have added *nam plah* (a very high-sodium fish sauce). This recipe has an excellent taste prepared without the chicken.

SERVES 6   SODIUM PER RECIPE: 612 MG
SODIUM PER SERVING: 102 MG

6 cups Maureen's Chicken Broth (page 48) (124.9)
1 stalk fresh lemongrass (2.01 mg)
5 thin slices fresh ginger (1.43 mg)
3 small fresh jalapeño chilies† (.42 mg)
¾ pound cabbage (64.3 mg)
8 ounces mushrooms (7.68 mg)
1 pound boneless, skinless chicken breast halves (306.8 mg)
1 medium sliced carrot (21.4 mg)
2 cloves garlic, chopped (1.02 mg)
½ 14.5-ounce can S&W no-salt-added stewed tomatoes with juice (52.5 mg)

*Sugars are in the sugar. Replace with Splenda.
†If you like hot and spicy, add one more chili.

¼ **cup freshly squeezed lemon juice (.61 mg) plus 1 medium lemon, cut into wedges (3.24 mg)**
2½ **cups hot, cooked rice (3.95 mg)**
3 **tablespoons thinly sliced or chopped green onions (3.2 mg)**
White pepper (trace)
1 **tablespoon white granulated sugar or Splenda (.126 mg)**
¾ **cup fresh chopped cilantro (18.6 mg) for garnish (optional)**

In a medium to large stockpot, over high heat, bring the homemade chicken broth to a boil.

While the broth mixture comes to a boil, peel and discard the outer layers of the lemongrass. Trim off and discard the stem ends. Cut the stalk into about 3-inch lengths. Using a large-blade veggie knife, lightly crush the lemongrass (to bring out the flavor) and the ginger.

Rinse and seed the chilies (you must wear rubber gloves because the oils are irritating to the skin if you don't) and cut one in half lengthwise. Finely chop the others, and set aside.

Add the lemongrass, ginger, and halved chilies to the boiling broth. Reduce the heat and simmer, covered, for about 25 to 30 minutes.

While the above is simmering, rinse the cabbage and cut into shreds about ¼ inch wide and about 2 to 3 inches in length. Lightly, rinse the mushrooms.† Trim the stem ends. Thinly slice lengthwise to about ¼ to ⅜ inch thick.

Rinse the chicken; cut into bite-size pieces.

With a slotted spoon, remove and discard the lemongrass, ginger, and chilies from the broth. (If you like spicy soup, leave some of the chilies in the broth.)

Add the mushrooms, carrot, cabbage, and garlic. Cover and bring to a boil over high heat. Reduce the heat and simmer until the carrot is tender, about 10 minutes.

Add the chicken and tomatoes. Cover and cook over high heat until the chicken is no longer pink in the center—about 4 to 5 minutes. Add the fresh lemon juice, sugar, and white pepper to taste.

In a soup bowl, serve the soup hot over the rice. Sprinkle with the green onions.

Caution: When preparing hot peppers such as jalapeños, make sure to wear rubber gloves and wash your hands thoroughly afterward. If you cut a jalapeño and then touch your eyes, you will appreciate this word of caution.

---

†Greenhouse-grown mushrooms generally don't need rinsing, but I do it anyway.

Nutrient Values per Serving:
*Calories: 276.2. Protein: 25.6 g. Carbohydrate: 36.7 g. Dietary Fiber: 4.915 g. Total
Sugars: 2.954 g. Total Fat: 3.605 g. Saturated Fat: .929 g. Monounsaturated Fat: 1.12 g.
Polyunsaturated Fat: .897 g. Cholesterol: 56.9 mg. Calcium: 88.5 mg. Iron: 2.748 mg. Iron:
2.748 mg. Potassium: 830.5 mg. Sodium: 102 mg. Vitamin K: 88.7 mcg. Folate: 62.3 mcg.*

❖ SWEET AND SOUR CABBAGE SOUP ❖

NOT ADAPTABLE FOR DIABETES UNLESS FLAVOR CHANGE IS
ACCEPTABLE. DIABETIC ADAPTABLE (WITH BROWN TWIN SUGAR)*

This soup is full of nutritional value. We think you'll really enjoy it.

SERVES 6 TO 8   SODIUM PER RECIPE: 515.7 MG
SODIUM PER SERVING (6): 85.9 MG
SODIUM PER SERVING (8): 64.5 MG

1   1½-pound fresh lean beef brisket, cooked in Crock-Pot
1   medium onion, quartered (for Crock-Pot) (2.2 mg) plus
   1 medium onion, chopped (for sautéing) (2.2 mg)
3   cups no-sodium bottled water (trace) plus 4 cups bottled
   water (trace)
1   tablespoon olive oil (trace)
6   tablespoons unpacked brown sugar (21 mg)
4   cups broth (from cooking brisket)† (167.8 mg)
4   cups no-sodium bottled water
1   cup fresh diagonally sliced carrots (42.7 mg)
⅓   cup packed golden raisins (6.593 mg)
1   14-ounce can no-salt-added diced tomatoes (105 mg)
3   tablespoons lemon juice (.45 mg)
3   tablespoons cornstarch (2.16 mg)
1   teaspoon garlic powder (.728 mg)
¼   cup red wine vinegar (.6 mg)
2   cups shredded cabbage (25.2 mg)
1½   cups cooked beef brisket (188.2 mg)

Prepare the brisket first. This will take about 6 hours in a Crock-Pot.
Quarter an onion and lay it in the Crock-Pot as a bed for the brisket.
Add 1½ cups water and the brisket. Cook on high setting for 5 to 6
hours. When done, remove the meat and onion and measure out 4 cups

---

*Sugars are in the brown sugar and the canned tomatoes.

broth. Defat the broth either with a spoon, by chilling it then scraping off the fat, or by using a defatter. Reserve this liquid for the soup. Then cut 1½ cups of brisket meat into small bite-sized pieces to be used for soup.

To prepare the soup, first sauté the chopped onion in a large stockpot on medium-high heat with the olive oil. Sauté until translucent. Add the brown sugar and caramelize. When the onion is ready, add 4 cups of the brisket broth, 1½ cups brisket, and the 4 cups of water.

Add the carrots, raisins, and tomatoes and bring to a low boil over medium-high heat.

Make a paste with the lemon juice and cornstarch. Add this to the soup and cook for 2 minutes at medium-high heat. Add garlic powder and vinegar, cook an additional 2 minutes on medium-high heat. Then add the cabbage; cover and simmer for 15 minutes.

Serve hot with a toasted low-sodium dinner roll.

Nutrient Values per Serving (6):
Calories: 262.9. Protein: 8.662 g. Carbohydrate: 32 g. Dietary Fiber: 2.916 g. Total Sugars: 10.5 g. Total Fat: 11.6 g. Saturated Fat: .683 g. Monounsaturated Fat: 1.683 g. Polyunsaturated Fat: .278 g. Cholesterol: 4.159 mg. Calcium: 43.3 mg. Iron: 1.507 mg. Potassium: 517.9 mg. Sodium: 85.9 mg. Vitamin K: 36.7 mcg. Folate: 24.5 mcg.

Nutrient Values per Serving (8):
Calories: 197.2. Protein: 6.496 g. Carbohydrate: 24 g. Dietary Fiber: 2.187 g. Total Sugars: 7.86 g. Total Fat: 8.701 g. Saturated Fat: .512 g. Monounsaturated Fat: 1.262 g. Polyunsaturated Fat: .208 g. Cholesterol: 3.119 mg. Calcium: 32.5 mg. Iron: 1.131 mg. Potassium: 388.5 mg. Sodium: 64.5 mg. Vitamin K: 27.5 mcg. Folate: 18.4 mcg.

SWEET AND SOUR ZINFANDEL SAUCE
❖ WITH MAUREEN'S CHICKEN BROTH ❖

DIABETIC ADAPTABLE

Scott Leysath, the Sporting Chef (TV, magazines, events), graciously adapted our first version of this sauce, found on page 176 of The No-Salt, Lowest-Sodium Cookbook, *just for this book. If you use the wine, make sure to check with your doctor to avoid any interaction with your medications. The alcohol should cook off, but just in case it all doesn't go away, you'll want to make sure with your physician. If wine is not possible, then exchange with unsweetened Concord grape juice (5 mg).*

SERVES 8   SODIUM PER RECIPE: 116 MG
WITH ZINFANDEL, SODIUM PER SERVING: 14.5 MG

4 cloves garlic, minced (2.04 mg)

⅓ cup yellow onion, diced fine (1.584 mg)

2 tablespoons extra virgin olive oil (trace)

¼ cup brown sugar, packed (21.5 mg)

2 cups Zinfandel (23.6 mg)

2 tablespoons balsamic vinegar (.3 mg)

1 cup Maureen's Chicken broth (page 48) (20.7 mg)

3 tablespoons no-salt-added tomato paste (43.3 mg)

2 tablespoons unsalted butter (3.124 mg)

Pepper to taste (trace)

In a medium saucepan over medium-high heat, sauté garlic and onion in oil for 2 to 3 minutes. Add brown sugar and cook until the sugar liquefies and caramelizes the onion and garlic. Add the remaining ingredients, except the unsalted butter and pepper. Reduce contents by boiling, uncovered, until there is approximately 1½ cups of liquid. Remove pan from heat and whisk in butter one tablespoon at a time until sauce is thickened. Season sparingly with pepper. If you need to heat the sauce at a later time, do so over low heat. Do not boil or sauce will separate.

Nutrient Values per Serving:
Calories: 124.2. Protein: .891 g. Carbohydrate: 10.6 g. Dietary Fiber: .507 g. Total Sugars: 6.669 g. Total Fat: 4.863 g. Saturated Fat: 2.097 g. Monounsaturated Fat: 2.18 g. Polyunsaturated Fat: .325 g. Cholesterol: 9.187 mg. Calcium: 19.6 mg. Iron: .625 mg. Potassium: 183.1 mg. Sodium: 14.5 mg. Vitamin K: 1.193 mcg. Folate: 5.382 mcg.

❖ GRILLED RED BELL PEPPER SAUCE ❖

The Sporting Chef, Scott Leysath, uses this sauce for many of his upland game recipes. You can use it for any fowl and pork roast in barbecued turkey burgers.

MAKES APPROXIMATELY 2 CUPS
SERVES 8 TO 12 SODIUM PER CUP: 6.78 MG
SODIUM PER SERVING: 1.133 MG

½ medium red onion, sliced into 2 rings (2.2mg)

1 clove garlic, minced (.5mg)

1 medium tomato, cut in half (5.5mg)

2 tablespoons olive oil (trace)

1 large or 2 small red bell pepper (3.28mg)

⅓ teaspoon dried red pepper flakes (.178mg)

1 tablespoon red wine vinegar (.15mg)

⅓ cup no-sodium water
2 tablespoons fresh basil, minced or 1 tablespoon dried
(.2 mg)
Pepper to taste (trace)

PREPARING VEGETABLES USING A BARBECUE:

Brush onion, garlic, and tomato with 1 tablespoon olive oil. On a greased barbecue grill over white-hot coals, place bell pepper over hottest part of grill. Place onion and tomato on grill and cook until grill marks appear on both sides. Remove and set aside. Place garlic on foil or small pan and cook until lightly browned. Cook bell pepper until blackened on all sides. Remove bell pepper from grill and place in a small paper bag. Close top of bag and allow to steam for 10 minutes. Remove bell pepper, pull out stem, tear along one side to open up pepper. Remove seeds. Place blackened side out on a flat serve and scrape skin off with the edge of a knife. A few bits of skin won't hurt the finished sauce.

PREPARING VEGETABLES USING A STOVETOP:

You can easily prepare this on your stovetop. Pan grill onion. Blanch bell pepper and tomato in steamer, peel skin from pepper.

Place all ingredients except fresh basil in a blender or food processor and puree until smooth. Transfer to small saucepan and heat to a boil. Add basil and cook over medium heat for 4 minutes.

Nutrient Values per Serving:
Calories: 28. Protein: .26 g. Carbohydrate: 1.901 g. Dietary Fiber: .463 g. Total Sugars: .027 g. Total Fat: 2.313 g. Saturated Fat: .313 g. Monounsaturated Fat: 1.665 g. Polyunsaturated Fat: .219 g. Cholesterol: 0 mg. Calcium: 3.373 mg. Iron: .126 mg. Potassium: 48.7 mg. Sodium: 1.133 mg. Vitamin K: 1.535 mcg. Folate: 5.024 mcg.

TOMATO SOUP

❖ WITH BASIL AND GARLIC ❖

AN ENTRÉE
DIABETIC ADAPTABLE*

As children we ate a lot of tomato soup because during WWII, coming out of the depression and with our father in the South Pacific, that's about all our mother could afford. Tomato soup often seemed like a staple. Maureen has enhanced the flavor of this tomato soup by using fresh basil and garlic cloves with a touch of chopped jalapeño. Serve it hot with our soup crackers or freshly made French Rolls.

SERVES 4 SODIUM PER RECIPE: 234.8 MG
SODIUM PER SERVING: 58.7 MG

1 teaspoon extra virgin olive oil (trace)
4 cloves garlic, minced (2.04 mg)
½ cup chopped onion (2.4 mg)
2 cups Maureen's Chicken Broth (page 48) (19.4 mg)
2 14.5-ounce cans no-salt-added stewing tomatoes with juice (210 mg)
½ cup thinly sliced or chopped fresh basil leaves (1 mg)
2 tablespoons chopped jalapeños† (about 1 small pepper) (.112 mg)
1 dollop light sour cream (9.145 mg)
fresh basil leaves (.03 mg) (optional)

In a large stockpot or large saucepan heat the oil over medium heat. Cook the garlic and onion in the oil, stirring, for 5 minutes or until the onion is translucent. Add the chilies and cook another 3 to 5 minutes. Add the broth and no-salt-added tomatoes with their juice, and bring to a boil. Reduce the heat and simmer for about 15 minutes.

Puree this with your handheld mixer or in a blender or food processor. If using a blender puree the mix in portions. Bring back to the stockpot or saucepan and stir in the fresh basil. A dollop of light sour cream (on each serving) (9.145 mg) increases this soup's attractiveness while adding another flavor. Garnish with fresh basil leaves. Serve hot.

Nutrient Values per Serving:
Calories: 76.2. Protein: 3.491 g. Carbohydrate: 10.3 g. Dietary Fiber: 2.502 g. Total Sugars: 5.25 g. Total Fat: 1.497 g. Saturated Fat: .249 g. Monounsaturated Fat: .903 g. Polyunsaturated Fat: .216 g. Cholesterol: 16.4 mg. Calcium: 20 mg. Iron: 6.018 mg. Potassium: 373.9 mg. Sodium: 58.7 mg. Vitamin K: .946 mcg. Folate: 30.8 mcg.

*Sugars are in the canned tomatoes.
†Caution: When preparing hot peppers such as jalapeños, make sure to wear rubber gloves and wash your hands thoroughly afterward. If you cut a jalapeño and then touch your eyes, you will appreciate this word of caution.

❊ TURKEY TORTILLA SOUP ❊

A DIFFERENT FLAVOR FOR TRADITIONAL TURKEY SOUP
DIABETIC ADAPTABLE*

Many Californians will tell you they "love" Mexican food. Native Californians also "love" avocados. This recipe includes a touch of each. Corn tortillas generally have no salt in them, although some may have higher amounts of sodium than others. USDA range varies from 2.5 to 16 mg per tortilla. Make sure you read the label to ensure you are buying a no-salt-added brand. Avocados have about 20 mg per avocado, but a few slices added as a garnish to this soup won't add much. If you don't care for avocados, this soup is also terrific without them. Garnish instead with cilantro. You can freeze some of this soup either in Mason jars or in plastic containers for up to 3 months. If you wish to make only half the recipe, you can cut each ingredient in half.

Note: Make the broth the day before you make the soup so you can chill the broth and skim off the fat.

MAKES 12 CUPS   SODIUM PER RECIPE: 751.4 MG
SODIUM PER CUP: 62.6 MG

⅓ cup chopped onion (1.584 mg)
3 cloves garlic, peeled and chopped (1.53 mg)
¾ teaspoon ground cumin (2.646 mg)
¾ teaspoon dried oregano (.169 mg)
¼ teaspoon Grandma's Chili Powder (trace)
¼ teaspoon pepper (.704 mg)
8 cups Turkey Broth (page 48) (77.6 mg)
1 14-ounce can no-salt-added diced tomatoes with juice (75 mg)
1 4-ounce can diced green chilies (80 mg)
10 corn tortillas (6 inches wide) (no salt in ingredient list of tortillas) (trace)
1½ pounds leftover turkey white meat (some dark meat okay) (432 mg)
1 firm ripe avocado, thinly sliced, for garnish (20.8 mg) (optional)
1 14-ounce can no-salt corn, drained, or one 10-ounce package frozen, unsalted corn (14.2 mg)

---

*Sugars are in the canned tomatoes.

2 tablespoons chopped fresh cilantro (5.184 mg)
8 ounces (approximately) low-sodium Cheddar† (80 mg)

In a 5- to 6-quart nonstick pan or other pan sprayed with olive oil, over medium heat, sauté the onion for 5 minutes or until translucent, then add the garlic, cumin, oregano, chili powder, and pepper until the spices are fragrant, about 1 minute. Add the Turkey Broth, tomatoes (including the juice), and green chilies. Cover and bring to a boil over high heat.

Meanwhile, stack the tortillas and cut into ⅛-inch-wide strips. Add to the boiling broth. Reduce the heat. Cover and simmer for 15 minutes, stirring occasionally.

Cut the cooked turkey meat into ½-inch pieces. Peel the avocado, if using; pit and thinly slice.

Add the turkey meat and the corn to the broth. Make sure the turkey gets heated through. Stir in the cilantro. Ladle into soup bowls, garnish with the avocado, pass the cheese at the table so guests can help themselves. You may freeze leftovers for future use.

Nutrient Values per Cup:
Calories: 220.7. Protein: 18.2 g. Carbohydrate: 19.1 g. Dietary Fiber: 2.532 g. Total Sugars: .635 g. Total Fat: 6.838 g. Saturated Fat: .712 g. Monounsaturated Fat: 1.764 g. Polyunsaturated Fat: .45 g. Cholesterol: 62.2 mg. Calcium: 76.2 mg. Iron: 8.057 mg. Potassium: 199.8 mg. Sodium: 62.6 mg. Vitamin K: .088 mcg. Folate: 47.3 mcg.

†At this writing low-sodium Cheddar is available from Heluva Good Quality Foods at www.heluvagood.com or from Healthy Heart Market at www.healthyheartmarket.com.

STOCKS AND BROTHS

Note: The bones used in making stocks most likely provide negligible amounts of any nutrients to the final food product. An unbleached bone, such as a whole chicken bone, provides the least nutrients. Fish bones may leach some calcium into a stock if an acid is present to dissolve the calcium from the bones. Only a bleached bone containing exposed marrow would provide any measurable nutrients at all, and the USDA doesn't have any information listed in the Standard Reference on marrow at this time.

The bottom line is that not much comes from bones when you make stock except flavor.

We allowed for sodium however with beef, turkey, and chicken, assuming some meat would be on the bones you use, to add to the flavor. If you use bones with no meat, then you can subtract the listed sodium data and probably the listed saturated fats from your recipe.

BROTH PRIMER

Broths are a liquid concentration of flavors. Beef, fowl, fish, and vegetables are what make the best broths. Because today's domestically raised animals are leaner (fat is where the flavor is), the best meats are cuts from the more exercised parts of the animal, such as the neck, shank, chuck, or bottom round. These will provide you with the best flavors. For fowl, which are also leaner these days, the best to use for chicken-based soups are stewing hens. Avoid the younger birds. For game stock, see *The No-Salt, Lowest-Sodium Cookbook,* or Scott Leysath's *The Sporting Chef's Favorite Wild Game Recipes,* available from www.sportingchef.com.

When using fish or shellfish make sure they are always fresh bones and meat. It is best to use lean white-fleshed fish, such as orange roughy, halibut, sole, cod, or flounder (and their bones). Avoid oily fish like salmon or tuna, which tend to lose freshness when subjected to high temperatures. Shellfish should always be cooked in their shells in a small amount of liquid.

For Vegetable Broth, any favorite combination of vegetables will make great broths if cooked properly. A combined selection of root vegetables will make a flavorful vegetable broth.

To make a basic broth (see: *The No-Salt, Lowest-Sodium Cookbook*), combine about 5 pounds of meat or poultry with 8 cups of cool no-sodium or bottled distilled water in a tall pot. (You'll find you may have to add some more water during cooking to keep the ingredients completely submerged.) Bring the broth to a slow simmer over low heat, skim frequently, and continue to simmer. Add your selection of spices and herbs, and pepper, until flavorful. The usual simmering time for basic broth is 80 minutes for fish, 3 hours for poultry, and 4 hours for beef.

For a sturdy vegetable broth a recipe that has been around a long time calls for about 6 pounds of vegetables cleaned and chopped (nearly 8 cups). Season these with your spices and simmer for about 1 hour, or until richly flavored. (There is another school of thought that teaches us to simmer vegetables at a very low heat [Crock-Pot level] for up to 8 hours to bring out the maximum flavor.)

Once the broth has simmered for the length of time you choose, strain it through a sieve or colander into a metal or glass bowl (avoid using plastic containers for liquids since plastic will insulate the broth and prevent rapid cooling). Set the bowl into a sink or larger bowl with ice water. Stir the broth occasionally to hurry cooling. Cover and refrigerate broths for up to three days in your refrigerator or place in freezer containers for longer storage. (Plastic is fine here.)

The primary vegetables used in soups are onions, leeks, carrots, and celery. However, you can include virtually any vegetable in your refrigerator or veggie basket in a soup. According to the experts at culinary institutes, aromatic vegetables containing high sulfur levels, such as onions, leeks, shallots, and garlic should be cooked first. This will prevent their strong flavor from overpowering the flavors of the other ingredients.

Vegetable soups are a wonderful way to use leftovers or "stragglers" in your refrigerator. Remember to cut the vegetables into sizes as uniform as possible. Equal-size vegetable pieces will cook at the same speed. It's important to remember that vegetables should always be added to the soup with their cooking times in mind. The hardier, bulkier root vegetables should be added first; the more delicate vegetables added later.

Your choice of herbs, spices, and other aromatic ingredients (lemongrass or chilies, for example) are added to soups to increase flavor. For our no salt lifestyle, these are what make a difference. Lemongrass is especially a good addition for replacing the usual salt flavor.

To add these items, tie in a sachet made from a large tea ball or make your own sachet by wrapping and tying flavorings in a piece of cheesecloth.

◈ FISH STOCK ◈

Here's another easy-to-make recipe from our Sporting Chef friend, Scott Leysath. Sportsmen and nonsportsmen alike can make this and use it with a clam chowder, fish chowder, or fish soup.

MAKES 2½ CUPS   SODIUM PER RECIPE: 5.54 MG
SODIUM PER ½ CUP: 1.108 MG

1   pound mild fish bones (trace)
1   quart no-sodium bottled water (trace)
1   bunch fresh parsley stems (2.24 mg)
1   medium onion, thinly sliced (3.3 mg)

Combine all the ingredients in a large saucepan. Bring to a boil. Cover, reduce the heat, and simmer 2 hours.

Pour the mixture through a wire mesh strainer, discarding the bones, parsley, and onion.

Nutrient Values per ½ Cup:
Calories: 8.648. Protein: .279 g. Carbohydrate: 1.949 g. Dietary Fiber: .422 g. Total Sugars: 0 g. Total Fat: .042 g. Saturated Fat: .007 g. Monounsaturated Fat: .007 g. Polyunsaturated Fat: .015 g. Cholesterol: 0 mg. Calcium: 5.504 mg. Iron: .098 mg. Potassium: 39 mg. Sodium: 1.108 mg. Vitamin K: 4.76 mcg. Folate: 5.396 mcg.

❖ TURKEY BROTH ❖

Use the leftover carcass and scraps of meat from your turkey dinner to make this wonderful soup.

MAKES 12 CUPS   SODIUM PER RECIPE: 394.1 MG
SODIUM PER CUP: 32.84 MG

1 **cooked turkey carcass* (217.9 mg)**
12 **ounces no-salt, cooked turkey meat attached to bones†**
    (135.7 mg)
1 **large onion, quartered (4.5 mg)**
3 **celery tops (34.8 mg)**
2 **teaspoons Don's Flavor Enhancer (page 177) (1.721 mg)**

Cover the turkey carcass with water in large stove-top pan. (Usually a 12-quart or larger pan is needed.) Bring to a boil, then simmer, covered, for about 2 to 3 hours. When done, cool and strip the meat from the bones. Throw the bones away. Cool in the refrigerator overnight. Separate the fat from the broth. (Make sure all the bones are removed so that very small bones don't show up later in the soup.) Use immediately to make terrific "Turkey Broth" soups. Store extra broth in quart-sized Mason jars in the refrigerator for up to 2 weeks. See our low-sodium Vegetable Stocks (page 49) for your first effort.

Nutrient Values per Cup:
Calories: 100.8. Protein: 8.186 g. Carbohydrate: 1.427 g. Dietary Fiber: .316 g. Total Sugars: 0 g. Total Fat: 6.729 g. Saturated Fat: 2.233 g. Monounsaturated Fat: 2.058 g. Polyunsaturated Fat: 1.917 g. Cholesterol: 46 mg. Calcium: 62.5 mg. Iron: .95 mg. Potassium: 140.1 mg. Sodium: 32.8 mg. Vitamin K: .65 mcg. Folate: 7.85 mcg.

❖ MAUREEN'S CHICKEN BROTH ❖

Chicken stock (broth) can be made many different ways. Often we find similar recipes in different cookbooks. At the beginning of our efforts to create soups and stocks, we tested the artificial bouillons and found them to be too heavily loaded with potassium chloride for many heart patients. Not only that, the potassium had a flavor (or taste) that might not agree with everyone. So, we have built a variety of broths in this book to be used with our

---

*Based on a 1-pound turkey frame, mechanically stripped.
†Estimated amount of turkey meat left on handpicked frame after serving the meat from the whole turkey.

recipes. This one started as Maureen's basic chicken broth and has evolved into a flavorful broth that works very well with all our soups.

MAKES 10 CUPS SODIUM PER RECIPE: 207 MG
SODIUM PER CUP: 20.7 MG

1 2½- to 3-pound fryer, whole* (87.9 mg)
4 quarts no-sodium bottled water (trace)
2 medium stalks celery, cut into 1-inch pieces (69.6 mg)
1 large onion, quartered (4.5 mg)
2 cloves garlic, minced (1.02 mg)
2 bay leaves (.091 mg)
2 medium carrots, cut into 1-inch pieces (42.7 mg)
8 black peppercorns (8 mg)
2 teaspoons Don's Flavor Enhancer (page 177) (1.721 mg)

Wash the chicken, put it into a large stockpot, and cover with the water. Bring all the ingredients to a boil over moderate heat. Lower the heat to a constant simmer and skim the fat and scum that rise to the top of the water. Continue to simmer (do not boil), skimming foam from the water during the cooking period. Cook for about 3 hours. When ready, remove and strain the ingredients through a sieve with a fine mesh. Discard the vegetables and bay leaves. Remove the chicken meat from the bones. The meat can be used in soups, casserole dishes, fried rice, etc. Cool the broth, then chill in the refrigerator. Remove the fat that rises to the surface. You can save the broth in canning jars in your refrigerator for future use; it will keep for up to a week. Or you can freeze the broth in vacuum-sealed bags or quart jars filled only two-thirds full for up to 3 months.

Nutrient Values per Cup:
Calories: 41.4. Protein: 2.764 g. Carbohydrate: 3.34 g. Dietary Fiber: .836 g. Total Sugars: 0 g. Total Fat: 1.956 g. Saturated Fat: .549 g. Monounsaturated Fat: .782 g. Polyunsaturated Fat: .437 g. Cholesterol: 11.3 mg. Calcium: 13.9 mg. Iron: .37 mg. Potassium: 116.6 mg Sodium: 20.7 mg. Vitamin K: 1.87 mcg. Folate: 11 mcg.

❖ VEGETABLE STOCK ❖

If you've ever made soup from scratch before, you probably do what we do when making a vegetable broth. Just clean out the vegetable drawers in the refrigerator and grab what's left in the vegetable bin or pantry. At least

---

*The sodium level has been figured after the meat has been removed.

with this recipe you'll know exactly how much sodium you're getting and many of the other nutrients you'll have.

MAKES 6 CUPS SODIUM PER RECIPE: *299.7* MG
SODIUM PER CUP: *49.9* MG

 3 **medium onions, chopped (9.9 mg)**
 4 **medium carrots, chopped (85.4 mg)**
 4 **medium stalks celery, chopped (139.2 mg)**
 1 **leek, chopped (17.8 mg)**
 2 **medium sweet potatoes, chopped (33.8 mg)**
 2 **medium red potatoes (8.55 mg)**
 5 **cloves garlic, minced (2.55 mg)**
 1 **dried bay leaf (.046 mg)**
 4 **sprigs of thyme (.576) mg)**
 4 **allspice berries (1.463 mg)**
12 **cups no-sodium bottled water (trace)**

Bring everything to a boil in the water in a large stockpot, over high heat. Reduce the heat and let simmer for about an hour or slightly more. The liquid should reduce about halfway. Strain the stock through a fine mesh, discarding the vegetables and especially the bay leaf. The broth may be used immediately or it can be refrigerated or frozen for up to 3 months, and thawed later.

Nutrient Values per Cup:
Calories: 111.8. Protein: 2.968 g. Carbohydrate: 25.7 g. Dietary Fiber: 5.377 g.
Total Sugars: 0 g. Total Fat: .46 g. Saturated Fat: .1 g. Monounsaturated Fat: .037 g.
Polyunsaturated Fat: .204 g. Cholesterol: 0 mg. Calcium: 65.8 mg. Iron: 1.529 mg.
Potassium: 549.3 mg. Sodium: 49.9 mg. Vitamin K: 8.41 mcg. Folate: 44.9 mcg.

❖ GAME STOCK ❖

Make good use of frequently discarded bones to create a marvelous game stock.

MAKES 1 QUART SODIUM PER RECIPE: *178.1* MG
SODIUM PER CUP: *44.5* MG

 2 **tablespoons extra virgin olive oil (trace)**
1½ **to 2 pounds big-game neck, back, and/or rib bones and bird carcasses (113.9 mg)**
 1 **medium onion, unpeeled and quartered (3.3 mg)**
 1 **large carrot, unpeeled and sliced into 1-inch-thick pieces (25.2 mg)**

2   medium celery stalks, cut in half (69.5 mg)
2   quarts no-sodium bottled water (trace)
1   dried bay leaf (.046 mg)
½   teaspoon coarsely ground black pepper (.462 mg)

Preheat the oven to 350°F. Rub the oil over the bones and/or carcasses and place in a roasting pan with the vegetables. Put the pan in the oven and roast until the bones and vegetables are browned, but not burnt. Transfer the contents, including the drippings, to a large stockpot. Add the water, bay leaf, and pepper. Bring to a boil over medium-high heat. Lower the heat to a simmer and cook, uncovered, for 6 to 8 hours. During cooking, keep enough liquid in pot to cover bones, adding additional water, if necessary. Strain (discard the bay leaf), cool, and refrigerate or freeze up to 3 months.

Nutrient Values per Cup:
Calories: 214.5. Protein: 13.1 g. Carbohydrate: 5.436 g. Dietary Fiber: 1.563 g. Total Sugars: 0 g. Total Fat: 15.6 g. Saturated Fat: 4.002 g. Monounsaturated Fat: 8.804 g. Polyunsaturated Fat: 1.635 g. Cholesterol: 33.8 mg. Calcium: 30.9 mg. Iron: 1.395 mg. Potassium: 285.8 mg. Sodium: 44.5 mg. Vitamin K: 7.158 mcg. Folate: 15.9 mcg.

❖ BEEF BROTH ❖

MAKES 8 CUPS   SODIUM PER RECIPE: 148.8 MG
SODIUM PER CUP: 18.6 MG

2   meaty beef bones (shank, short ribs, or shin bones) (53.6 mg)
2   pounds cracked beef bones (trace)
2   stalks celery, chopped (69.6 mg)
2   large onions, chopped (9 mg)
10 cups no-sodium bottled water (trace)
2   tablespoons dried parsley flakes (11.8 mg)
2   peppercorns (2 mg)
2   teaspoons onion powder (2.268 mg)
4   cloves garlic, minced (2.04 mg)
½   teaspoon dried thyme leaves (.036 mg)
1   dried bay leaf (.046 mg)
1   teaspoon Don's Flavor Enhancer (page 177) (.861 mg) or
    more onion powder to taste (optional)

Place all the bones in a large roasting pan and roast at 450°F degrees for 30 minutes. Add the celery and onions and roast for 45 minutes longer, or until the bones are deep brown. Stir about every 15 minutes.

Place the roasted ingredients in an 8- to 10-quart stockpot. Spoon off the fat in the roasting pan. Add 2 cups of the water to the roasting pan, heat and scrape to loosen the browned drippings.

Add this to the stockpot, along with the remaining 8 cups of water. Bring all to a boil, then reduce the heat and simmer, partly covered, for about 30 minutes. Skim off any residue and fat that might rise to the surface. Add the rest of the ingredients and simmer, partially covered, for another 5 to 6 hours or until the liquid is thicker and meets your tastes.

Strain the broth after removing the bones and the bay leaf. Add Don's Flavor Enhancer or more onion powder, if needed. Cool, uncovered, in the refrigerator. Skim all fat from the broth before using.

Will store for 3 days in your refrigerator in a sealed container. Will freeze up to 3 to 4 months in a sealed container.

Nutrient Values per Cup:
Calories: 34.7. Protein: 3.052 g. Carbohydrate: 4.757 g. Dietary Fiber: 1.032 g. Total Sugars: 0 g. Total Fat: .518 g. Saturated Fat: .154 g. Monounsaturated Fat: .211 g. Polyunsaturated Fat: .056 g. Cholesterol: 4.146 mg. Calcium: 23.8 mg. Iron: .767 mg. Potassium: 152.8 mg. Sodium: 18.6 mg. Vitamin K: 1.95 mcg. Folate: 12.4 mcg.

WILD GAME SOUPS

❖ ❖ ❖ ❖ ❖ ❖ ❖ ❖

❖ FISH CHOWDER ❖

Scott Leysath, the Sporting Chef, provided us with this wonderful chowder recipe. In this original he uses no salt. You can use Don's Flavor Enhancer lightly or to taste along with some black pepper to kick this up a bit.

SERVES 6   SODIUM PER RECIPE: 699.4 MG
SODIUM PER SERVING: 116.6 MG

1   **large yellow onion, diced (4.5 mg)**
2   **medium carrots, diced (42.7 mg)**
3   **medium stalks celery, diced (104.4 mg)**
1   **cup Maureen's Chicken Broth (page 48) (20.7 mg)**
½   **cup dry white wine* (8 mg)**
    Dash of Worcestershire sauce (11.7 mg)
2   **cups peeled, diced red potatoes (½-inch cubes), cooked firm
    (24 mg)**
¼   **cup minced fresh parsley (8.4 mg)**
2   **cups half and half (198.4 mg)**
18 **ounces fresh, skinless fish fillets (362.1 mg)**
2   **cups Maureen's Chicken Broth (page 48) or Vegetable Stock
    (page 49) (41.3 mg)**
    Don's Flavor Enhancer (page 177) to taste
    Black pepper to taste (trace)

In a medium stockpot over medium heat, sauté onions, carrots, and celery. Increase heat to medium-high and cook for 3 to 4 minutes. Add 2 cups chicken broth, white wine, and Worcestershire. Cover and simmer for 10 minutes. Reduce heat to a low medium, add potatoes, parsley, and half and half and the fish. If fish is not covered with liquid, add the balance of chicken broth until it is. Cook until fish is just cooked and potatoes are warmed throughout. Season to taste with Don's Flavor Enhancer and black pepper.

---

*Use wine only if your doctor has cleared you. Even cooked wine doesn't always dissipate the alcohol. Exchange with a mild white grape juice if wine is out.

Nutrient Values per Serving:
Calories: 223. Protein: 19.7 g. Carbohydrate: 10.6 g. Dietary Fiber: 2.373 g. Total Sugars: .425 g. Total Fat: 10.2 g. Saturated Fat: 5.953 g. Monounsaturated Fat: 2.902 g. Polyunsaturated Fat: .659 g. Cholesterol: 63.2 mg. Calcium: 118.2 mg. Iron: 1.352 mg. Potassium: 820.1 mg. Sodium: 116.6 mg. Vitamin K: 29.5 mcg. Folate: 40 mcg.

❈ HEARTY BOAR SOUP ❈

This soup, inspired by French Master Chef Paul Bocuse, makes good use of boar bones and frequently discarded scraps. If you can hot-smoke the bones and meat rather than roasting them, so much the better!

SERVES 8 SODIUM PER RECIPE: 1,112MG
SODIUM PER SERVING: 139 MG

3 pounds wild boar bones and joints with some meat attached (estimated: 765 mg)

1 cup dried pinto beans, soaked overnight in 1 quart bottled water (19.3 mg)

1 cup dried white or navy beans, soaked overnight in 1 quart bottled water (25.8 mg)

3 quarts no-sodium bottled water (trace)

1 teaspoon Don's Herbes de Provence Spice Mix (page 175) (1.2 mg)

¼ teaspoon Don's Flavor Enhancer (page 177) (.43 mg)

¼ teaspoon freshly ground black pepper (.231 mg)

1 cup washed, diced leeks, white part only (17.8 mg)

1½ cups diced carrots, (¼-inch cubes) (64.1 mg)

1½ cups diced zucchini, (¼-inch cubes) (5.58 mg)

1 cup cut-up green beans, strings removed (½-inch pieces) (6.6 mg)

2 cups diced potatoes, (½-inch cubes) (21 mg)

6 cloves garlic, minced (3.06 mg)

1 cup fresh basil leaves (1.696 mg)

¾ cup olive oil (trace)

2 cups chopped fresh ripe tomatoes (peeled, seeded, chopped, and drained) (32.4 mg)

3½ ounces dry small elbow macaroni pasta (20.9 mg)

4 ounces low-sodium or low-sodium Cheddar (Heluva Good or Rumiano) (127.9 mg)

Preheat the oven to 375°F. Place the boar bones and joints in a roasting pan and roast in the oven until well browned. Place the soaked beans, browned boar bones and joints, and the water in a large stockpot and bring to a boil. Reduce the heat to low, add Don's Herbes de Provence Spice Mix, Don's Flavor Enhancer, and the pepper and simmer for 1 hour while skimming any foam or fat that rises to the surface. Add the leeks, carrots, zucchini, green beans, and potatoes, and continue simmering for an additional hour. Meanwhile, place ½ cup of the liquid from the stockpot with the garlic and basil in a food processor or blender. Blend for 10 seconds. While processing at low speed, add the oil in a thin stream until emulsified. Add the tomatoes and process for 2 to 3 seconds. Add the pasta and cook until tender, about 15 minutes. Remove the boar bones and joints. Take the stockpot from the heat and stir in the mixture from the processor. Let stand for 10 minutes. Serve in bowls and top each with low-sodium Cheddar cheese.

Nutrient Values per Serving:
Calories: 744.2. Protein: 63.6 g. Carbohydrate: 52 g. Dietary Fiber: 16 g. Total Sugars: .319 g. Total Fat: 31.4 g. Saturated Fat: 6.936 g. Monounsaturated Fat: 18.6 g. Polyunsaturated Fat: 3.38 g. Cholesterol: 143.7 mg. Calcium: 261.2 mg. Iron: 7.407 mg. Potassium: 1903 mg. Sodium: 139 mg. Vitamin K: 18 mcg. Folate: 306.2 mcg.

◆ NEW MEXICO VENISON CHILI ◆

The perfect cure for a winter chill. This version is a bit spicy, so reduce the chipotle and/or jalapeño chilies if you prefer a milder version.

SERVES 8   SODIUM PER RECIPE: 915.2 MG
SODIUM PER SERVING: 114.4 MG

3 **pounds (or less) venison shoulder, sirloin, or rump roast, cut into 1-inch cubes (694 mg)**
½ **teaspoon cumin (1.764 mg)**
¾ **teaspoon Grandma's or other no-salt chili powder (trace) plus 3 tablespoons (trace)**
4 **tablespoons extra virgin olive oil (trace)**
1 **large yellow onion, diced (4.5 mg)**
2 **Anaheim peppers, seeded and diced* (.28 mg)**
1 **medium red bell pepper, seeded and chopped (2.38 mg)**
1 **jalapeño pepper, seeded and very finely diced (.14 mg) (see Caution below)**
5 **cloves garlic, minced (2.55 mg)**
¼ **teaspoon dried oregano flakes (trace)**

*Caution: When preparing hot peppers such as jalapeños, make sure to wear rubber gloves and wash your hands thoroughly afterward. If you cut a jalapeño and then touch your eyes, you will appreciate this word of caution.

1 tablespoon ground cumin (10.1 mg)
¼ teaspoon dried red pepper flakes (9.135 mg)
4 cups drained canned Eden Organic Pinto Beans (120 mg)
3 cups drained, no-salt-added canned diced tomatoes (72 mg)
¼ cup chopped fresh cilantro (6.21 mg)
   Don's Flavor Enhancer to taste (page 177)
   Pepper to taste (.861 mg)

In a paper bag or large bowl, toss the venison with the cumin and ¾ tea-spoon chili powder. Heat the oil in a large skillet over medium heat and brown the seasoned meat evenly. Add the onion, peppers, and garlic. Cook 3 to 4 more minutes or until the onions become translucent, but not browned. Transfer the contents of the skillet to a large stockpot over medium heat and add the remaining ingredients except the cilantro, flavor enhancer, and pepper. Cover and cook until the chili begins to bubble, stirring occasionally. Reduce the heat to a simmer, cover and cook until the meat is tender, about 1½ hours. Stir in the cilantro. Season with Don's Flavor Enhancer and the pepper.

Nutrient Values per Serving:
Calories: 341.6. Protein: 46.7 g. Carbohydrate: 26.1 g. Dietary Fiber: 7.916 g. Total Sugars: 0 g. Total Fat: 4.57 g. Saturated Fat: 1.667 g. Monounsaturated Fat: 1.302 g. Polyunsaturated Fat: .939 g. Cholesterol: 144.6 mg. Calcium: 55.5 mg. Iron: 7.123 mg. Potassium: 1198 mg. Sodium: 114.4 mg. Vitamin K: .375 mcg. Folate: 24.7 mcg.

❈ PORTUGUESE VENISON STEW ❈

DIABETIC ACCEPTABLE

Real linguica sausage is what makes this "Portuguese." However, we can't have linguica so we're using Don's Sweet Italian Sausage and it works great. Top with garlic croutons.

SERVES 8   SODIUM PER RECIPE: 605.6 MG
SODIUM PER SERVING: 75.7 MG

½ pound Don's Sweet Italian Sausage (page 60) (128.4 mg)
½ cup finely chopped red onion
½ cup coarsely chopped green bell pepper (1.49 mg)
½ cup coarsely chopped red bell pepper (1.49 mg)
1 pound venison stew meat, cut into 1-inch cubes (231.3 mg)
1 cup peeled, cubed russet potato (cut into 1-inch cubes) (10.5 mg)
4 cups low-sodium Game Stock (page 50) (194.2 mg) or low-sodium Beef Broth (page 51) (74.4 mg)

3 cloves garlic, minced (1.53 mg)
1 teaspoon dried oregano flakes (.255 mg)
1 tablespoon finely dried fresh rosemary (.442 mg)
2 dried bay leaves (.091 mg)
½ teaspoon freshly ground black pepper (.462 mg)
2 cups diced fresh, ripe tomatoes (32.4 mg)
   Don's Flavor Enhancer (page 177) and white pepper to taste
      (trace)

In a large stockpot over medium-high heat, cook Don's Italian Sausage recipe until browned. Add the onion and peppers and cook for an additional 3 minutes. Add the venison and brown evenly. Stir in the potato, stock, and garlic. Bring to a boil and reduce the heat to a simmer. Add the oregano, rosemary, bay leaves, and pepper. Cover and cook until the venison is tender, about 1 hour, depending on the quality of the meat. Remove the bay leaves and add the tomato.

Season with white pepper (trace) to taste.

Nutrient Values per Serving (Figured with Game Stock):
Calories: 319.3. Protein: 23.3 g. Carbohydrate: 9.052 g. Dietary Fiber: 2.636 g. Total Sugars: .159 g. Total Fat: 21.1 g. Saturated Fat: 6.816 g. Monounsaturated Fat: 10.1 g. Polyunsaturated Fat: 2.316 g. Cholesterol: 89.5 mg. Calcium: 44.4 mg. Iron: 3.542 mg. Potassium: 663.2 mg. Sodium: 75.7 mg. Vitamin K: 8.853 mcg. Folate: 31.9 mcg.

❖ RABBIT MULLIGATAWNY SOUP ❖

Scott Leysath told me this was, "Always one of my favorite year-round soups. Try it with light-fleshed game birds as well." Domestic, wild, or domestically grown wild work with this recipe.

Try adding a dash of white pepper and Don's Herbes de Provence Spice Mix (page 175) (trace) to taste to this recipe.

SERVES 8   SODIUM PER RECIPE (CHICKEN STOCK): 355.1 MG
SODIUM PER RECIPE (GAME STOCK): 466.3 MG
SODIUM PER SERVING (CHICKEN BROTH): 44.4 MG
SODIUM PER SERVING (GAME STOCK): 58.3 MG

¼ cup all-purpose white unbleached flour (.625 mg)
1 teaspoon garlic powder (.728 mg)
1 teaspoon Don's Flavor Enhancer (page 177) (.861 mg)
½ teaspoon freshly ground black pepper (.462 mg)
2 cups ½-inch cubes cottontail rabbit or hare or 12 ounces
   (170.1 mg)

3 tablespoons extra virgin olive oil (trace)
¼ cup dry white wine* (8 mg) (optional)
2 tablespoons unsalted butter (3.124 mg)
½ cup diced carrot (22.4 mg)
½ cup diced celery (52.2 mg)
⅓ cup diced red onion (1.598 mg)
2 teaspoons curry powder (2.08 mg)
1 quart Game Stock (page 50) (194.2 mg) or Maureen's Chicken
    Broth (page 48) (83 mg)
2 cloves garlic, minced (1.02 mg)
1 pinch of coriander (.05 mg)
1 teaspoon freshly grated ginger (.26 mg)
⅔ cup cubes Granny Smith apple (¼-inch cubes) (trace)
1 cup cooked basmati rice (trace)
½ cup diced fresh tomato (.01 mg)

Combine the flour, garlic powder, Don's Flavor Enhancer (page 177), and black pepper. Place in a bag, add the rabbit pieces, and toss to coat thoroughly. Over medium-high heat, in a medium-size stockpot, heat the oil and sauté the rabbit until browned. Deglaze the pot with the wine, scraping up any bits that have stuck to the pan. Add the butter and sauté the carrot, celery, and onion for 3 minutes. Sprinkle the curry powder over the contents of the pan and stir to blend. Add the stock, garlic, coriander, and ginger. Bring to a boil, stir and reduce the heat to low. Cover and simmer for 20 minutes. Add the apple cubes and rice. Cook 6 to 7 minutes more. Add the diced tomato and serve hot.

Nutrient Values per Serving if Using Chicken Broth:
Calories: 207.3. Protein: 12.1 g. Carbohydrate: 15 g. Dietary Fiber: 1.796 g.
Total Sugars: 0 g. Total Fat: 10.2 g. Saturated Fat: 3.097 g. Monounsaturated Fat: 5.288 g.
Polyunsaturated Fat: 1.037 g. Cholesterol: 47.9 mg. Calcium: 28.8 mg. Iron: 2.757 mg.
Potassium: 359.4 mg. Sodium: 44.4 mg. Vitamin K: 5.524 mcg. Folate: 19.9 mcg.

Nutrient Values per Serving if Using Game Stock:
Calories: 334.8. Protein: 15 g. Carbohydrate: 16.1 g. Dietary Fiber: 2.159 g.
Total Sugars: 0 g. Total Fat: 22.6 g. Saturated Fat: 6.821 g. Monounsaturated Fat: 11.9 g.
Polyunsaturated Fat: 2.209 g. Cholesterol: 63.2 mg. Calcium: 38.9 mg. Iron: 3.031 mg.
Potassium: 455 mg. Sodium: 58.3 mg. Vitamin K: 8.168 mcg. Folate: 22.7 mcg.

*Because of health and medication reasons, check with your doctor before drinking or cooking with any alcoholic beverage.

Guaranteed to bring good luck for the New Year and a great way to utilize a variety of game meats. Stew can be prepared a day or two ahead.

SERVES 10   SODIUM PER RECIPE: *851* MG
SODIUM PER SERVING: *85.1* MG

- 1 cup all-purpose white unbleached flour (2.5 mg)
  Don's Flavor Enhancer (page 177) (trace)
  Black pepper to taste (trace)
- ⅔ pound varietal game meat, waterfowl, and/or game birds, boned and cut into bite-size pieces (283.4 mg)
- ¼ cup extra virgin olive oil
- 2 stalks celery, chopped (34.8 mg)
- 1 medium onion, chopped (3.3 mg)
- 2 medium green bell peppers, chopped (4.76 mg)
- 1 medium carrot, diced (21.4 mg)
- ½ pound sparerib meat, sliced into bite-size pieces (172.4 mg)
- 2 jalapeño peppers, seeded and finely diced* (.28 mg)
- 2 tablespoons minced garlic (4.59 mg)
- 1 16-ounce can no-salt-added diced or stewed tomatoes with juice (105 mg)
- 2 10-ounce packages frozen black-eyed (cowpea) peas (34 mg)
- 3 cups Game Stock (page 50) (144.9 mg) or Beef Broth (page 51) (55.7 mg)
- 1 tablespoon low-sodium Worcestershire sauce (4 mg)
- ½ teaspoon chili flakes (.27 mg)
- ¼ teaspoon dried red pepper flakes (9.135 mg)
- 2 dried bay leaves (.828 mg)

Season the flour with Don's Flavor Enhancer and black pepper to taste. Coat game meat with the seasoned flour. Heat the oil in a large, heavy stockpot on medium high and add all meat. Cook until evenly browned. Remove the meat, and cook until crispy. Add the celery, onion, peppers, and carrot and until the onion becomes translucent. Add the remaining ingredients, cover, and cook over low heat until the meat is tender, about 2 to 3 hours. Remove the bay leaves before serving.

*Caution: When preparing hot peppers such as jalapeños, make sure to wear rubber gloves and wash your hands thoroughly afterward. If you cut a jalapeño and then touch your eyes, you will appreciate this word of caution.

❧ DON'S SWEET ITALIAN SAUSAGE ❧

This authentic Italian sausage is a favorite of mine. If you stuff casings you'll really love these. If not, then patty or ball them, and freeze them separated from each other by wax or baking paper—or serve freshly made (cooked). Serve with pasta of any sort or add slices of this sausage (pre-cooked) to your favorite meat-based pasta sauce and, of course, to Don's Hero Sandwich (Page 78).

MAKES 1 POUND   SODIUM PER RECIPE: 256.8 MG
SODIUM PER OUNCE: 16.1 MG

1   **pound lean ground pork (253.1 mg) or turkey burger (428.6 mg)**
1½ **teaspoons Don's Flavor Enhancer (1.291 mg)**
1¼ **teaspoons white or black pepper (trace)**
¼   **tablespoon wild fennel seeds or anise seeds**
½   **tablespoon parsley, chopped (1.064 mg)**

Mix all ingredients by hand. Knead for about 3 minutes until you think everything is well blended. Cook links the way you always would. Fry patties in fry pan in very light spritz of olive oil until cooked through.

Nutrient Values per Ounce:
Calories: 75.7. Protein: 4.827 g. Carbohydrate: .259 g. Dietary Fiber: .088 g. Total Sugars: 0 g. Total Fat: 6.017 g. Saturated Fat: 2.227 g. Monounsaturated Fat: 2.683 g. Polyunsaturated Fat: .547 g. Cholesterol: 20.3 mg. Calcium: 6.236 mg. Iron: .313 mg. Potassium: 85.4 mg. Sodium: 16.1 mg. Vitamin K: .641 mcg. Folate: 1.764 mcg.

SANDWICHES

❖ ❖ ❖ ❖ ❖ ❖ ❖ ❖

THE HISTORY OF THE SANDWICH

It would be pretentious of me to attempt to write the history of the sandwich. Yet, one is tempted to reflect upon the history of the sandwich in our own lives. That is: Was peanut butter and jelly the first sandwich or was it one laced with potato chips, or just a piece of bread smothered in mayonnaise?

Gross, you declare?

Well, when I put the question on megaheart.com that I was seeking the "best sandwich you ever made or ate" for this short verse, I hardly expected to receive back what, well, what came back as sandwiches.

"Cut a diagonal groove into a banana lengthwise and fill it with peanut butter. Then roll bread over that and eat with great pleasure."

"Pickles and peanut butter, mmm, my favorite."

"Mustard, pickles and onions on rye. No meat."

"Black olives, sliced, diced, crushed, I don't care. Mix with cream cheese and spread on a huge piece of white bread and slap it together with another. Best darned sandwich I ever ate."

And so on. Oh, of course I received the ubiquitous hamburger recipes, lettuce, tomato, and avocado, and bacon (pre–heart disease), but it was the wilder the better that got me.

Then I had to reflect upon my own theories of what a great sandwich was when I was a youngster. Of course I remember the peanut butter and jam or jelly, but there were others back then, too. The crazy sandwiches were when mother was not there to take care of our lunch. While she was off shopping or helping others we'd hit the kitchen and grab whatever there was, slam it between bread and call it a sandwich. That could include graham crackers, potato chips, even peanuts. Throw in some jam or peanut butter and *that's* a sandwich.

Or so we thought.

So, where did the sandwich come from? Who actually put the

first one together? We've heard of "the Earl of Sandwich," and indeed there's even a town in the U.K. named after the earl. But was he the first?

Some believe it was a rabbi named Hillel, who conveniently or out of frustration pressed some chopped nuts, apples, spices, and other things available between two matzos to eat with bitter herbs during Passover. That was B.C. time.

Around 1762, though, some scribes in London did in fact record John Montagu's (fourth earl of Sandwich) putting together some cheese, bread, and meat while gambling. He was hungry; he called for the ingredients (probably without thinking of a sandwich). He needed one hand free, so he held the food together with two pieces of bread and continued playing cards with the free hand. The other players liked the looks of his meal so much they too ordered what "Sandwich" has. This little event put Montagu down as a recognized place in history.

In 1827, it is recorded, an Englishwoman, Eliza Leslie, wrote a cookbook for Americans and gave a recipe for "ham sandwiches as a main dish."

By 1900, commercial bakeries began producing loaves of soft white bread for retail sale. By the 1920s, children were carrying sandwiches to school in metal lunch pails, forerunners of the "lunch box." What was most popular then? Ham and eggs.

Along came a small restaurant in 1921 in Wichita, Kansas, known as White Castle. It became America's first hamburger chain.

Wonder Bread arrived in the 1930s with a soft white loaf of bread presliced for sandwiches. This bread revolutionized sandwich making and thus began the phrase, "the best thing since sliced bread."

Remember *Blondie,* the comic strip? Remember Dagwood's giant sandwich? And there was Blimpie, too, another comic character. Dagwood Bumstead, however, made it a habit to raid the icebox to build giant stacks of fillings that were not compatible. The Dagwood sandwich probably influenced my brothers, sisters, and me. It certainly influenced the *Webster's New World Dictionary* because it made it into that serious book.

Our GIs invented PB&J it is said during WWII. Now, I ate those same C rations a few years later. What you found in there was what we called John Wayne Biscuits (a very hard cookie-shaped biscuit), peanut butter as old as the history of sandwiches, and some jam. The GIs would slam the jam, peanut butter, and John Wayne cookie together and call them PB&Js. After returning home, they continued the habit. I remember my mother making us peanut butter and jam sandwiches some time after we became involved in that war.

I confess to having made a lot of peanut butter and banana sandwiches back then. Yet, some historians claim it was Elvis Presley who invented the banana/peanut butter sandwich. I don't accept that since I ate them years before Elvis hit the scene. I believe he simply presented the sandwich in his movie *Blue Suede Shoes*, and that brought it national attention.

Picnics were another great place (and still are) to present new inventions for sandwiches. However, at picnics, as a child, I always demanded egg salad or "deviled egg" sandwiches. To me there wasn't anything else for a picnic. Once again though, this type of sandwich always presented a challenge. You had to keep them chilled because of the eggs and mayonnaise in them. Today you can find a very low-sodium version in this book (page 75). It's not the same high oil, high-sodium sandwich, but it tastes great, especially if you're picnicking on a nice spring day in the mountains or along a waterside.

MREs have replaced C rations for our military men and women. And thanks to chemicals, preservatives, and vacuum packaging, we can serve these troops a meal that is actually a lot tastier than the John Wayne biscuits and aged peanut butter. (By the way, the C rations always had a small package of four cigarettes in them. What a way to hook our youth back then.)

MREs now have sandwiches of pepperoni, barbecued chicken, and other varieties that store without refrigeration for up to three years. Ummmm, ummm, delicious! ☺

When I first began building the sandwich section for this book, I naturally tested my own concoctions first. Then I did some research and found other popular sandwiches . . . but many had way too much sodium in them. I was amazed at how much sodium can be poured into one little lunch. I found sandwich recipes with more than 3,000 mg of sodium and some with so much fat that "heart attack" should have been included in their names. (A famous monthly magazine nearly always features a huge sandwich with enough sodium to force us to dial 911.)

Take the Reuben sandwich for instance. It has been claimed that this high-sodium sandwich was "invented" by more than one sandwich maker of note. One story goes that a landmark delicatessen in Manhattan named Reuben's was responsible. The owner's daughter declares that her father (Arnold) created the sandwich in 1914 to feed Annette Seelos, Charlie Chaplin's hungry leading lady. Yet others claim that in Omaha a wholesale grocer named Reuben Kulakofsky created the sandwich at the city's Blackstone Hotel in 1925 (or 1922 in other versions)—to feed late-night poker players. (Seems gambling has played a large role in sandwich development.)

It doesn't end there. In 1956, Fern Snider, a waitress at the Omaha bowling alley The Rose Bowl entered the recipe in a national sandwich competition and won. Documentation that the sandwich also was featured at the Cornhusker Hotel in Lincoln, Nebraska, back in 1937 also exists. That one was built like the Reuben we know today. Corned beef (or pastrami), sauerkraut, Swiss cheese on Russian rye with a Russian-type dressing and lots of butter to fry them in.

So, after all this somewhat questionable history concerning the Reuben, is it the highest in sodium? Close. (See answer at the end of this article.) A "standard" Reuben contains more than 2,293 milligrams of sodium. Worse, it has 50 grams of fat, half of those saturated. Make a regular lunch of that sandwich and you'll get to know your cardiologist or paramedics real well.

The sandwiches in this book are all low in sodium and most are low in fat with many adaptable for diabetics and vegetarians.

One of my favorites is a sandwich I have since discovered has many different names and slightly different ingredients. It uses fresh basil, fresh mozzarella (no salt), tomatoes, olive oil, and vinegar and any of my sandwich or bread recipes in this book. It's easy to put together, healthy, and very low in sodium.

The only sandwich in this book that I would make only once a year is my Hero Sandwich. There are just some things we can't give up although we do have to alter the recipe and adapt the flavor. A hero or a big boy, or whatever you like to call it, uses sausage. So, I've put together a good sausage recipe for you that is included here (page 31), so you can make this sandwich. Just cut it in half and serve it to two of you and you'll be okay.

I have included some new bread recipes just for the sandwiches in this book and some spice mixes, sauces, a new mayonnaise substitute, and other recipes that you can use for sandwiches. I've also re-created the bread enhancer that I've used previously. If you own a copy of *The No-Salt, Lowest-Sodium Baking Book*, just exchange the orange zest in recipes with Sure-Jell Ever-Fresh. Sure-Jell Ever-Fresh has pure citric acid in it, which has proved nearly impossible to buy in a retail outlet. Diabetics may want to stick with the sugarless orange zest. Sure-Jell has 12 grams of sugars per tablespoon. For more information about our salads and soups, see the articles directed toward them.

What's the highest-sodium "homemade" sandwich I've seen? It's called Turkey Pastrami on Irish Soda Bread. It's rated at 4,710 milligrams of sodium per sandwich. It also has 126.1 grams of fat, 22.4 of those saturated. The sandwich contains 2,041 calories. The National Turkey Federation posts it on the Internet.

Note: None of the above data includes or refers to fast-food restaurants, and all refer only to homemade recipes. Fast-food shops often exceed homemade varieties.

Note: There are more than a few towns in the United States named Sandwich.

❖ BAKED SALMON SALAD SANDWICH ❖

DIABETIC ACCEPTABLE*

When you cook too much fresh salmon for yourself or your guests and the refrigerator contains the leftovers, here's one way to use up that delicious and very healthy meat. Use baked, poached, or barbecued salmon for this sandwich mix. If you don't have close to a pound of leftovers, then just cut this recipe in half.

MAKES 4 TO 6 SANDWICHES   SODIUM PER RECIPE: 271.8 MG
SODIUM PER SANDWICH (4): 68 MG
SODIUM PER SANDWICH (6): 45.3 MG

15 ounces leftover baked† salmon (195.5 mg)
⅓ cup plain lowfat or regular yogurt (56.8 mg)
⅓ cup sliced (or diced) mushrooms (.924 mg)
⅓ cup chopped green onions (5.28 mg)

*Most of the sugars are in the bread. Make the bread with Splenda to reduce the sugars to near zero.
†Baked, poached, or barbecued salmon will work.

1 tablespoon fresh lemon juice (.15 mg)
   White pepper to taste (.15)
   Don's Flavor Enhancer to taste (page 177) (trace)
8 to 12 slices Don's White Sandwich Bread* (page 123) (13.4 mg)

Cut the salmon into bite-size pieces. In a medium or large mixing bowl, stir in the yogurt, mushrooms, onions, and lemon juice.

Season with the white pepper or Don's Flavor Enhancer.

Toast the bread; spread one piece with the salmon mixture and cover with the other. Serve immediately.

Nutrient Values per Sandwich (4)
Calories: 486.6. Protein: 34 g. Carbohydrate: 58.7 g. Dietary Fiber: 4.866 g. Total Sugars: 2.339 g. Total Fat: 12.7 g. Saturated Fat: 2.385 g. Monounsaturated Fat: 6.22 g. Polyunsaturated Fat: 2.935 g. Cholesterol: 49 mg. Calcium: 101.3 mg. Iron: 4.157 mg. Potassium: 724.4 mg. Sodium: 68 mg. Vitamin K: 2.481 mcg. Folate: 136.1 mcg.

Nutrient Values per Sandwich (6):
Calories: 324.4. Protein: 22.7 g. Carbohydrate: 39.1 g. Dietary Fiber: 3.244 g. Total Sugars: 1.559 g. Total Fat: 8.46 g. Saturated Fat: 1.59 g. Monounsaturated Fat: 4.147 g. Polyunsaturated Fat: 1.957 g. Cholesterol: 32.7 mg. Calcium: 67.5 mg. Iron: 2.771 mg. Potassium: 482.9 mg. Sodium: 45.3 mg. Vitamin K: 1.654 mcg. Folate: 90.7 mcg.

❧ BARBECUED TURKEY SANDWICH ❧

NOT ADAPTABLE FOR DIABETICS WITHOUT AFFECTING FLAVOR

You can use leftover turkey from Thanksgiving or start fresh with a new turkey breast. If using cooked leftover turkey, then heat with the ingredients below and serve. Quick, easy, and delicious.

MAKES 4 SANDWICHES   SODIUM PER RECIPE: 405.6 MG
SODIUM PER SANDWICH: 101.4 MG

1 cup Don's Quick Barbecue Sauce† (page 171, *No-Salt, Lowest-Sodium Cookbook*) (60.4 mg)
¼ cup cider vinegar (.6 mg)
¼ cup natural maple syrup‡ (7.088 mg)
1 pound uncooked turkey breast, packaged without salt or added sodium (254.2 mg)
4 Don's Tasty Burger Buns, toasted (page 119) (82.3 mg)
½ cup freshly cooked cranberry sauce§ (1.077 mg)

*Based on twelve slices.
†Page 171, *The No-Salt, Lowest-Sodium Cookbook*.
‡Natural means not artificial like Log Cabin and other commercial varieties.
§Page 303, *The No-Salt, Lowest-Sodium Cookbook*.

Mix together Don's Quick Barbecue Sauce and the vinegar and syrup.

Barbecue the turkey breast (or broil if no barbecue is handy). While cooking, swath the meat with the barbecue sauce. If broiling, let the breast cook three-quarters through before swabbing with the sauce. Let cook for about 5 minutes, then turn once and swab the other side until the breast is done.

Serve on toasted sandwich rolls, topped with 2 tablespoons of freshly made cranberry sauce. (More if you like.)

Serve.

Nutrient Values per Sandwich:
Calories: 503.8. Protein: 38.1 g. Carbohydrate: 73.4 g. Dietary Fiber: 2.501 g. Total Sugars: 39.1 g. Total Fat: 7.043 g. Saturated Fat: 1.392 g. Monounsaturated Fat: 3.926 g. Polyunsaturated Fat: .88 g. Cholesterol: 94.6 mg. Calcium: 84.2 mg. Iron: 8.048 mg. Potassium: 689.5 mg. Sodium: 101.4 mg. Vitamin K: 2.683 mcg. Folate: 84.2 mcg.

FRESH BASIL SANDWICH
❂ WITH MOZZARELLA AND TOMATO SLICES ❂

DIABETIC ADAPTABLE*

One of the pleasures of life is that we can adapt many healthy foods to great-tasting combinations. No longer do we need the high-sodium fast foods when we have flavors like fresh basil, fresh tomatoes, and low-sodium mozzarella. Use our fresh, low-sodium sandwich bread or French Garlic Rolls (page 104) and this treat will become a habit.

This recipe uses a low-sodium mozzarella cheese from Trader Joe's and other supermarkets. This same mozzarella can be used in my Lasagna (page 113, No-Salt, Lowest-Sodium Cookbook), instead of the roux. There are other brands of low-sodium mozzarella available, but often they are found in specialty stores and not in general supermarkets.

MAKES 1 SANDWICH   SODIUM PER RECIPE: 28.8 MG

1 **Fresh baguette bun (page 113) (6.081 mg)**
6 **leaves fresh basil (.12 mg)**
2 **thin slices from large tomato (2.43 mg)**
3 **mozzarella balls, cut in half (20 mg)**

*Most of the sugars are in the bread. Make the bread with Splenda to reduce the sugars to near zero.

½ tablespoon olive oil (trace)
1 tablespoon raspberry vinegar (.15 mg)

In a toaster oven, lightly toast the "interior" side of the bread after slicing. Layer the basil, tomato, and cheese on one side. Lightly toast the layered section until the cheese just begins to melt.

Stir together the olive oil and vinegar and spritz the other half of the sandwich.

Nutrient Values per Serving:
Calories: 269. Protein: 9.746 g. Carbohydrate: 28 g. Dietary Fiber: 1.515 g. Total Sugars: 1.027 g. Total Fat: 9.739 g. Saturated Fat: 1.047 g. Monounsaturated Fat: 5.198 g. Polyunsaturated Fat: 1.021 g. Cholesterol: 10 mg. Calcium: 25.4 mg. Iron: 2.036 mg. Potassium: 146.9 mg. Sodium: 28.8 mg. Vitamin K: 4.988 mcg. Folate: 69.1 mcg.

BRUSCHETTA
❈ WITH TOMATOES AND MOZZARELLA ❈

DIABETIC ADAPTABLE*

While working in Italy, I grabbed a "quick" sandwich from a local restorante. It turned out to be the best sandwich I ate on that trip. It was called a Bruschetta, which in Italian means, "Garlic bread with tomatoes and herbs." Mine had Parmesan or Romano but you can make it with any low-sodium cheese. You can also pick your own herbs. I like to use a pinch of Don's Herbes de Provence Spice Mix (page 175) or sometimes just a pinch of fresh oregano. The mozzarella can be mixed with a low-sodium Swiss or Muenster. Either way, this is a delicious and easy-to-make sandwich.

MAKES 4   SODIUM PER RECIPE: 39.6 MG
SODIUM PER TOASTED SLICE: 9.891

3 plum tomatoes, finely chopped (24.6 mg)
½ red onion, finely chopped (2.4 mg)
2 cloves garlic, minced (1.02 mg)
¼ cup chopped fresh basil (.424 mg)
¼ pound fresh-packed in water mozzarella, either grated, finely chopped, or thinly sliced (7.345 mg)
2 tablespoons balsamic or red wine vinegar (.3 mg)
4 tablespoons olive oil (trace)

*Most of the sugars are in the bread. Make the bread with Splenda to reduce the sugars to an acceptable level.

¼ teaspoon Don's Flavor Enhancer (page 177) (.215 mg) or a
   spice or mix of spices of your choice
4 slices Italian Milano Bread* toasted (3.291 mg)

Preheat the broiler. In a large bowl combine the tomatoes, onion, garlic, basil, and mozzarella. Stir in the balsamic vinegar and olive oil. Season with Don's Flavor Enhancer. Top the toasted bread with the mixture and place on a baking sheet. Broil until the cheese melts. Serve hot.

Nutrient Values per Slice:
Calories: 266.8. Protein: 5.765 g. Carbohydrate: 27.7 g. Dietary Fiber: 2.069 g. Total Sugars: 1.663 g. Total Fat: 15.3 g. Saturated Fat: 2.674 g. Monounsaturated Fat: 10.4 g. Polyunsaturated Fat: 1.397 g. Cholesterol: 3.814 mg. Calcium: 71 mg. Iron: 2.287 mg. Potassium: 255.2 mg. Sodium: 9.891 mg. Vitamin K: 11.1 mcg. Folate: 68.2 mcg.

❖ DON'S CALIFORNIA BEACH SANDWICH ❖

DIABETIC ADAPTABLE[†]

On a hot summer afternoon an airy light sandwich is called for. Every time I make this sandwich I am reminded of those childhood happy days on the beaches of Southern California when we either picnicked on this sandwich or my mother's deviled egg sandwiches. This one often had a "sand" taste for us younger types since we had a tough time holding it together with our smaller hands . . . but as I aged, I came to appreciate it for its healthy lightness and the juxtaposition of flavors not always found elsewhere. At least you don't have to eat it on a blanket stretched out on the sand.

**MAKES TWO 8-INCH SANDWICHES   SODIUM PER RECIPE: 140.4 MG
SODIUM PER SANDWICH: 70.2 MG**

2 Don's Sandwich Buns (page 116) (3.198 mg)
2 tablespoons low-fat or light sour cream[‡] (12.3 mg)
½ cup mashed avocado (about ¾ avocado) (15.6 mg)
1 medium fresh tomato, chopped (about ½ cup) (8.1 mg)
¼ cup B&G Unsalted Crunchy Kosher Dills (trace)[§] (optional)

---

*See page 247 of *The No-Salt, Lowest-Sodium Cookbook*, or use the Tuscan Bread (page 122) in this book and slice it into sandwich-size buns.
[†]Most of the sugars are in the bread. Make the bread with Splenda to reduce the sugars to near zero.
[‡]Sodium levels vary from brand to brand. (see Glossary sour cream)
[§]Available from www.healthyheartmarket.com.

4 **thin slices cooked chicken breast (76.7 mg)**
1 **slice low-sodium Swiss cheese (8.61 mg)**
½ **cup shredded romaine or butterhead lettuce (2.24 mg)**
6 **thin slices red onion (1.62 mg)**
2 **tablespoons balsamic vinegar (.3 mg)**

Toast the sandwich buns.

Puree the sour cream and avocado together and use as a spread on each sliced half of sandwich bun.

Mix together the chopped tomato and pickles, if you are using them.

Layer the sandwich buns with the chicken, cheese, lettuce, and onion. Sprinkle the tomato/pickle mix over this and then spritz with the balsamic vinegar. You may serve the sandwich cut in half.

Nutrient Values per Sandwich:
Calories: 446.3. Protein: 25.1 g. Carbohydrate: 50.7 g. Dietary Fiber: 7.99 g. Total Sugars: 1.386 g. Total Fat: 18 g. Saturated Fat: 4.912 g. Monounsaturated Fat: 9.224 g. Polyunsaturated Fat: 2.089 g. Cholesterol: 49 mg. Calcium: 209.9 mg. Iron: 6.698 mg. Potassium: 1267 mg. Sodium: 70.2 mg. Vitamin K: 3.561 mcg. Folate: 190.5 mcg.

❄ CHICKEN SALAD SANDWICH ❄

DIABETIC ACCEPTABLE*

Always a refreshing lunch during a warm spring day.

MAKES 4 SANDWICHES   SODIUM PER RECIPE: 326 MG
SODIUM PER SANDWICH: 81.5 MG

2 **cooked boneless, skinless chicken breast halves**
   Approx ½ pound (153.4 mg)
1 **large stalk celery (55.7 mg)**
½ **medium onion (1.65 mg)**
1 **hard-boiled egg (63 mg)**
¼ **cup homemade mayonnaise† (31.4 mg) or Don's Sandwich**
   Vinaigrette
½ **teaspoon oregano (.112 mg)**
⅛ **teaspoon white pepper (trace)**
4 **Don's Sandwich Buns (page 116) (6.395 mg)**
1 **medium tomato, cut into 8 thin slices (11.1 mg)**
4 **leave butterhead or romaine lettuce (3.2 mg)**
   low sodium honey mustard to taste (trace) (optional)

*Most of the sugars are in the bread. Make the bread with Splenda to reduce the sugar to near zero.
†See page 306, *No-Salt, Lowest-Sodium Cookbook* for homemade recipe. Also, start with only 2 tablespoons. If that's enough, then don't add the full ¼ cup (4 tablespoons).

Coarsely chop the cooked chicken, celery, onion, and egg and mix with the homemade mayonnaise or with Don's Sandwich Vinaigrette, the oregano, and the pepper. (You may use a food processor for this but click on and off only about three or four times to get the right consistency.)

Slice each bun in half. Lightly toast the open side. Spread the chicken mixture on one side of the bread; add two tomato slices, one leaf of lettuce, and top with the second half of the bun.

Nutrient Values per Sandwich:
Calories: 296.1. Protein: 22 g. Carbohydrate: 37.5 g. Dietary Fiber: 2.81 g. Total Sugars: .693 g. Total Fat: 6.17 g. Saturated Fat: 1.867 g. Monounsaturated Fat: 2.394 g. Polyunsaturated Fat: 1.112 g. Cholesterol: 90.6 mg. Calcium: 58.6 mg. Iron: 3.148 mg. Potassium: 434 mg. Sodium: 81.5 mg. Vitamin K: 4.847 mcg. Folate: 112.1 mcg.

❖ HOT "TO GO" CHILI PEPPER BURGERS ❖

DIABETIC ADAPTABLE*

I'm not sure where the first Togo's sandwich shop was. Legend in Hollywood has it that it began on Gower and Hollywood Boulevard across from the old ABC studios. Production assistants would order sandwiches from the shop there, and then pick them up. They began calling them to-goes. You can figure the rest out. One of the sandwiches from that shop (before it was named Togo's) was a hot chili burger. I figured the first time I ordered it that it would be chili beans. Nope, it was deli beef with hot chilies and it was great! Here's my interpretation, using fresh ground beef.

**MAKES 4 CHILI PEPPER BURGERS   SODIUM PER RECIPE: 275.6 MG
SODIUM PER BURGER: 68.9 MG**

⅓ cup chopped green onion (5.328 mg)
1 red serrano pepper, seeded and finely chopped† (1.22 mg)
   plus 2 additional red serrano peppers, chopped (1.22 mg)
1 pinch of Don's Flavor Enhancer (page 177) (trace)
¾ pound lean ground beef (223.7 mg)
2 cloves garlic, minced (.61 mg)
1 medium tomato, thinly sliced (11.1 mg)
½ red onion, thinly sliced (1.65 mg)

*Most of the sugars are in the bread and honey mustard. Make the bread with Splenda to reduce the sugars to an acceptable level. Leave the mustard out if the sugar level is too high.
†You can add one more serrano pepper (.61 mg) if you like really hot burgers.

4 **Don's Place Burger Buns, toasted* (page 111) (9.92 mg)**
2 **tablespoons no-salted-added ketchup (6 mg) (optional)**
1 **tablespoon honey mustard (15 mg) (optional)**

Caution: When preparing hot peppers such as serranos, make sure to wear rubber gloves and wash your hands thoroughly afterward. If you cut a serrano and then touch your eyes, you will appreciate this word of caution.

In a large mixing bowl, combine the green onion, garlic, one chopped serrano pepper, and Don's Flavor Enhancer. Add the beef; mix well. Shape the meat mixture into four equal-size patties.

Grill on your barbecue for about 15 minutes or until done.

Serve the burgers on grilled or toasted buns or on bread with the tomato slices, red onion slices, and the remaining chopped serrano peppers. Mix ketchup with the honey mustard and spread the mixture evenly on the bun.

Nutrient Values per Burger:
Calories: 492.3. Protein: 24.8 g. Carbohydrate: 57.6 g. Dietary Fiber: 4.026 g. Total Sugars: 3.579 g. Total Fat: 17.7 g. Saturated Fat: 6.222 g. Monounsaturated Fat: 8.059 g. Polyunsaturated Fat: 1.165 g. Cholesterol: 58.5 mg. Calcium: 34.4 mg. Iron: 5.058 mg. Potassium: 529.2 mg. Sodium: 68.9 mg. Vitamin K: 3.314 mcg. Folate: 129.9 mcg.

❖ CUBE STEAK HUNGER STRIKE ❖

DIABETIC ADAPTABLE[†]

Ever get really hungry for some protein but feel too lazy to make a sandwich containing what your taste buds are demanding? Here's a great solution for you. Pick up a package of 3- to 4-ounce cube steaks. Freeze them on a cookie sheet, keeping them separated, and then stack in a Ziploc bag. Store the steaks in your freezer. Pull one out when you want it. They thaw in a hurry since they're only about ⅛ to ¼ inch thick—or you can microwave-thaw them. They cook in a pan with very little oil in about 3 minutes over medium-high heat, turning once. Use your favorite bread or bun, white or whole wheat.

---

*You can also use your favorite no-salt-added sandwich bread, toasted. Another recommendation is Don's Sandwich Buns (page 116) (2.007 mg per bun).
[†]Most of the sugars are in the bread and honey mustard. Reduce the mustard to very low level and make the bread with Splenda to reduce its sugars to near zero.

1 3- to 4-ounce cube steak (49.3 mg)
¼ onion, thinly sliced (.825 mg)
1 ounce low-sodium Cheddar cheese* (10 mg)
2 slices Don's White Sandwich Bread† (page 123) (2.235 mg)
1 tablespoon honey mustard‡ (15 mg)
1 tablespoon no-salt-added ketchup (3 mg)
1 leaf iceberg or romaine lettuce, chilled (.72 mg)

Sauté the cube steak on medium-high with the onion. Heat the cheese on top of the meat near completion of the cooking.

Spread the bread with the mustard and ketchup; put the lettuce and sautéed onion on top of the bread. Place the hot meat on the other piece of bread and close the sandwich. Serve it hot. Check your liquid refreshment for the sodium level to add up your total lunch count.

Nutrient Values per Sandwich:
Calories: 491.6. Protein: 32.1 g. Carbohydrate: 50 g. Dietary Fiber: 3.844 g. Total Sugars: 7.559 g. Total Fat: 17.4 g. Saturated Fat: 2.072 g. Monounsaturated Fat: 4.283 g. Polyunsaturated Fat: .781 g. Cholesterol: 76.9 mg. Calcium: 228.8 mg. Iron: 4.728 mg. Potassium: 554.2 mg. Sodium: 81.1 mg. Vitamin K: 2.204 mcg. Folate: 97.3 mcg.

❁ CUCUMBER AVOCADO SANDWICH ❁

Cucumbers are one of the easiest vegetables to grow in your home garden. You can grow them for salads, sandwiches, and your own homemade pickles. You can make this in a long Baguette roll (double ingredients to make 4 sandwiches).

MAKES 2 SANDWICHES   SODIUM PER RECIPE: *27.8 MG*
SODIUM PER SANDWICH: *13.9 MG*

2 3-inch cuts from Don's French-Style Picnic Rolls
   (page 112) (1.767 mg)
¾ cup thinly sliced cucumber (1.785 mg)
1 medium tomato, thinly sliced (11.1 mg)
½ ripe California avocado (10.4 mg)
½ teaspoon Grandma's chili powder (trace)

---

*Heluva Good & Rumiano are making low-sodium Cheddar at this writing. Contact Heluva Good at www.heluvagood.com or Rumiano cheese at www.rumianocheese.com.
†Or use your favorite low-sodium bread.
‡East Shore, Mendocino, Grey Poupon—all the honey mustards have same low-sodium rating.

1 **teaspoon fresh lemon juice (.05 mg)**
2 **leaves romaine or iceberg lettuce (1.6 mg)**
4 **thin slices onion (1.08 mg)**
   white pepper to taste

Slice bread for sandwiches and lay out on countertop.

Clean and skin cucumber. Slice thinly. Clean and slice thinly the tomato.

Mash avocado with chili and lemon juice using a fork and spread each bread slice with mashed avocado. Arrange the cucumber slices on top of the avocado. Sprinkle cucumbers very lightly with white pepper.

Then arrange the tomatoes and onion slices over the cucumbers and pepper. Lay on the lettuce. Cover the cucumber, tomatoes, and lettuce with the remaining avocado spread slices.

Place the sandwiches on a serving plate and wrap with plastic wrap. Place in refrigerator to chill for 30 minutes and serve.

Picnicking & Tailgating: Place chilled sandwich platter into an ice chest. When ready to serve, unwrap and serve.

Nutrient Values per Sandwich:
Calories: 190.6. Protein: 4.779 g. Carbohydrate: 25.6 g. Dietary Fiber: 4.564 g. Total Sugars: .534 g. Total Fat: 8.855 g. Saturated Fat: 1.315 g. Monounsaturated Fat: 5.47 g. Polyunsaturated Fat: 1.178 g. Cholesterol: 0 mg. Calcium: 25.9 mg. Iron: 2.008 mg. Potassium: 577.4 mg. Sodium: 13.9 mg. Vitamin K: 4.418 mcg. Folate: 97.6 mcg.

❈ CUCUMBER SANDWICH ❈

DIABETIC ADAPTABLE*

Cucumbers are great when they first come in. Crisp them well in ice water for best flavor and enjoyment. This sandwich can be cut in half and served to two people. The Seven-Grain Bread recipe can be found in our No-Salt, Lowest-Sodium Baking Book. *It's a great recipe and works well with this sandwich.*

MAKES 1 SANDWICH   SODIUM PER SANDWICH: 34.2 MG

1 **tablespoon honey mustard (East Shore, Grey Poupon, or Mendocino) (trace)**
2 **thick slices Seven-Grain Bread† (10.2 mg)**

---

*All the sugars are in the bread. Make the bread with Splenda to reduce the sugars to zero.
†The recipe is on page 66 of *The No-Salt, Lowest-Sodium Baking Book*. To cut the calories in half or more, either use only one slice or cut them thinner. Four hundred of the calories in this sandwich are in the bread and 150 calories are in the avocado.

6 slices fresh, peeled, chilled cucumber (.84 mg)
2 tablespoons fresh alfalfa sprouts, washed (.36 mg) (optional)
1 teaspoon extra virgin olive oil (trace)
1 teaspoon red wine vinegar (trace)
1 slice low-sodium Swiss cheese (8.61 mg)
1 small tomato, sliced (8.19 mg)
1 leaf iceberg or romaine lettuce (.8 mg)
¼ avocado, mashed (5.2 mg)

Spread the mustard on the surface of the top slice of bread.

On the same top slice, lay three cucumber slices in a single layer. Do the same with the other top slices. Cover each top slice with half the sprouts, then sprinkle both top slices with the oil and vinegar. On each top slice, layer the cheese, tomato slices, and one lettuce leaf. Spread the other two slices of bread with the mashed avocado. Close the sandwich and serve immediately. You may also slice each sandwich into halves and serve one half along with a bowl of any soup in this book.

Nutrient Values per Sandwich:
Calories: 691.9. Protein: 19.2 g. Carbohydrate: 91.4 g. Dietary Fiber: 10.7 g. Total Sugars: 14 g. Total Fat: 30.2 g. Saturated Fat: 6.901 g. Monounsaturated Fat: 17.9 g. Polyunsaturated Fat: 3.251 g. Cholesterol: 17.9 mg. Calcium: 274.2 mg. Iron: 5.111 mg. Potassium: 989.1 mg. Sodium: 34.2 mg. Vitamin K: 13.1 mcg. Folate: 191.8. mcg.

❖ DEVILED EGG SANDWICH ❖

DIABETIC ADAPTABLE*

When I was growing up, this was one of my favorite picnic sandwiches. It probably had more salt in it than we needed, but this version will prove that you can make a great sandwich without salt. You can add your own flavors if you like, but please don't add the sand we used to get from our surfside picnics. Sand makes these just a bit too crunchy.

MAKES 4 SANDWICHES   SODIUM PER RECIPE: 235.6 MG
SODIUM PER SANDWICH: 58.9 MG

3 large whole eggs, hard-boiled (189 mg)
2 tablespoons Homemade Mayonnaise Substitute (page 306,
  No-Salt, Lowest-Sodium Cookbook) (36.8 mg)
  Sprinkle of paprika† (.714 mg) plus more to taste (optional)

---

*The sugars in this recipe are in the bread. Make the bread with Splenda to reduce the sugars to zero.
†Nutrient Values measured for 1 teaspoon paprika.

8 slices of your favorite no-salt sandwich bread (8.941 mg)
2 tablespoons chopped celery (13.1 mg) or 2 tablespoons chopped homemade dill pickle or B&G no-salt pickles (6.1 mg) (optional)

Shell the eggs and chop them; place into a small mixing bowl.

Stir in the homemade mayonnaise substitute. Use more paprika if you like.

Chill for about 2 to 3 hours before making the sandwiches. Spread the deviled eggs evenly on one side of bread, then cover with the other slice.

Serve immediately or wrap for a picnic and chill until served.

Nutrient Values per Sandwich:
Calories: 290.7. Protein: 11.8 g. Carbohydrate: 39 g. Dietary Fiber: 3.18 g. Total Sugars: 1.559 g. Total Fat: 9.918 g. Saturated Fat: 2.805 g. Monounsaturated Fat: 4.802 g. Polyunsaturated Fat: 1.181 g. Cholesterol: 163 mg. Calcium: 56.6 mg. Iron: 2.932 mg. Potassium: 206.7 mg. Sodium: 58.9 mg. Vitamin K: 1.932 mcg. Folate: 98.4 mcg.

❖ DON'S CALIFORNIA SWITCH ❖

DIABETIC ACCEPTABLE*

Remember the BLT? In California we used to call them "BLATs" an acronym for: Bacon, Lettuce, Avocado, and Tomato. No more bacon, that's for sure. So, I had to adapt this favorite sandwich somewhat extensively for my own tasty use and here it is now, for you as well. You can make this open-faced or standard.

MAKES 4 OPEN-FACED SANDWICHES   SODIUM PER RECIPE: 91.2 MG
SODIUM PER OPEN-FACED SANDWICH: 22.8 MG

1 medium ripe avocado, peeled and seeded (20.1 mg)
2 tablespoons light sour cream (25 mg)
1 teaspoon Grandma's No-Salt Chili Powder† (trace)
¼ cup chopped onion (1.2 mg)
   1 to 2 teaspoons lemon juice (.3 mg)
½ teaspoon Don's Herb Chicken Spices (1.0 mg) (See page 184 in *The No-Salt, Lowest-Sodium Cookbook*)

---

*The sugars are in the sour cream and English muffins. Make the muffins using Splenda to reduce the sugars.
†See pages 113–114 in *The No-Salt, Lowest-Sodium Baking Book*.

2 **Don's English Muffins, split and toasted (pages 113–114,**
   No-Salt, Lowest-Sodium Cookbook) **(19.4 mg)**
4 **slices tomato (7.2 mg)**
2 **slices low-sodium Swiss cheese, halved‡ (17.2 mg)**

Mash the avocado and sour cream with a fork; stir in the chili powder, onion, lemon juice, and Don's Herb Chicken Spices. Spread four muffin halves with the avocado mixture. Top with tomato and cheese.

Place the muffin halves on broiler rack in oven (preheat the broiler) or if you have a countertop toaster oven place the halves on a rack on the toaster's pan and broil. If there's enough room, toast the plain halves as well but don't over-toast them. Broil about 2 to 4 minutes or just until the cheese melts. Join the halves into a sandwich and serve immediately. Or, use just two muffins and serve half as an open-faced sandwich along with our Red Pepper with Carrot Soup (page 30).

Nutrients per Sandwich with 4 Muffins used:
Calories: 240.7. Protein: 8.043 g. Carbohydrate: 29.5 g. Dietary Fiber: 4.468 g. Total Sugars: .916 g. Total Fat: 11.4 g. Saturated Fat: 3.36 g. Monounsaturated Fat: 5.634 g. Polyunsaturated Fat: 1.214 g. Cholesterol: 17.4 mg. Calcium: 179.6 mg. Iron: 2.211 mg. Potassium: 556.4 mg. Sodium: 22.8 mg. Vitamin K: 21.5 mcg. Folate: 83.4 mcg.

DON'S SPECIAL CRANBERRY SANDWICH
❖ ## WITH LOW-SODIUM CHEDDAR CHEESE ❖

DIABETIC ADAPTABLE (WHEN MAKING CRANBERRY SAUCE)

You really want to make this with freshly cooked and chilled cranberry sauce. Ummmm, good. Canned cranberries will work but won't have the same great cranberry flavor, as the fresh will give you.

MAKES 4 SANDWICHES   SODIUM PER RECIPE: 106.8 MG
SODIUM PER SANDWICH: 26.7 MG

4 **Don's Secret Bread Recipe* buns, toasted (80.8 mg)**
1 **cup fresh whole cranberry sauce (2.155 mg)**
4 **ounces low-sodium Cheddar or Colby cheese, grated†**
   (23.8 mg)

‡Nutrient values are based on USDA low-sodium figures for the average of all products.
*Recipe in *The No-Salt, Lowest-Sodium Baking Book*, pages 82–83
†At this writing we have two low-sodium Cheddars available to us. One is from Heluva Good Quality Foods (www.heluvagood.com), and the other is from Rumiano Cheese Company (www.rumianocheese.com).

Make the bread according to the recipe in the *No-Salt, Lowest Sodium Baking Book*.

Prepare fresh cranberries per package instructions, leaving out any salt called for. Chill

Spread the cranberry sauce on the bottom half of a toasted bun. (Toast only the open side.) Sprinkle the cheese evenly on the cranberry sauce.

Place the bun cranberry-Cheddar side up on a pan and put the pan under a toaster-oven broiler or your main oven broiler (preheat the broiler). Broil for about 2 to 3 minutes or until the cheese is melted. Place the top of each bun on the cranberry-Cheddar half. Serve immediately.

Nutrient Values per Sandwich:
Calories: 368.6. Protein: 12.3 g. Carbohydrate: 55.3 g. Dietary Fiber: 2.549 g. Total Sugars: 23.3 g. Total Fat: 12 g. Saturated Fat: 6.534 g. Monounsaturated Fat: 3.876 g. Polyunsaturated Fat: .612 g. Cholesterol: 42.6 mg. Calcium: 239 mg. Iron: 6.275 mg. Potassium: 114.2 mg. Sodium: 26.7 mg. Vitamin K: .754 mcg. Folate: 76.6 mcg.

❖ DON'S HERO SANDWICH ❖

DIABETIC ACCEPTABLE*

My first trip to New York City was typical of the small country boy eyeballing those "really tall buildings." But I drove into the city very early and thought it was a ghost town. I stood outside my car wondering where everyone was. I heard a rattling noise, a thundering sort of sound, and all of a sudden doors banged open and people came up out of stairwells. I was young, headed for duty at Quantico, Virginia, and wanted to see the big city first. The subway train had arrived and New York seemed to fill in minutes. That same day I was introduced to my first submarine sandwich from a street vendor. These sandwiches are also known as grinders, hoagies, poor boys, or heroes. Essentially, the hero sandwich consists of a large oblong roll or even a small loaf of Italian or French bread. The bottom half is often dug out and stacked with layers of your choice of thinly sliced deli or freshly cooked meats, cheeses (low-sodium for us), tomatoes, pickles, lettuce, peppers, well, anything

*No sugars in this recipe.

you're in the mood for. So, read this recipe and change, alter, or add anything you want, or just enjoy it the way it is. Make sure your ingredients are salt-free and low in sodium. You can replace the Italian sausage with your favorite meat or leave it out and make this hero a vegetarian delight—which will cut a great many of the calories out.

MAKES 8 SANDWICHES   SODIUM PER RECIPE: 330.4 MG
SODIUM PER SANDWICH: 41.3 MG

2 tablespoons extra virgin olive oil (trace)
4 teaspoons red wine vinegar (TK mg)
¾ pound cooked Don's Sweet Italian Sausage† (page 60)
   (189.8 mg)
8 thin slices medium fresh red onion (4.5 mg)
3 cloves garlic, minced (1.53 mg)
½ fresh red bell pepper cut into thin strips (TK mg)
4 long French rolls‡ (23.3 mg)
½ cup fresh tomato, chopped (8.1 mg)
4 mozzarella balls, packed in water§ (26.6 mg)
8 medium fresh basil leaves (.166 mg)
4 level tablespoons Homemade Mayonnaise Substitute
   (page 306 in *The No-Salt, Lowest-Sodium Cookbook* or
   from Health Heart Market, www.healthyheartmarket.com)
   (73.7 mg)

Combine 1 tablespoon olive oil and red wine vinegar and shake well.

Place meat patties into nonstick pan with 1 tablespoon of oil and brown on both sides. Cook over medium heat for another 15 minutes turning once halfway.

In medium hot oil, sauté the onion with garlic until limp. Add the bell peppers and cook over medium heat until they are tender, about 10 minutes. Add the cooked sausage to reheat.

Split the rolls in half lengthwise. Hollow out the bottom leaving a ½-inch shell; discard the bread crumbs. Layer the bottom of each roll with the mayonnaise, onion, garlic, tomato, pepper mix, one ball of mozzarella, thinly sliced, two basil leaves, and either three links or one sausage patty.

---

†May also make with Don's Sweet Italian Sausage mix when made with turkey burger.
‡They're long, so you can cut them into two or even three sandwiches.
§Fresh mozzarella packed in water is available in most grocery store deli areas.

Sprinkle the olive oil red wine vinegar mix over the top of the bun. Join and enjoy.

(May add honey mustard or other no-salt condiment you like to the top of the bun.) Serve hot.

Nutrient Values per Sandwich:
Calories: 489.5. Protein: 18.3 g. Carbohydrate: 66 g. Dietary Fiber: 3.531 g. Total Sugars: 0 g. Total Fat: 15.8 g. Saturated Fat: 5.024 g. Monounsaturated Fat: 7.461 g. Polyunsaturated Fat: 1.588 g. Cholesterol: 35.8 mg. Calcium: 55 mg. Iron: 6.73 mg. Potassium: 360.3 mg. Sodium: 41.3 mg. Vitamin K: 3.944 mcg. Folate: 186.9 mcg.

❂ DON'S MUSHROOM BURGER ❂

DIABETIC ADAPTABLE*

Not large, just a bit messy. This burger came about a long time ago and I return to it once or twice a year. I love it with barbecued turkey burger for the added flavor the coals give. (I don't barbecue over gas flames. Isn't that like drinking a nonfat, decaf latte?) Sauté the mushrooms and onions in a nonstick pan to help cut the fat down. Mix the mustard sauce for the burgers and spread on a toasted sandwich bun. This burger will become one of your favorites.

MAKES 1 BURGER   SODIUM PER RECIPE: 75.7 MG

⅓ sweet or white onion (1.099 mg)
8 medium to large mushrooms (5.76)
1 teaspoon no-salt-added ketchup† (approximately) (trace)
1 teaspoon honey mustard (approximately) (5 mg)
1 Don's Sandwich Buns (page 116) (1.599 mg)
1 ounce Heluva Good or Rumiano Cheddar cheese‡ (10 mg)
3 ounces very lean ground turkey or ground beef (7 percent lean) (56.1 mg)
   Spritz of olive oil from PAM or similar spray can (trace)
1 leaf fresh romaine lettuce (.8 mg)

*The sugars are in the bread and mustard only. Bread has .693, mustard has 2 g.
†Read the labels. Some no-salt-added ketchup contains potassium chloride, yet the label doesn't show how much. If potassium chloride is a problem for you, then search for the no salt-added variety that doesn't contain it.
‡At this writing we have two low-sodium Cheddars available to us. One is from Heluva Good Quality Foods (www.heluvagood.com) and the other is from Rumiano Cheese Company (www.rumianocheese.com).

Thinly slice the onion. Wash the mushrooms and slice in half through the stems.

Mix together the ketchup and mustard; set aside.

Slice your sandwich bun to make a sandwich. Set the cheese on the top layer; place both in a toaster oven but hold until the meat and onion/mushrooms are ready.

In a nonstick pan or on your barbecue, cook the burger meat through, but don't let it burn.

When the meat is close to being ready, in a small to medium nonstick fry pan, spritz the bottom with olive oil and sauté the onion and mushrooms for about 4 to 5 minutes, stirring often.

Toast the bun. Spread the ketchup mix on the bottom layers of the bun (not the side with the melted cheese). Lay the cooked meat on the cheese, the mushrooms and onions on the meat, and the lettuce on top. Put the bun halves together and serve.

Nutrient Values per Burger:
Calories: 421.5. Protein: 31.9 g. Carbohydrate: 44.3 g. Dietary Fiber: 4.231 g. Total Sugars: 2.693 g. Total Fat: 25.3 g. Saturated Fat: 11.7 g. Monounsaturated Fat: 7.072 g. Polyunsaturated Fat: 1.425 g. Cholesterol: 53.8 mg. Calcium: 32.5 mg. Iron: 5.276 mg. Potassium: 1056 mg. Sodium: 75.7 mg. Vitamin K: 1.497 mcg. Folate: 120.7 mcg.

DON'S OPEN-FACE CHEESE
❖ AND GARLIC SANDWICH ❖

DIABETIC ADAPTABLE*

I created this sandwich more than 45 years ago. I was a first lieutenant in the Marines at the time, living a bachelor's life in the Officers Quarters. The food in our mess wasn't always the most pleasant so I bought a small toaster oven that by today's standards was fairly primitive, and a double hot plate. I cooked many of my own meals right there. This sandwich was a favorite since it was easy, quick, and I didn't exactly get an hour for a lunch break. I've adapted it for our lifestyle and hope you like it.

MAKES 1 OPEN-FACE SANDWICH SODIUM PER SANDWICH: 25.2 MG

1 teaspoon honey mustard (5 mg)
1 half-inch thick slice Don's Cheese & Garlic Bread
   (page 109) or Don's Garlic Bread (page 105) (3.874 mg)

---

*The sugars are in the mustard with .52 in the bread.

3 **very thin slices medium to large onion (.81 mg)**
3 **very thin slices large tomato (4.05 mg)**
 White pepper or garlic powder to taste‡ (trace)
1 **ounce Heluva Good Low-Sodium Cheddar Cheese grated
  (10 mg)**
2 **large mushroom caps (1.44 mg)**

Spread the mustard on bread. Layer with the onion and tomatoes and sprinkle the grated cheese over them. Top with the mushroom caps. Place in toaster oven to toast both sides; toast at low setting.

 Serve hot.

Nutrient Values for Sandwich Using Cheese and Garlic Bread:
Calories: 140.3. Protein: 12.5 g. Carbohydrate: 27.1 g. Dietary Fiber: 2.299 g. Total Sugars: 2.26 g. Total Fat: 11 g. Saturated Fat: 6.59 g. Monounsaturated Fat: .7 g. Polyunsaturated Fat: .299 g. Cholesterol: .28 mg. Calcium: 20.5 mg. Iron: 1.905 mg. Potassium: 478 mg. Sodium: 25.2 mg. Vitamin K: 3.661 mcg. Folate: 70.2 mcg.

Nutrient Values for Sandwich Using Garlic Bread:
Calories: 139.2. Protein: 11.8 g. Carbohydrate: 27.2 g. Dietary Fiber: 2.273 g. Total Sugars: 2.52 g. Total Fat: 10.4 g. Saturated Fat: 6.199 g. Monounsaturated Fat: .686 g. Polyunsaturated Fat: .299 g. Cholesterol: 0 mg. Calcium: 16.1 mg. Iron: 1.855 mg. Potassium: 457.3 mg. Sodium: 22.4 mg. Vitamin K: 3.661 mcg. Folate: 62.8 mcg.

DON'S PHILLY STEAK
WITH HOMEMADE
❖ FRENCH GARLIC ROLLS ❖

DIABETIC ADAPTABLE*

Did you ever catch that Jack in the Box TV commercial where the boss tells "Fred" to go to Philly and learn about their Philly steak? In the next scene Fred is totally wiped out and has changed his looks, his personality, and oh, confirmed the existence of the Philly steak. Funny stuff. But the Philly steak isn't funny, it's just darned good-tasting. Problem is when it's served, the bread is usually loaded with a lot of fat and calories. I turned my Philly steak into a Philly sandwich. It's leaner and just as tasty and great fun to make.

**MAKES 4 SANDWICHES   SODIUM PER RECIPE: 218.3 MG
SODIUM PER SANDWICH: 54.6 MG**

---

‡Definitely optional.
*The sugars are in the bread. Make the bread with Splenda to reduce the sugars to near zero.

¾ **pound lean round steak, ⅛-inch trim cut into 3 × ½-inch strips (183.7 mg)**

1 **tablespoon olive oil (trace)**

½ **large green or red bell pepper, thinly sliced lengthwise (1.64 mg)**

1 **pound button, baby bellas, or shiitake mushrooms, sliced (14 mg)**

½ **large red onion, thinly sliced (2.25 mg)**

3 **cloves garlic, minced (1.53 mg)**

½ **teaspoon Don's Herbes de Provence Spice Mix (page 175) (.622 mg)**

⅛ **teaspoon ground sage (.01 mg)**

   Pepper to taste (trace)

4 **Don's Garlic Rolls (44.8 mg)**

In a Teflon or nonstick pan, brown the meat on medium-high heat for about 10 minutes (either before or after slicing).

Add the olive oil and then add the remaining ingredients except the rolls. Lower the heat to medium and sauté for about 10 to 15 minutes until you have a sauce.

Toast or warm Don's French Garlic Rolls. Slice the bread lengthwise. Evenly place the meat on one half of the four rolls; then spread the sauce mix on the other half of each sandwich and close. Before serving, microwave or heat in the oven at 350°F for a few minutes.

Nutrient Values per Sandwich:
Calories: 492.9. Protein: 28.5 g. Carbohydrate: 61 g. Dietary Fiber: 4.146 g. Total Sugars: 4.078 g. Total Fat: 14.6 g. Saturated Fat: 4.568 g. Monounsaturated Fat: 6.971 g. Polyunsaturated Fat: 1.104 g. Cholesterol: 52.7 mg. Calcium: 38.6 mg. Iron: 6.275 mg. Potassium: 806.7 mg. Sodium: 54.6 mg. Vitamin K: 2.046 mcg. Folate: 160.8 mcg.

❖ DON'S PIZZA SANDWICH ❖

CALZONE DOUGH*
DIABETIC ADAPTABLE*

Warning: This is delicious! That said, let's talk. Commercial pizza was a favorite of mine before I had to adopt this new no-salt lifestyle. So, one of the first things I "invented" was a no-salt, very, very low-sodium pizza. It has been as successful as any of my recipes, if not the most popular. Well, here we go again. Here's my latest tasty bit

---

*The sugars are in the pizza dough and the pasta sauce. Make your own pasta sauce and dough with Splenda to reduced the sugars to near zero.

of Italy and I use ingredients already made up for you except for the dough. Try it; I think you'll really enjoy it.

MAKES 8 PIZZA SANDWICHES   SODIUM PER RECIPE: 289.6 MG
SODIUM PER PIZZA SANDWICH: 36.2 MG

  1 **Calzone Dough recipe (page 108) (12.9 mg)**
 ½ **pound lean ground beef† (149.2 mg)**
  1 **cup Enrico's Low-Sodium Pasta Sauce‡ or your own
        low-sodium marinara/pizza sauce (50 mg)**
  3 **cloves garlic, minced (1.53 mg)**
  1 **teaspoon Don's Herbes de Provence Spice Mix (page 175)
        (1.244 mg)**
 12 **large mushrooms, sliced (11 mg)**
  1 **small onion, thinly sliced (2.1 mg)**
  6 **ounces Heluva Good low-sodium Cheddar cheese (60 mg)**
 ½ **sweet red bell pepper, thinly sliced and chopped (1.64 mg)**

Preheat the oven to 375°F. Lightly grease a cookie sheet. Roll out the dough in a large square shape. Spread the ingredients evenly on half the dough, then fold the dough over, and pinch it closed. Bake on the prepared cookie sheet for about 20 minutes.

Nutrient Values per Sandwich:
Calories: 298. Protein: 17.8 g. Carbohydrate: 41.5 g. Dietary Fiber: 2.386 g. Total Sugars: 4.309 g. Total Fat: 16 g. Saturated Fat: 6.986 g. Monounsaturated Fat: 4.648 g. Polyunsaturated Fat: .733 g. Cholesterol: 19.5 mg. Calcium: 24.3 mg. Iron: 3.43 mg. Potassium: 419.1 mg. Sodium: 36.2 mg. Vitamin K: 1.836 mcg. Folate: 97.9 mcg.

◆ DON'S PLACE BURGER ◆

DIABETIC ADAPTABLE*

Have I mentioned Don's Place to you before? It was located in Burbank, California, and was popular with the film crowd. No, not the "film crowd" always in the news. Instead, the people who put the shows together, the grunts, the real-time workers. We headed there for lunch to reenergize, and the burgers at Don's Place, although probably

---

†Figured on 17 percent lean, raw. The USDA does not provide for leaner beef, but we suggest 7 percent fat if your local market has it.
‡Available from www.healthyheartmarket.com
*The sugars are in the bun and the burger sauce. Make each with Splenda to lower the sugars to zero.

*not as healthy as we would like today, were huge with en-
ergy. Onions about a quarter inch thick, enough lettuce to
feed a battleship of sailors, and ground beef? I'm sure it
would suffice for a week. And the fries? A foot long and foot
thick it seemed. All served with a delicious sauce and lots
of ketchup and a good cold beer. Those days are over if we
want to hang around much longer. Besides, I haven't been
there for a few years now and a friend informed me that
Don's Place burned down. Something about hot sauce . . .
Anyway, here's my best bet to replace that wonderfully en-
ticing and hugely popular burger. By the way, the meat
will be quite a bit lower in volume here.*

MAKES 1 BURGER[†]   **SODIUM PER RECIPE: 139.1 MG**

> **2 tablespoons Don's Burger Sauce (page 86) (25.7 mg)**
> **½ teaspoon Don's Curry Mix (page 180) (.8 mg)**
> **1 onion (1.14 mg)**
> **1 tomato (2.43 mg)**
> **3 leaves very fresh, chilled iceberg lettuce (2.16 mg)**
> **4 ounces lean ground beef (72.4 mg)**
> **1 ounce low-sodium Cheddar or low-sodium Swiss (5.954 mg)**
> **1 Don's Place Burger Buns (page 111) (2.48 mg)**

Prepare Don's Burger Sauce ahead of time. The recipe calls for more than
you need, so store the rest in the refrigerator in a tightly sealed jar. It will
last about 2 weeks in the fridge or may be frozen.

Preheat the grill or the broiler. If you don't have Don's Curry Mix on
hand, make a bunch, and put it into an empty spice jar. Store it on a shelf
in a dark cool place, tightly closed for future use. Works extremely well
with all the meat dishes.

Slice the onion and tomato to quarter-inch thickness (or thicker if
you're really into this). Set aside and chill in the refrigerator.

Wash the iceberg lettuce; don't break the leaves up.

Work Don's Curry Mix into the meat. Barbecue the meat if you can.
Otherwise broil it. Use 4 ounces of lean meat in the patty. When the patty
is nearly done, melt the cheese on the patty, but not all the way.

Toast the open side of the sliced bun lightly. Spread Don's warmed
Burger Sauce liberally on both bun halves. Place the meat on the lower
bun. Lay the onion and tomato on top of the meat and cheese and the lettuce leaves on top of that. Close the burger and enjoy.

[†]Just multiply the ingredients by the number of burgers you want to make at a single
sitting.

❖ DON'S BURGER SAUCE ❖

DIABETIC ADAPTABLE*

Commercial meat sauces usually come in bottles with a lot of salt, soy sauce, and other high-sodium ingredients. For years I have toyed with varieties of the below. I confess I never mix a burger "sauce" or burger "spread" the same each time. It's more fun for me to play around with them when I barbecue burgers. I rarely make a burger in the kitchen since I enjoy the barbecue flavor a lot more. Lightly toast the inside of the buns before spreading any sauce on them.

**MAKES 1 CUP   SODIUM PER RECIPE: 206.4 MG
SODIUM PER TABLESPOON: 12.9 MG**

1 **6-ounce can Contadina or other no-salt-added tomato paste (100 mg)**
1 **8-ounce can no-salt-added tomato sauce (70 mg)**
1 **tablespoon apple cider vinegar (.15)**
1 **tablespoon extra virgin olive oil (trace)**
4 **large mushrooms, washed and diced (3.68 mg)**
½ **cup chopped onion (2.4 mg)**
⅛ **teaspoon ground cloves (.638 mg)**
½ **teaspoon Mustard Powder (trace)**
¼ **cup unpacked brown sugar (28.3 mg)**
½ **teaspoon coriander (.315 mg)**
½ **teaspoon ground thyme (.385 mg)**

Over medium heat, cook the tomato paste and sauce, stirring until well mixed. Add the vinegar and oil and heat for 1 minute. Add the rest of the ingredients and stir for 2 minutes. Bring to a very light boil, turn the heat down, and let simmer for about 10 minutes, stirring frequently.

*The sugars are in the brown sugar. Try using Splenda or Sugar Twin brown sugar substitute to lower the sugars to zero.

Store in a sealed bottle. Heat the sauce before using. You may also place the sauce on the burger meat while barbecuing or broiling. May be stored frozen up to 3 months.

Nutrient Values per Tablespoon:
Calories: 42.3. Protein: .877 g. Carbohydrate: 7.959 g. Dietary Fiber: .517 g. Total Sugars: 5.333 g. Total Fat: .906 g. Saturated Fat: .124 g. Monounsaturated Fat: .641 g. Polyunsaturated Fat: .091 g. Cholesterol: 0 mg. Calcium: 6.683 mg. Iron: 1.485 mg. Potassium: 47.3 mg. Sodium: 12.9 mg. Vitamin K: .515 mcg. Folate: 1.82 mcg.

EGG SALAD SANDWICH
❧ WITH LAVENDER ❧

DIABETIC ADAPTABLE*

I use lavender in some of my spice mixes. Here's a great way to use it in a sandwich also. You can buy lavender at most natural food stores. Or, if you have it growing in your yard, you can use that, too.

MAKES 4 SANDWICHES   SODIUM PER RECIPE: 301.2 MG
SODIUM PER SANDWICH: 75.3 MG

2　tablespoons sour cream (12.7 mg)
2　tablespoons plain yogurt (23.2 mg)
1　teaspoon dried dill (2.08 mg)
½　teaspoon extra virgin olive oil (trace)
2　teaspoons curry powder† (2.08 mg)
2　tablespoons lavender buds (trace)
4　eggs, hard-boiled, chopped (252 mg)
8　slices Don's White Sandwich Bread (page 123) (8.941 mg)
　B&G Unsalted Sweet Relish‡ (optional)

Mix the sour cream, yogurt, dill, olive oil, curry powder, and lavender buds together. Mix in the chopped eggs.

Chill for about 2 hours.

Spread on plain or toasted sandwich bread. Close and serve.

*The sugars are in the bread. Make the bread with Splenda to lower the sugars to zero.
†You may use Don's Curry Mix (page 180) if you have it on hand.
‡You may add B&G Unsalted Sweet Relish, if you like. It can be purchased at www.healthyheartmarket.com

Nutrient Values per Sandwich:
Calories: 314.4. Protein: 13.5 g. Carbohydrate: 39.5 g. Dietary Fiber: 3.408 g. Total Sugars: 1.559 g. Total Fat: 11.6 g. Saturated Fat: 3.075 g. Monounsaturated Fat: 5.731 g. Polyunsaturated Fat: 1.379 g. Cholesterol: 215.3 mg. Calcium: 68.9 mg. Iron: 3.387 mg. Potassium: 231.6 mg. Sodium: 75.3 mg. Vitamin K: 2.264 mcg. Folate: 105.2 mcg.

❊ HUMMUS PITA SANDWICH ❊

DIABETIC ACCEPTABLE

This recipe comes to us from river-raft guide Becky Gaz-zaniga (my baby sister). She loves hummus and makes up a variety of mixtures. This one is particularly good.

**MAKES 4 PITA SANDWICHES   SODIUM PER RECIPE: 84.4 MG
SODIUM PER PITA SANDWICH: 21.1 MG**

1   **can Eden Organic (no-salt-added) Garbanzo Beans, drained*
      (35 mg)**
2   **tablespoons unsalted tahini†, plus more to taste (34.5 mg)**
½   **teaspoon ground cumin (1.764 mg)**
5   **cloves garlic (2.55 mg)**
      Juice of 1 medium fresh lemon (.47 mg)
¼   **teaspoon Don's Flavor Enhancer (page 177) (.215 mg)**
1   **teaspoon extra virgin olive oil (trace)**
4   **pitas (pages 251–252, *No-Salt, Lower-Sodium Cookbook*)
      (7.082 mg)**
4   **leaves iceberg or romaine lettuce (2.88 mg)**

I use a Braun 550 Handblender to puree this mixture. You can also used a food processor or a blender. In a food processor, using the steel blade, puree together the olive oil, beans, tahini, cumin, garlic, and lemon juice. Get it all smooth and creamy like. Taste as you go with the tahini. Don't put it all in at once. Make sure you're not overdoing or, for that matter, un-derdoing it. Add more than the recipe calls for if it's not enough for you.

Open one of the pitas, place a leaf of lettuce inside as a sheath or "wall," and then spoon in the hummus, adding your vegetable choices (see below) as you go.

MAKE IT YOUR WAY:
You can add any veggies you like, chopped, diced, sliced, or minced. Tuck a leaf of lettuce into the pita in such a way that it form: a shell inside the pita.

*If not available locally, you can obtain from www.healthyheartmarket.com
†Tahini is available made from toasted and untoasted tahini seeds. Test before buying or trying. May exchange with unsalted peanut butter.

I like to add thinly sliced and quartered cucumbers and sometimes radishes. I don't like sprouts but if you do, they work nicely here, too. You can even add chopped unsalted walnuts or chopped carrots. It's all your choice.

Note: Hummus also makes a great party dip. Add a bit of Grandma's chili or some cayenne pepper or a dash more tahini for the party.

Nutrient Values per Sandwich:
Calories: 313.5. Protein: 12.5 g. Carbohydrate: 48.5 g. Dietary Fiber: 7.589 g. Total Sugars: 0 g. Total Fat: 8.196 g. Saturated Fat: .959 g. Monounsaturated Fat: 3.299 g. Polyunsaturated Fat: 2.17 g. Cholesterol: 0 mg. Calcium: 52.3 mg. Iron: 6.823 mg. Potassium: 177.7 mg. Sodium: 21.1 mg. Vitamin K: 1.097 mcg. Folate: 93.2 mcg.

❈ MILANESE TURKEY SANDWICH ❈

DIABETIC ADAPTABLE*

While filming in Milan we were treated to some very excellent Italian cuisine, prepared mostly by our host, the local subject of our film, from risotto osso bucco to this sandwich. Grill the veggies quickly, so that they hold some of their crispness, and you'll fall in love with the results.

MAKES 2 SANDWICHES   SODIUM PER RECIPE: 98.4 MG
SODIUM PER SANDWICH: 49.2 MG

4 ounces fresh turkey breast meat, cooked without salt,† (54.4 mg)
4 slices Tuscan bread bread‡ (4.224 mg)
2 ¾-ounce slices low-sodium Swiss cheese§ (17.2 mg)
4 teaspoons East Shore or other honey mustard (20 mg) (optional)
¼ large red bell pepper (.82 mg)
¼ large green bell pepper (.82 mg)
¼ large onion (1.125 mg)
½ medium zucchini (2.94 mg)
1 tablespoon extra virgin olive oil‖ (trace)

---

*The sugars are in the mustard with a neglible amount in the bread. Leave the mustard out or replace it with low-sodium mustard that is not a honey mustard to reduce the sugars near zero.

†You cannot use deli turkey because of its high sodium.

‡See page 247 of the *No-Salt, Lowest-Sodium Cookbook* or try the Tuscan Bread (page 122) in this book. Just make it into a round loaf instead of a baguette, or slice the baguette into three or four sandwich-size buns.

§Grey Poupon, Mendocino, and East Shore each make delicious honey mustard.

‖Or use 1 teaspoon in a nonstick pan and cut the fat.

Cut the freshly baked turkey meat into four thin slices.

Toast four slices of the Tuscan Bread with cheese on two pieces and set aside on serving plates. If using the mustard, spread it on the slices without the cheese.

Cut the peppers into long thin strips. Thinly slice the onion. Slice the zucchini into thin chips. Heat the olive oil in a nonstick pan and sauté the vegetables quickly.

Place the vegetables evenly on two pieces of the toast, close the sandwiches, and serve hot.

Nutrient Values per Sandwich:
Calories: 334.2. Protein: 21.4 g. Carbohydrate: 17.9 g. Dietary Fiber: 2.151 g. Total Sugars: 4.13 g. Total Fat: 19.4 g. Saturated Fat: 5.358 g. Monounsaturated Fat: 11.5 g. Polyunsaturated Fat: 1.486 g. Cholesterol: 52.3 mg. Calcium: 184.5 mg. Iron: 1.786 mg. Potassium: 454 mg. Sodium: 49.2 mg. Vitamin K: 10.5 mcg. Folate: 53.3 mcg.

LAMB BURGER
❖ WITH MINT ❖

DIABETIC ADAPTABLE*

To this day my favorite red meat is lamb. Beef is okay, but lamb is what I like on my birthday and Christmas. After these meals, while growing up, my mother used to grind up the lamb and make lamb burgers. With mint jelly! *They were my favorite and here's the very closest I can come to her recipe—which she never wrote down. The difference here is you will grill raw lamb burger and not use previously baked lamb. Ground lamb is usually available, but if not, ask your butcher to grind some. He'll use the cuttings from the legs and shanks he's worked on.*

**MAKES 4 SANDWICHES SODIUM PER RECIPE: 280.6 MG
SODIUM PER SANDWICH: 70.2 MG**

2 **tablespoon chopped onion (.6 mg)**
1 **clove garlic, minced (.51 mg)**
¼ **teaspoon ground or dried rosemary (.15 mg)**
¾ **pound lean ground lamb† (200.7 mg)**
3 **tablespoons liquid mint jelly, or regular apple mint jelly (.585 mg)**

*Sugars are in the mint jelly. Make homemade mint sauce and use 3 tablespoons (2.715 mg) (Mint sauce recipe follows.)
†You can always use leftover lamb, and finely chop or slice it.

2 large homemade no-salt, low-sodium pita bread rounds, halved (pages 251–252, *No-Salt, Lowest-Sodium Cookbook*)‡ (3.541 mg)
4 medium leaves lettuce (2.88 mg)
½ medium cucumber, thinly sliced (2.01 mg)
1 small tomato, halved and sliced (8.19 mg)
½ cup plain yogurt or low-fat (light) sour cream (60.9 mg) (optional)

In a medium mixing bowl combine the onion, garlic, and rosemary. Add the ground lamb and mix well. Shape into four equal sized patties.

Preheat an uncovered barbecue grill. Directly over medium coals, grill, the patties on the first side for about 5 to 8 minutes. Flip and brush with mint jelly. Grill for another 5 minutes; turn over again and brush the other side with the jelly. Grill for another 5 to 8 minutes, brush again with mint jelly. (You may also broil these in your oven in the same way for about the same amount of time—preheat the oven first.) Line the insides of each pita with a lettuce leaf and a few cucumber and tomato slices. Place the patties in pita bread halves with the lettuce, cucumber, tomato, and yogurt or sour cream.

Nutrient Values per Sandwich:
Calories: 394.3 Protein: 17.9 g. Carbohydrate: 20 g. Dietary Fiber: 1.816 g. Total Sugars: 2.062 g. Total Fat: 26.9 g. Saturated Fat: 12.6 g. Monounsaturated Fat: 10.4 g. Polyunsaturated Fat: 2.001 g. Cholesterol: 74.7 mg. Calcium: 62 mg. Iron: 4.525 mg. Potassium: 394.4 mg. Sodium: 70.2 mg. Vitamin K: 2.028 mcg. Folate: 70.9 mcg.

HOMEMADE MINT SAUCE
❖ FOR LAMB BURGERS ❖

DESIGNED FOR DIABETICS
GOOD FOR 2 SANDWICHES   SODIUM PER RECIPE: 5.43 MG
SODIUM PER SANDWICH: 2.715 MG

3 tablespoons chopped fresh mint (5.13 mg)
3 tablespoons boiling water (trace)
2 tablespoons fresh lemon juice (.3 mg)
1 tablespoon Splenda (trace)

‡You can also use four small pita breads, capped (see Pages 251–252 *No-Salt, Lowest-Sodium Cookbook*.) Any toasted bun can be used for this recipe, such as the Don's Place Burger Bun (page 111)

Chop mint until it's as finely cut as you can make it.

In a small bowl, pour boiling water over the mint, stir.

Add the lemon juice and Splenda. Taste test, add more Splenda if bite is too harsh. Let it stand for about five minutes. You can right away.

Nutrient Values per Sandwich:
Calories: 7.512. Protein: .338 g. Carbohydrate: 2.014 g. Dietary Fiber: .641 g. Total Sugars: 0 g. Total Fat: .062 g. Saturated Fat: .016 g. Monounsaturated Fat: .002 g. Polyunsaturated Fat: .034 g. Cholesterol: 0 mg. Calcium: 18.1 mg. Iron: 1.019 mg. Potassium: 57.8 mg. Sodium: 2.715 mg. Vitamin K: 0 mcg. Folate: 10.9 mcg.

❈ PINEAPPLE BURGER ❈

DIABETIC ADAPTABLE*

Hawaii here we come! I was doing a film in Hawaii when we ended up on a pineapple farm. It was the first time I saw pineapples growing and learned that each pineapple takes two years to mature. Two years! Of course the area was full of pineapple this and pineapple that. But when I ran into a pineapple burger that did me in. I thought a peanut butter burger might be a bit weird although very tasty—but pineapple? When I got home I created my own pineapple burger with a California flavor. Try this; you'll really enjoy it for a change.

MAKES 4 BURGERS   SODIUM PER RECIPE: 351.2 MG
SODIUM PER BURGER: 87.8 MG

PINEAPPLE MIX FIRST
1   8-¼ ounce can crushed pineapple in water, drained
     (2.46 mg)
½   cup chopped red or green sweet bell pepper (1.49 mg)
¼   cup thinly sliced green onions (4 mg)
2   tablespoons snipped fresh cilantro or parsley (5.184 mg)
2   cloves garlic, minced (1.02 mg)
1   small jalapeño or serrano pepper, seeded and finely
     chopped† (.61 mg)

AND NOW THE MEAT
¾   pound uncooked lean ground chicken, beef, or turkey
     (319.8 mg)

---

*The sugars are in the bread. Use Splenda to make the bread lowering the sugars to zero.

†Caution: When preparing hot peppers such as jalapeños, make sure to wear rubber gloves and wash your hands thoroughly afterward. If you cut a jalapeño and then touch your eyes, you will appreciate this word of caution.

¼ cup thinly sliced green onions (4 mg)
2 teaspoons Don's Herbes de Provence Spice Mix (page 175) (2.488 mg)
¼ teaspoon Don's Flavor Enhancer (page 177) (.215 mg)
4 Don's Place Burger Buns (page 111) (9.92 mg)

FIRST THE PINEAPPLE MIX

In a medium bowl, mix together the first 6 ingredients. Cover and chill for at least 8 hours.

NOW, THE MEAT

Preheat your outdoor grill or broiler. In another medium bowl combine green onions, herbes de Provence, and Don's Flavor Enhancer. Add the ground chicken or turkey; mix well. Shape into four ¾-inch-thick patties. A variety of ways to grill meat are available. But I like to grill the patties uncovered on the barbecue grill, turning once or twice until done. You may also broil these in your oven about four to five inches from the heat for 10 to 12 minutes.

FINALLY, THE BURGER

Spread the pineapple mix over one bun; lay the burger on the mix and close the sandwich.

Nutrient Values per Burger:
Calories: 424.1. Protein: 23.9 g. Carbohydrate: 59.1 g. Dietary Fiber: 4.926 g. Total Sugars: 2.079 g. Total Fat: 10.3 g. Saturated Fat: 2.402 g. Monounsaturated Fat: 4.419 g. Polyunsaturated Fat: 2.258 g. Cholesterol: 67.2 mg. Calcium: 80.3 mg. Iron: 5.775 mg. Potassium: 506.5 mg. Sodium: 87.8 mg. Vitamin K: 1.133 mcg. Folate: 134 mcg.

❖ DON'S PITA DELIGHT ❖

DIABETIC ACCEPTABLE*

You can use my pita recipe for many different sandwiches. This one is quick, refreshing, and healthy.

MAKES 6 PITA SANDWICHES   SODIUM PER RECIPE: 234 MG
SODIUM PER PITA SANDWICH: 39 MG

2 4-ounce boneless, skinless chicken half breasts (153.4 mg)
½ tablespoon extra virgin olive oil or spray from can (PAM) (trace)
1 cup (about 5 to 6 balls) sliced and diced *Bocconcini*
Fresh mozzarella or other no-salt mozzarella cheese in fresh pasteurized water (29.4 mg)

*The sugars are negligible.

½ cup drained Eden Organic (no-salt-added) Black Beans
  (15 mg)
½ medium green bell pepper, seeded and diced (.19 mg)
½ cup sliced thinly mushrooms (1.4 mg)
1 medium red onion, peeled and thinly sliced (3.3 mg)
8 tablespoons Don's Italian Dressing (page 166) (2.77 mg)
6 homemade Pita Bread (pages 251–252, *No-Salt, Lowest-Sodium Cookbook*) (10.6 mg)
6 medium leaves Boston/Bibb or other lettuce, washed, butterhead sliced, or broken (2.25 mg)

Sauté the chicken breast meat in oil-sprayed pan over medium-high heat until thoroughly cooked.

In a bowl combine the mozzarella cheese, black beans, green bell pepper, mushrooms, red onion, and vinaigrette. When the chicken is cool, slice and dice the meat into smaller than bite-size pieces. Toss the chicken with the ingredients in the bowl. Slice the pita pockets in half. Fill with 1 medium lettuce leaf and the chicken and cheese mixture. Serve immediately.

Nutrient Values per Pita Sandwich:
Calories: 521.1. Protein: 25.6 g. Carbohydrate: 63.1 g. Dietary Fiber: 7.067 g. Total Sugars: 0 g. Total Fat: 19 g. Saturated Fat: 4.273 g. Monounsaturated Fat: 11.7 g. Polyunsaturated Fat: 1.823 g. Cholesterol: 33 mg. Calcium: 174.6 mg. Iron: 12.5 mg. Potassium: 514.4 mg. Sodium: 39 mg. Vitamin K: 18.1 mcg. Folate: 180 mcg.

APPLE SALAD SANDWICH
❖ WITH CHICKEN IN A PITA ❖

DIABETIC ACCEPTABLE

You can find this pita bread recipe in The No-Salt, Lowest-Sodium Cookbook, *on page 251. This sandwich was "discovered" on a trip to the northwest. Somewhere in mid-Washington state a small café we pulled into was making use of the apples from their own orchard. Mid-Washington is apple country. We thought it was tasty and worth replicating here.*

MAKES 4 PITA SANDWICHES   SODIUM PER RECIPE: 331.2 MG
SODIUM PER PITA SANDWICH: 82.8 MG

2 half chicken breasts, cooked and cubed or cut into bite-size pieces (153.4 mg)
2 medium Washington Delicious apples, cored, chopped (skin on) (trace)

1 8-ounce can crushed pineapple packed in its own juice,
   drained (2.49 mg)
⅓ cup chopped celery (34.5 mg)
¼ cup Don's Mayonnaise substitute (page 306, *No-Salt,
   Lowest-Sodium Cookbook*) (73.7 mg)
⅓ cup low-fat lemon yogurt (57.3)
   About 2 teaspoons celery seed (optional)
4 pitas (7.082 mg)
4 leaves iceberg or romaine lettuce (2.88 mg)

Mix the chicken together with the chopped apples, pineapple, and celery. In another bowl, stir together the Don's Mayonnaise substitute, yogurt, and celery seeds, if you are using them. Toss until well mixed.

Line the pitas with lettuce leaves and spoon the mixture into each pita evenly. Serve. Do not store the dressing.

Nutrient Values per Pita Sandwich:
Calories: 350.2. Protein: 21.2 g. Carbohydrate: 51.8 g. Dietary Fiber: 4.935 g. Total Sugars: 0 g. Total Fat: 7.143 g. Saturated Fat: 2.826 g. Monounsaturated Fat: 2.78 g. Polyunsaturated Fat: .751 g. Cholesterol: 42.7 mg. Calcium: 119.6 mg. Iron: 6.736 mg. Potassium: 552.5 mg. Sodium: 82.8 mg. Vitamin K: 2.296 mcg. Folate: 100 mcg.

SCOTT'S HELUVA GOOD CHEESE

❖ VENISON BURGER ❖

DIABETIC ADAPTABLE*

With permission from my good friend and cooking ace "The Sporting Chef" (Scott Leysath—www.sportingchef .com), I have adapted his venison burger recipe to our no-salt, low-sodium lifestyle. Scott has received complaints from many sportsmen who have some of their venison turned into ground meat—they say it's flavorless. Scott's advice was to wait and grind the meat just before using it. Frozen ground venison is known to lose its freshness and flavor quickly. Also, overcooking the meat will cast out all flavor. Scott's recipe did indeed flavor venison but the sodium level was just a bit too high for us. Here then is my interpretation (after years of working with venison) of a good low-sodium venison burger.

*The sugars are in the bread. Make the bread with Splenda to lower the sugars to zero.

1 tablespoon extra virgin olive oil (trace)
1 medium onion, finely diced (3.3 mg)
3 cloves garlic, minced (1.53 mg)
2 cups coarsely chopped mushrooms (7.68 mg)
1¼ pounds fresh ground venison† (289.2 mg)
4 ounces Heluva Good white or yellow low-sodium Cheddar‡ (40 mg)
2 tablespoons bread crumbs from Don's crouton recipe§ (page 114) (.138 mg)
1 tablespoon Don's Herbes de Provence Spice Mix (page 175) (3.733 mg)
1 teaspoon mint
⅛ teaspoon white pepper (trace)
4 Don's Place Burger Buns (page 111) (9.92 mg)
4 large fresh, chilled lettuce leaves (3.2 mg)
4 slices large tomato (65.5 mg)

In a nonstick skillet over medium heat, in the olive oil, sauté the onion and garlic until translucent. Stir in the mushrooms and sauté until soft. Transfer to a medium bowl and allow to cool. Add to the mushroom mix the ground venison, Heluva Good cheese, bread crumbs, Don's Herbes de Provence, mint, and pepper and mix well with your hands to blend. Form into four equal patties. Grill, pan-fry, or broil the patties until browned. Add to the buns with the lettuce, tomato, and your choice of other condiments.

Nutrient Values per Burger:
Calories: 505.7. Protein: 51.5 g. Carbohydrate: 65.9 g. Dietary Fiber: 7.268 g. Total Sugars: 2.098 g. Total Fat: 16.5 g. Saturated Fat: 7.969 g. Monounsaturated Fat: 2.864 g. Polyunsaturated Fat: 1.527 g. Cholesterol: 120.5 mg. Calcium: 92 mg. Iron: 11 mg. Potassium: 1403 mg. Sodium: 106.1 mg. Vitamin K: 12.6 mcg. Folate: 170.8 mcg.

†Venison is practically fat free—1½ pounds has nearly the same total fat (16.5 g) as a tablespoon of olive oil.
‡Heluva Good and Rumiano are making low-sodium Cheddar at this writing. Contact Heluva Good at www.helluvagood.com or Rumiano Cheese at www.rumianocheese.com.
§If not available dry any of our white breads and use the crumbs.

TORTILLA SPINS
❧ AKA SANDWICH ❧

DIABETIC ADAPTABLE*

This sandwich is just right for a lunch or for your children. You can use anything for the insides from a spinach salad mix to burger makings. I've even been known to roll up hot applesauce and melted Cheddar to make a "quickie apple pie."

MAKES 4 SANDWICHES SODIUM PER RECIPE: 82 MG
SODIUM PER SANDWICH: 20.5 MG

8 tablespoons no-salt-added refried beans (37.1 mg)
4 Whole-Wheat Flour Tortillas† (page 120) (10.3 mg)
2 ounces low-sodium Cheddar‡ (20 mg)
4 leaves lettuce (romaine or iceberg), shredded (1.8 mg)
1 medium tomato, chopped or diced (11.1 mg)
½ onion, chopped (1.65 mg)

Heat the refried beans in a pan on your stove top.

Spread the hot unsalted refried beans on each tortilla.†

Lay the cheese on that.

To each tortilla, add one quarter of the shredded lettuce, chopped tomato, and chopped onion.

Roll the tortilla up tightly. You can eat it this way or cut the roll into slices (spins) to serve your children or your guests or for that matter yourself.

Note: If you want to add ground turkey (26.8 mg) or beef (18.7 mg) then add about 1 ounce sautéed in very light oil.

Nutrients Values per Sandwich:
Calories: 458.3 Protein: 16.1 g. Carbohydrate: 58 g. Dietary Fiber: 12.3 g. Total Sugars: .347 g. Total Fat: 19.3 g. Saturated Fat: 2.042 g. Monounsaturated Fat: 10.2 g. Polyunsaturated Fat: 1.632. g. Cholesterol: 12.5 mg. Calcium: 239.2 mg. Iron: 4.395 mg. Potassium: 826.2 mg. Sodium: 20.5 mg. Vitamin K: 13.3 mcg. Folate: 220.5 mcg.

*The sugars are in the tortillas. For diabetics, make tortillas with Splenda.
†See page 95 in *The No-Salt Lowest-Sodium Baking Book* for white Flour Tortillas.
‡Heluva Good and Rumiano are making low-sodium Cheddar at this writing. Contact Heluva Good at www.heluvagood.com or Rumiano Cheese at www.rumianocheese.com

DIABETIC ADAPTABLE*

A calzone is a baked or fried Italian turnover made of pizza dough and filled with vegetables, meat, cheese, or a either or a combination of all. I like to bake mine, to help cut out the fat from frying. This one is a terrific calzone with lots of flavor and nutrition. There's enough dough in our Calzone Dough recipe to make six to eight if you desire. A similar commercial calzone would have about 2,131 mg of sodium.

SERVES 8   SODIUM PER RECIPE: 133.6 MG
SODIUM PER SERVING: 16.7 MG

1 **Calzone Dough (page 108) (12.9 mg)**
8 **tablespoons homemade spaghetti or marinara sauce†**
   (22.7 mg)
¾ **cup mushrooms, sliced (2.1 mg)**
¾ **cup zucchini, halved lengthwise and thinly sliced (2.543 mg)**
¼ **cup diced green bell pepper (.745 mg)**
2 **cloves garlic, minced (1.02 mg)**
¼ **cup sliced green onions (4 mg)**
1 **teaspoon Don's Herbes de Provence Spice Mix (page 175)**
   (1.244 mg)
8 **thin slices fresh, no-salt-added mozzarella cheese in water**
   (17.9 mg)
1 **egg white, beaten (54.8 mg)**

Preheat the oven to 425°F.

Prepare the dough and spaghetti/marinara sauce first.† Set aside.

Spritz a large cookie sheet with olive oil spray (PAM), or wipe on extra virgin olive oil from a bottle.

In a medium bowl combine the mushrooms, zucchini, pepper, garlic, and onions. Sprinkle with Don's Herbes de Provence Spice Mix and mix together.

Roll the dough into a large square on the cookie sheet to about a thick-

---

*Sugars are in the calzone dough. Make the dough with Splenda instead of sugar and lower the sugar to near zero.
†See pages 143, 146, 147, and 148 for your choice of sauce, in *The No-Salt, Lowest-Sodium Cookbook*. Or use bottled Enrico's no-salt added (NSA) pasta sauce with the added punch of some cloves, oregano, and basil. Enrico's pasta sauce is available from www.healthyheartmarket.com. Use 1 to 2 tablespoons per calzone.

ness of ⅛ inch or slightly thicker. Cut into four equal squares. Place 2 tablespoons sauce and a quarter of the vegetable mixture on each square, cover with two slices of the mozzarella cheese. Leave about a ½ inch edge around three sides of each square for folding and sealing (half each square should empty).

Fold the dough in half over the filling. Press the edges with a fork to seal. Brush each calzone with some of the beaten egg white. Punch holes into them after sealing with a fork three or four times. Let rest 5 minutes.

Bake 12 to 15 minutes or until golden brown. Cool on a rack. Cut in half to serve. Serve hot or reheated. You may freeze for up to a month in Ziploc freezer bag and reheat.

Nutrient Values per Serving:
Calories: 270.5. Protein: 11.1 g. Carbohydrate: 39 g. Dietary Fiber: 2.401 g. Total Sugars: 1.559 g. Total Fat: 7.499 g. Saturated Fat: 2.209 g. Monounsaturated Fat: 3.923 g. Polyunsaturated Fat: .67 g. Cholesterol: 8.392 mg. Calcium: 135.2 mg. Iron: 2.995 mg. Potassium: 244.2 mg. Sodium: 16.7 mg. Vitamin K: 2.18 mcg. Folate: 99.2 mcg.

SANDWICH BREADS

❖ ❖ ❖ ❖ ❖ ❖ ❖ ❖

ABOUT NO-SALT BREAD-MAKING

I have written about making no-salt bread in both *The No-Salt, Lowest-Sodium Cookbook* and *The No-Salt, Lowest-Sodium Baking Book*.

Since completing each of those books I have learned even more about no-salt bread-making. I have passed much of that fresh knowledge on to visitors at www.megaheart.com. Here is much of what I have learned:

Many manufacturers and suppliers have products known as bread enhancers, dough relaxers, and such, but you won't need those for the recipes in this book. Each recipe has a minimum combination of the right ingredients to make up what would be considered a bread enhancer. As to dough relaxers you won't need them either for any of the recipes in this book. Generally they are used only for pizza dough if you want it as thin as humanly possible.

However, each recipe requires just a bit more or a bit less of each ingredient, so I have put in what that recipe best tested with.

In the Glossary of this book, you can read about bread enhancers and about gluten/vital wheat gluten. These and ascorbic acid or citric acid (they are essentially the same thing), are generally the main ingredients of any bread enhancer. Ascorbic acid is literally vitamin C.

In order for bread to rise without the use of salt, the enhancers are important. Previously I used orange juice or orange zest to serve as the citric acid. This works, but many wrote and said they weren't fond of the orange flavor. Thus, we have successfully reconstructed the combination of ingredients (which will be reflected in future reprints of the previous two books), to help make bread rise perfectly each time.

Some breads don't need enhancers though. Especially flat breads like pita bread, tortillas, some pizza doughs, some calzone doughs, etc.

If your bread doesn't rise as high as you suspect it should, it could be the flour you are using. Flour varies in its level of gluten and you may have to add more to our recipes if you discover your flour is a low gluten product. To fix the flour, start by adding just 1 tablespoon of gluten and 1 teaspoon of our citric-acid product (Sure-Jell Ever Fresh or Fruit Fresh). If the recipe you are using doesn't call for sugar, add at least one teaspoon as well, otherwise the existing sugar will work. This combination is known as a "bread enhancer."

By the way, always make sure before altering a recipe, that your yeast is alive. Test it before proceeding with any changes. To test the yeast, put a ½ teaspoon into a ½ cup of room temperature water with ¼ teaspoon of sugar. Stir to dissolve and wait 5 minutes. If it's alive it'll sponge up. If nothing happens, then your yeast is not good.

Citric acid is not generally available in your market. It is available in some locations but you may find yourself faced with buying it by the barrel. So, we have experimented with and been highly successful with using Sure-Jell Ever-Fresh or Fruit-Fresh, two products that are mostly citric acid. These products are easily available in any market. There may be other products out there for keeping fruit fresh—with the same ingredients—but as of this writing, we haven't found them. Diabetics, these products have 4 grams of carbohydrate/sugar per teaspoon.

To enhance existing recipes in our *No-Salt, Lowest-Sodium Cookbook,* and in our *No-Salt, Lowest-Sodium Baking Book,* just add 1 tablespoon of Sure-Jell/Fruit Fresh for each bread recipe that contains vital wheat gluten and sugar (or Splenda).

Softness is also a desired trait for many breads—buns, sandwich breads, etc. If your recipe isn't "soft" enough the first time, add 1 tablespoon of olive oil. Up to 3 tablespoons total can be used in any recipe with between 3 and 6 cups of flour. Keep an eye on the kneading process to make sure the dough isn't sticky or too wet after adding the oil. One tablespoon shouldn't affect it, but two might. Remember that adding the oil adds 14 grams of fat per tablespoon for the entire recipe—and no sodium. Olive oil and canola oil have no cholesterol.

All of the bread recipes in our previous two books work well. These suggestions are simply updates that help make them work just a bit better and without the flavor of orange if you find that distasteful.

The bread recipes in this book were designed to go along with our soups and salads, and to help make great sandwiches.

Visit www.megaheart.com often to see what other new recipes we make available.

As always remember www.megaheart.com is there to help you with recipes and to understand sodium and what we can do to return to good health. If you haven't already signed on for the newsletter, then visit MegaHeart and click on the newsletter sign-up button. We send out newsletters once a month.

We are also available daily to help answer questions about recipes and to support this book and the two before it.

DOUGH RISE TIMES CHART

In our recipes we use the phrases "let rise in a warm place" and "let rise in room temperature."

Rise times for most dough can vary depending upon the temperature in the spot you choose for your dough to rise.

Here is a chart that we worked out by testing times with our bread recipes. If you live in an area where your house is kept at 60°F let's say, your rise-time requirements may be lengthier than someone living in a hot clime.

Here then are suggested rise times to apply to each bread recipe in this book, in *The No-Salt, Lowest-Sodium Baking Book* and at www.megaheart.com We usually suggest 45 minutes. At that point preheat your oven and then put the dough in for baking. A longer time (or less time) may be required; knowledge you'll gain with your first effort or two.

TEMPERATURE	SUGGESTED RISE TIME
60°F	1 hour 15 minutes
65°F	1 hour 10 minutes
70°F	1 hour
75°F	55 minutes
80°F	50 minutes
Above 85°F	45 minutes

These are only suggested since your climate may be either humid or dry. Humidity may make the rising time longer, dry air less time.

See our altitude chart on page 26 of *The No-Salt, Lowest-Sodium Baking Book* for further help.

Do remember this: Never put your bread dough in an area where a draft is possible. An opening door allowing a draft of cooler air over the dough may cause it to collapse or stop rising. Never bump rising dough and when carrying it to the oven, use extra caution that you don't set it down hard or bump the baking sheet. Always keep rising dough covered with something light and that will hold the dough's heat in.

❈ FRENCH GARLIC ROLLS ❈

BREAD MACHINE KNEAD—OVEN BAKE*
DIABETIC ADAPTABLE[†]

I use cider vinegar in many bread recipes, but for this one I use white distilled. You can, of course, use white wine vinegar or white distilled vinegar in any bread recipe. White distilled vinegar gives this bread a real tasty kick, which works well with the garlic, onion powder, and basil. Great for sandwiches, bruschetta, or Don's Open-Face sandwich (page 81). Just before toasting this under your broiler or toaster oven, you might want to lightly spray the open surface with olive oil or even "liquid butter."

MAKES 1 LOAF OR 6 SANDWICH ROLLS   SODIUM PER RECIPE: 21.87 MG
SODIUM PER SANDWICH ROLL: 3.645 MG

1 **cup warm bottled/distilled water (110°F to 115°F)**
2 **tablespoons extra virgin olive oil (trace)**
1 **tablespoon white distilled vinegar (.15 mg)**
3 **to 3¼ cups best for bread flour (7.5 mg)**
1 **tablespoon Sure-Jell Ever-Fresh (4.992 mg)**
1½ **teaspoons vital wheat gluten (1.62 mg)**
1 **tablespoon white sugar (.126 mg) or Splenda substitute (trace)**

*May also bake in bread machine to make a loaf for sliced bread. Set at white bread, two-pound loaf, medium crust.
[†]Use Splenda instead of sugar to adapt for diabetics.

1½ teaspoons garlic powder (1.092 mg)
1½ teaspoons onion powder (1.701 mg)
1½ teaspoons dried basil (.039 mg)
2½ teaspoons bread machine yeast (4.8 mg)

Place ingredients into bread machine pan in order given or per your manufacturer's instructions. Set on dough.

When dough is ready, roll out onto lightly floured bread board and press down gently. Form a rectangle about 10 inches long. Using your hands, roll the dough into a log. Cut the log in half lengthwise. Stretch each new log to about 12 inches. Cut into three four-inch lengths and place on lightly greased baguette baking pan. Do this with each log. Run a sharp knife lengthwise down each roll about a ¼ inch deep. Set aside in a warm place, covered by wax paper or a very light cloth. Let rise for about 45 minutes to an hour.

Preheat oven to 375°F. Lightly spritz each bun using a spray can with olive oil. Bake rolls for 10 to 15 minutes or until golden brown.

Cool on a rack.

Nutrient Values per Roll:
Calories: 258.1. Protein: 7.934 g. Carbohydrate: 53.5 g. Dietary Fiber: 2.129 g. Total Sugars: 4.079 g. Total Fat: .713 g. Saturated Fat: .108 g. Monounsaturated Fat: .096 g. Polyunsaturated Fat: .264 g. Cholesterol: 0 mg. Calcium: 13.1 mg. Iron: 3.205 mg. Potassium: 112.3 mg. Sodium: 3.645 mg. Vitamin K: 0 mcg. Folate:. 134.7 mcg.

❖ DON'S GARLIC BREAD AND ROLLS ❖

BREAD MACHINE BAKE OR FOR SANDWICH ROLLS
BREAD MACHINE KNEAD/HAND SHAPE
DIABETIC ADAPTABLE

This recipe is a basic garlic bread I put together one day for a "sudden" visitation of guests "who love garlic bread." You can add the suggested ingredients to this* or make it exactly as is. You may also make garlic rolls with this recipe by setting the machine to Dough, then shaping the dough into the rolls you want and baking them in the oven.

MAKES 1 LOAF OR 6 TO 8 ROLLS   SODIUM PER LOAF: 17.4 MG
SODIUM PER SLICE (16): 1.09 MG
SODIUM PER ROLL (6): 2.411 MG

*You may add ½ cup chopped onion or 2 teaspoons onion powder. You may also add 1 teaspoon celery seed.

1 cup no-sodium bottled water, warmed to 110°F to 115°F (trace)
1 tablespoon apple cider vinegar (.15 mg)
1 tablespoon extra virgin olive oil (trace)
1 teaspoon Sure-Jell (1.6664 mg)
3 cups white bread machine flour (7.5 mg)
1 tablespoon vital wheat gluten (2.25 mg)
1 teaspoon garlic powder (.728 mg)
1 tablespoon white granulated sugar or Splenda (.126 mg)
3 cloves garlic, peeled, minced, or thinly sliced (1.53 mg)
2¼ teaspoons bread machine yeast (3.5 mg)

Place the ingredients into the bread machine pan in order. If you are making bread, set the machine to White Bread, Medium Crust, 2 pounds. When the bread is done, cool it on a rack.

If you are making rolls, place the machine on Dough. When the dough is ready, shape it into buns/rolls, place on a lightly greased cooking sheet, and let rise under a cloth or wax paper in a warm place for about 45 minutes. (See Rise Times Chart.)

When you are ready to proceed, preheat the oven to 425°F. Bake for about 6 to 8 minutes or until golden brown. Lightly butter the top of each bun when the rolls come out of oven to "soften" the top crust. Cool on rack.

Nutrient Values per Slice (16):
Calories: 101.8. Protein: 3.013 g. Carbohydrate: 19.6 g. Dietary Fiber: .754 g. Total Sugars: 1.03 g. Total Fat: 1.106 g. Saturated Fat: .154 g. Monounsaturated Fat: .654 g. Polyunsaturated Fat: .17 g. Cholesterol: 0 mg. Calcium: 5.018 mg. Iron: 1.184 mg. Potassium: 39 mg. Sodium: 1.09 mg. Vitamin K: .413 mcg. Folate: 46.4 mcg.

Nutrient Values per Roll (6):
Calories: 102.2 Protein: 3.901 g. Carbohydrate: 19.7 g. Dietary Fiber: .761 g. Total Sugars: 1.03 g. Total Fat: 2.232 g. Saturated Fat: .904 g. Monounsaturated Fat: .654 g. Polyunsaturated Fat: .17 g. Cholesterol: 0 mg. Calcium: 5.494 mg. Iron: 1.187 mg. Potassium: 57.7 mg. Sodium: 2.411 mg. Vitamin K: .413 mcg. Folate: 46.6 mcg.

Don's Best Barbecue
❖ Hamburger Buns ❖

Bread Machine Knead/Hand Shape
Diabetic Adaptable

This bun will go great with your barbecue. It will hold your BBQ sauce, the large hunk of lettuce, onion, tomato, and no-salt-added pickles. It will freeze well, serve well, and taste terrific. You can double this recipe.

Makes 6 large hamburger buns   Sodium per Recipe: 109.5 mg
Sodium per Bun with Sesame Seed Topping: 18.2 mg

¾ cup plus 2 tablespoons no-sodium bottled water heated to
    105°F to 115°F (trace)
3 cups white best for bread machine flour (7.5 mg)
1 tablespoon apple cider vinegar (.30 mg)
1 tablespoon extra virgin olive oil (trace)
1 tablespoon vital wheat gluten (2.25 mg)
1 tablespoon dry buttermilk powder (33.6 mg)
1 teaspoon Sure-Jell Ever-Fresh* (1.664 mg)
1 tablespoon white granulated sugar or Splenda (.126 mg)
½ cup chopped onion (2.4 mg)
3 cloves garlic, diced or minced (1.53 mg)
2¼ teaspoons bread machine yeast (3.5 mg)

THE GLAZING
   When the buns have been shaped:
1 large egg white (54.8 mg)
2 tablespoons sesame seed (1.98 mg)

Place all the ingredients except for the egg white and sesame seed (for glazing) in the bread machine pan and set the machine for Dough.

Prepare the egg by beating it until frothy.

When the dough is ready, roll it out onto a lightly floured breadboard. Pull off six balls of dough. Pull the edges around to meet at the bottom. Place this on a lightly greased cooking sheet and press down a bit to form a bun shape.

When ready, brush on the egg white. Sprinkle all the buns with sesame seed, making sure they "stick" to the egg white.

Let rise in a warm place under oil-sprayed wax paper for about 45 minutes. (See Rise Times chart.)

When you are ready to proceed, preheat the oven to 375°F. Bake for up to 20 minutes or until golden brown. Cool on a rack.

Nutrient Values per Bun:
Calories: 299.1 Protein: 9.601 g. Carbohydrate: 54.2 g. Dietary Fiber: 2.558 g. Total Sugars: 2.746 g. Total Fat: 4.519 g. Saturated Fat: .66 g. Monounsaturated Fat: 2.327 g. Polyunsaturated Fat: 1.115 g. Cholesterol: .747 mg. Calcium: 58.1 mg. Iron: 3.615 mg. Potassium: 158.9 mg. Sodium: 18.2 mg. Vitamin K: 1.61 mcg. Folate: 129.7 mcg.

*Or Fruit-Fresh. Diabetics, use 2 level tablespoons minced orange zest (use garlic press for help).

CALZONE DOUGH

⊠ OR USE FOR PIZZA SANDWICHES ⊠

HAND KNEAD, OVEN BAKE

Use this dough with our Veggie Calzones sandwich (page 98) and our Pizza Sandwich (page 83). It's easy to make by hand. It also makes a great crust for a low-sodium pizza.

MAKES 1 MEDIUM LARGE CRUST   SODIUM PER RECIPE: 12.9 MG
SODIUM PER QUARTER OF RECIPE (4 SERVINGS): 3.233 MG
SODIUM PER SLICE (BASED ON 8 SLICES): 1.616 MG

2¼ teaspoons active dry yeast (3.5 mg)
 1 cup warm distilled or no-sodium bottled water (trace)
 1 tablespoon white granulated sugar or Splenda (.126 mg)
 2 tablespoons extra virgin olive oil (trace)
 1 tablespoon vital wheat gluten (2.25 mg)
 1 tablespoon minced orange zest (.18 mg)
2¾ cups white bread flour or all-purpose unbleached flour
     (6.875 mg)

In a medium to large mixing bowl, dissolve the yeast in 1 cup of warm (110°F, no hotter) bottled or no-sodium water.

Mix in the sugar until both the sugar and yeast are dissolved. Let rest for about 5 minutes.

Add all other ingredients to the yeast/sugar mix. Knead for about 5 minutes, then let rest and rise in large warm bowl covered with a light kitchen towel for 30 minutes at room temperature (75°F to 95°F).

For Calzones: Bring out and roll to a flat square-shaped crust keeping in mind four calzones.*

For Pizza Crust: Roll out circle and place on pizza baking pan.

Preheat the oven to 425°F about 15 minutes before you are ready to proceed. Bake on middle rack for 12 to 15 minutes or until golden brown for pizza sandwiches and calzones. To bake the crust by itself, bake at 425°F for 8 minutes.

Nutrient Values per Quarter of Recipe:
Calories: 398.8. Protein: 11 g. Carbohydrate: 70.1 g. Dietary Fiber: 2.847 g. Total Sugars: 3.118 g. Total Fat: 7.707 g. Saturated Fat: 1.055 g. Monounsaturated Fat: 5.095 g. Polyunsaturated Fat: .923 g. Cholesterol: 0 mg. Calcium: 16.5 mg. Iron: 4.318 mg. Potassium: 130.2 mg. Sodium: 3.233 mg. Vitamin K: 3.308 mcg. Folate: 173.7 mcg.

---

*Can also make smaller calzones up to eight. Good to freeze and use for lunches or picnics or work. Keep refrigerated in a picnic cooler and heat before eating or eat chilled.

❖ DON'S CHEESE & GARLIC BREAD ❖

BREAD MACHINE BAKE
DIABETIC ADAPTABLE

This makes a great garlic toast for parties. You can slice it into small pieces and toast it with a spray of your own garlic mix. Makes a good salad side when bread is needed. The cheese can be doubled in this recipe.

MAKES 1 LOAF   SODIUM PER LOAF: 41.9 MG
SODIUM PER SLICE (16): 2.619 MG

1 cup no-sodium bottled water, warmed to 110°F to 115°F (trace)
1 tablespoon white distilled vinegar (.15 mg)
1 tablespoon extra virgin olive oil (trace)
1 tablespoon Sure-Jell Ever-Fresh* (4.992 mg)
3 cups white bread machine flour (7.5 mg)
1 tablespoon vital wheat gluten (2.25 mg)
1 teaspoon garlic powder (.728 mg)
1 teaspoon onion powder† (1.134 mg)
1 tablespoon white granulated sugar or Splenda (.126 mg)
3 cloves garlic, peeled and minced or thinly sliced (1.53 mg)
2 ounces Heluva Good low-sodium Cheddar, yellow or white (20 mg)
2¼ teaspoons bread machine yeast (3.5 mg)

Place the ingredients in the bread machine pan in order listed, or according to your manufacturer's instructions. Always set bread machine on a dry area before starting machine. Set the machine to White Bread, Medium Crust, 2 pounds.

Cool on a rack.

Nutrient Values per Slice:
Calories: 104.7. Protein: 3.901 g. Carbohydrate: 20.2 g. Dietary Fiber: .761 g. Total Sugars: 1.53 g. Total Fat: 2.232 g. Saturated Fat: .904 g. Monounsaturated Fat: .654 g. Polyunsaturated Fat: .17 g. Cholesterol: 0 mg. Calcium: 5.494 mg. Iron: 1.187 mg. Potassium: 57.7 mg. Sodium: 2.619 mg. Vitamin K: .413 mcg. Folate: 46.6 mcg.

*Or Fruit-Fresh. Diabetics, use 2 level tablespoons of grated orange zest instead (use garlic press for help).
†You may add ½ cup chopped onion or 2 teaspoons onion powder. You may also add 1 teaspoon celery seed.

CROUSTADES
❈ FOR YOUR STEWS AND SOUPS ❈

DIABETIC ADAPTABLE

A croustade is a container for soups, vegetable mixes, creamed meats, and other food servings, including shell-fish salads, etc. These will hold up during the course of a short or long dinner meal and you'll find yourself and your guests eating the bread when all of you finish the stew or other serving.

**MAKES 4 OR 6 SMALL CROUSTADES SODIUM PER RECIPE: 26 MG
SODIUM PER CROUSTADE: 6 MG**

2 **cups warmed (80°F to 90°F) no-sodium distilled water (trace)**
1 **tablespoon grated lemon peel (.36)**
6 **cups white, unbleached, or best for bread machine flour (15 mg)**
2 **tablespoons white granulated sugar or Splenda (.252 mg)**
2 **level tablespoons vital wheat gluten (4.5 mg)**
1 **tablespoon bread machine yeast (6 mg)**

Place all the ingredients in the bread machine pan in the order listed. Set bread machine for Dough cycle.

The dough may rise completely before the buzzer sounds. If the dough reaches the top, close to the lid, remove to a lightly floured breadboard. Cut into eight equal size "balls." Form each into a ball, tucking underneath and pinching each one shut. Place bottom side down on a lightly oiled/greased baking sheet and make four cross slices at the top with a very sharp knife.

Cover with light cloth and let rise in a warm place for about 45 minutes to an hour or until double in size.

About fifteen minutes before you will be ready to continue the recipe, preheat the oven to 425°F when you are ready to proceed. Bake on the middle oven rack for 18 to 25 minutes or until golden brown.

Cool on a rack. Cut a hole in the top, pull out the warm bread and let those Super Bowl watchers eat the insides with some dripping honey or strawberry jam. When ready to serve your soup, pour into croustade bowls and serve hot.

Nutrient Values Based on per Serving or Piece of a Croustade Cut into Eight Sections After Use:
Calories: 91.4. Protein: 2.927 g. Carbohydrate: 18.9 g. Dietary Fiber: .731 g.
Total Sugars: .78 g. Total Fat: .255 g. Saturated Fat: .039 g. Monounsaturated Fat: .03 g.
Polyunsaturated Fat: .097 g. Cholesterol: 0 mg. Calcium: 4.015 mg. Iron: 1.152 mg.
Potassium: 32.9 mg. Sodium: .816 mg. Vitamin K: 0 mcg. Folate: 44.9 mcg.

DON'S PLACE BURGER BUNS
✦ TEXAS-SIZE BURGER BUNS ✦

BREAD MACHINE PREPARATION, OVEN BAKE
DIABETIC ADAPTABLE*

MAKES 12 TEXAS-SIZE BURGER BUNS   SODIUM PER RECIPE: 32.64 MG
SODIUM PER BUN: 2.72 MG

2   **cups warmed (105°F to 115°F) no-sodium distilled water (trace)**
1   **tablespoon white distilled vinegar (.15 mg)**
1   **tablespoon extra virgin olive oil (trace)**
2   **teaspoons Sure-Jell Ever-Fresh* (3.328 mg)**
5   **cups white, unbleached, or best for bread flour (12.5 mg)**
1   **cup whole-wheat pastry flour (6 mg)**
4   **teaspoons white granulated sugar or Splenda (.168 mg)**
2   **tablespoons vital wheat gluten (4.5 mg)**
1   **tablespoon bread machine yeast (6 mg)**

Place all the ingredients in the bread machine pan in the order listed. Set the bread machine for Dough cycle.

The dough may rise completely before the buzzer sounds. If the dough reaches the top, close to the lid, remove it to a lightly floured breadboard. You will now shape/form twelve large burger buns. Cut the dough ball into twelve equal pieces. Roll with your hands by pulling the dough down to a bottom spot and pinching at bottom. Place six pieces on dough on two separate lightly greased baking sheets, pinched side down. Lightly press on them to make the shape bun you want. Cover with a light cloth and let rise for about 45 minutes to an hour or until double in size.

Fifteen minutes before you are ready to proceed, preheat the oven to 425°F for a standard oven, and 400°F for a convection oven. When ready, bake on a rack in the lower third of the oven for 8 to 20 minutes or until golden brown. (The time depends on each oven. When you learn the time it takes your oven to bake any bread, write it down in the recipe in the cookbook to remind you for the next time.)

Cool the buns on a rack. Serve the same day for the best flavors.

Nutrients Values per Bun:
Calories: 250.3. Protein: 8.092 g. Carbohydrate: 49.8 g. Dietary Fiber: 2.836 g. Total Sugars: 2.053 g. Total Fat: 1.889 g. Saturated Fat: .271 g. Monounsaturated Fat: .923 g. Polyunsaturated Fat: .388 g. Cholesterol: 0 mg. Calcium: 11.9 mg. Iron: 2.983 mg. Potassium: 117.5 mg. Sodium: 2.72 mg. Vitamin K: .551 mcg. Folate: 108 mcg.

*Diabetics may exchange the Sure-Jell (12 g sugars) with 3 level tablespoons minced orange zest.

❖ DON'S FRENCH-STYLE PICNIC ROLLS ❖

BREAD MACHINE KNEAD, OVEN BAKE
DIABETIC ADAPTABLE*

This versatile recipe will make sandwich rolls, buns, sliced bread, long loaves or dinner rolls. Make the dough and shape that you want to bake.

**MAKES 18 SANDWICH BUNS OR ROLLS† SODIUM PER RECIPE: 31.8 MG
SODIUM PER BUN (18): 1.768 MG**

2 **cups no-sodium bottled water (trace)**
1 **cup whole-wheat pastry flour (6 mg)**
5 **cups white, unbleached, or best for bread machine flour (12.5 mg)**
1 **tablespoon white wine vinegar (.15 mg)**
2 **tablespoons extra virgin olive oil (trace)**
1½ **tablespoons white granulated sugar or Splenda (.189 mg)**
2 **teaspoons onion powder (2.268 mg)**
2 **tablespoons vital wheat gluten (4.5 mg)**
1 **tablespoon Sure-Jell Ever-Fresh***
1 **tablespoon bread machine yeast (6 mg)**

Place the ingredients into the bread machine pan in the order listed or in the order your machine manufacturer lists. Set the machine to Dough.

When the dough is done, roll it out onto a lightly floured breadboard and slice it in half. Press or roll out the dough until it is about ¾ inch thick. Slice with sharp knife to make nine long buns. Use a baguette pan with troughs to hold the bun shape while rising and baking. Cover with lightly oiled wax paper and set in a warm place or room temperature spot with no draft possible.

Do the same with other half. Let both of the doughs rise for 45 minutes to an hour.

Preheat the oven to 375°F, 15 minutes before you are ready to proceed. Bake the buns for up to 12 minutes, or take them out when they are golden brown.

Nutrient Values per Bun:
Calories: 172.7. Protein: 5.418 g. Carbohydrate: 33.1 g. Dietary Fiber: 1.904 g. Total Sugars: 1.067 g. Total Fat: 2.012 g. Saturated Fat: .282 g. Monounsaturated Fat: 1.169 g. Polyunsaturated Fat: .322 g. Cholesterol: 0 mg. Calcium: 8.809 mg. Iron: 1.998 mg. Potassium: 80.5 mg. Sodium: 1.768 mg. Vitamin K: .735 mcg. Folate: 72.4 mcg.

*Diabetics may exchange the Sure-Jell (12 g sugars) with 3 level tablespoons minced orange zest.
†May make twelve super buns if you prefer.

❧ FRENCH BAGUETTES ❧

This recipe was designed especially to provide a baguette treat for our entrée salads such as the shrimp scampi salad and others. It's based on a special baguette I used to enjoy while filming in the French Protectorate, Tahiti. Only 33 calories per slice and very low total fat.

MAKES 3 LOAVES OR 48 SLICES OR 12 SANDWICH-LENGTH BUNS
SODIUM PER RECIPE: 73 MG
SODIUM PER SLICE (⅜ INCH): 1.52 MG

THE BREAD
1 **cup less 2 tablespoons no-sodium bottled water warmed to 105°F to 115°F (trace)**
1 **tablespoon white wine vinegar (.15 mg)**
3 **cups white, unbleached best for bread machine flour (7.5 mg)**
1 **tablespoon vital wheat gluten (2.25 mg)**
2 **teaspoons white granulated sugar or Splenda (.084 mg)**
1 **teaspoon Sure-Jell Ever-Fresh* (1.664 mg)**
1 **teaspoon onion powder (1.134 mg)**
2¼ **teaspoons bread machine yeast (3.5 mg)**

THE GLAZE
1 **egg white, beaten (54.8 mg)**
½ **tablespoon poppy seed (.924 mg)**
1 **tablespoon sesame seed (1.485 mg)**

Place the bread ingredients in the bread machine pan in order listed, or according to your manufacturer's instructions. Always set bread machine yeast on a dry area before starting the machine. Set the machine on Dough and let it run through a cycle.

Just before the dough is ready, beat the egg white until it's fluffy.

When the dough is ready, roll it out onto a lightly floured breadboard. Slice or break the dough into three equal-size pieces. Using your hands, roll a log from the first piece until it's about 12 to 13 inches long. Lay into a trough of a lightly greased baguette pan (Use a triple trough baguette pan). Do the same with the other two sections.

Make three or four diagonal slices in the loaves.

*Diabetics may exchange the Sure-Jell (12 g sugars) with 3 level tablespoons minced orange zest.

Using a basting brush, brush the egg white on all three loaves. Sprinkle an even mix of the poppy seed and sesame seed along each loaf. They won't amount to more than one or two more milligrams of sodium for the whole recipe.

Cover the dough with lightly greased wax paper and let it rise in a warm place for about 30 to 40 minutes.

Preheat the oven to 375°F, about 15 minutes before you are ready to proceed.

Bake for 12 to 15 minutes or until golden brown.

This freezes well in Ziploc bags. Defrost on a countertop or covered with wax paper in the microwave using the defrost setting.

Nutrient Values per Slice (⅝ inch):
Calories: 32.7. Protein: 1.11 g. Carbohydrate: 6.433 g. Dietary Fiber: .275 g. Total Sugars: .257 g. Total Fat: .22 g. Saturated Fat: .031 g. Monounsaturated Fat: .052 g. Polyunsaturated Fat: .102 g. Cholesterol: 0 mg. Calcium: 4.642 mg. Iron: .426 mg. Potassium: 14.5 mg. Sodium: 1.52 mg. Vitamin K: .015 mcg. Folate: 15.8 mcg.

❖ DON'S SALAD CROUTONS ❖

BREAD MACHINE RECIPE
1½-POUND LOAF
DIABETIC ADAPTABLE

Croutons are great with some salads, like our Caesar Salad (page 131). But they also work with other salads like a spinach salad or even with a mixed green salad with a raspberry vinaigrette. You'll like these. They taste pretty much like the commercially produced garlic croutons, which usually have 30 times more mg of sodium.*

MAKES 150 TO 200 CROUTONS   SODIUM PER RECIPE: 22.1 MG
SODIUM PER 10 CROUTONS (150 COUNT): .147 MG
SODIUM PER 10 CROUTONS (200 COUNT): .11 MG

1 **cup warmed no-sodium bottled water (110°F to 115°F) (trace)**
1 **tablespoon apple cider vinegar (.15 mg)**
1 **tablespoon extra virgin olive oil (trace)**

---

*You can adapt this recipe to a sourdough crouton if you exchange ⅓ cup of Sourdough Starter (page 118) for ⅓ cup of water. Keep an eye on the basket while the machine kneads, to make sure it isn't too dry or too wet. Fix if that happens with a bit more water or a bit more flour, whichever is called for.

2 **cups white bread flour (5 mg)**
1 **cup whole-wheat pastry flour (6 mg)**
2 **teaspoons garlic powder (1.456 mg)**
2 **teaspoons Oregon Flavor Rack Garlic Lover's Garlic†**
   (.952 mg)
¼ **teaspoon dried thyme leaves (trace)**
2 **teaspoons dried rosemary (1.2 mg)**
1 **tablespoon vital wheat gluten (2.25 mg)**
1 **tablespoon white granulated sugar or Splenda (.126 mg)**
1 **tablespoon minced orange zest‡ (.18 mg)**
2¼ **teaspoons bread machine yeast (3.5 mg)**

PREPARING CROUTONS FOR THE OVEN
   (After the bread is baked)
2 **tablespoons extra virgin olive oil (trace)**
4 **large cloves garlic, minced (2.04 mg)**

Place the ingredients into your bread machine in the order listed or according to your manufacturer's instructions. Keep the yeast dry. Set the machine to 1½ pound loaf, medium crust, white bread.

When the bread is done, roll it out onto a rack and cut it in half with sharp serrated bread knife. Let cool for about an hour.

Slice the bread into ½ inch to slightly larger slices. When all the slices are ready, lay them flat and cross cut so you end up with a lot of "crouton"-size pieces. Let them dry on a cutting board for about 2 hours.

When you are ready to proceed, preheat the oven to 350°F. Lightly oil a cookie sheet. Using a large frying pan or skillet, sauté 1 tablespoon of the oil and 2 cloves of garlic, stirring so the garlic doesn't burn. Heat for about a minute. Stir in half the croutons and toss for about another minute. Place these on the prepared cooking sheet. Now, toss the second half of the croutons in the skillet with the second tablespoon of olive oil and the remaining garlic cloves.

Put all the croutons on the baking sheet and place in your preheated oven for 15 minutes. Every 5 minutes stir and toss a bit to keep the bottom croutons from burning. Take the croutons out at 15 minutes and let cool on a rack. You can serve the croutons right away or let them cool and bag them for freezing (for up to 3 months).

---

†The Web site for Oregon Flavor Rack is www.spiceman.com. Sodium levels not listed by manufacturer or by USDA. We have chosen to include some as raw garlic for sauce amount.
‡Orange zest is intentional in this recipe and should not be replaced with Sure-Jell or Fruit-Fresh.

❈ DON'S SANDWICH BUNS ❈

BREAD MACHINE KNEAD, OVEN BAKE
DIABETIC ADAPTABLE

This recipe produces a delicious sandwich bun that is unlike a hamburger bun. Elongated rather than round, it contributes to the flavors of the sandwiches in this book where it is recommended. Of course, it will also work for your own sandwiches. You may cut this recipe in half, but if you do, use 2¼ teaspoons yeast.

MAKES 18 BUNS SODIUM PER RECIPE: 30.96 MG
SODIUM PER BUN: 1.72 MG

 2 cups warmed (105°F to 115°F) no-sodium bottled distilled water (trace)
 1 tablespoon apple cider vinegar (.15 mg)
 1 tablespoon extra virgin olive oil (trace)
 2 teaspoons Sure-Jell Ever-Fresh* (3.328 mg)
 ⅛ teaspoon Don's Flavor Enhancer (page 177) (.108 mg)
 5½ cups white, unbleached, or best for bread flour (13.8 mg)
 ½ cup whole-wheat pastry flour (3 mg)
 1 level tablespoon white granulated sugar or Splenda (.126 mg)
 2 tablespoons vital wheat gluten (4.5 mg)
 1 tablespoon bread machine yeast (6 mg)

Place the ingredients in the bread machine pan in the order listed. Set the machine for the Dough cycle.

---

*Diabetics may exchange the Sure-Jell (12 g of sugars) with 3 level tablespoons minced orange zest.

When ready, bring the dough out onto a lightly floured breadboard. Cut the dough in half. Work with one at a time. Press or roll down to about ¾ inch thick. With a sharp knife, cut six to nine elongated bun shapes. About 2 × 5 to 6 inches.

Place on a lightly greased baking sheet or in the troughs of a double or triple baguette pan. Cover with a very lightly floured cloth or lightly oiled wax paper and set in a warm place to rise for 45 minutes to an hour.

When the rising is almost done, preheat the oven to 450°F.

Bake in the hot oven for up to 8 to 10 minutes or until golden brown. Cool on a rack.

Nutrient Values per Bun:
Calories: 167.4. Protein: 5.299 g. Carbohydrate: 33.2 g. Dietary Fiber: 1.579 g. Total Sugars: 1.137 g. Total Fat: 1.232 g. Saturated Fat: .175 g. Monounsaturated Fat: .611g. Polyunsaturated Fat: .247 g. Cholesterol: 0 mg. Calcium: 7.401 mg. Iron: 2.022 mg. Potassium: 68.7 mg. Sodium: 1.72 mg. Vitamin K: .368 mcg. Folate: 75.9 mcg.

Don's Sourdough Baguette
❈ Sandwich Bread ❈

Bread Machine Knead, Oven Baked
Diabetic Adaptable

Make your sourdough a week ahead of time and follow the starter instructions for storing. Then make this bread and hmmm, it is good. You must use baguette pans to help shape this bread. This is also a very good bread to serve with salads, thinly sliced (½ inch thick), and lightly toasted. You can cut the fat if you leave out the olive oil. The bread will be a bit less soft if you do.

MAKES 2 BAGUETTES   SODIUM PER RECIPE: 63.9 MG
SODIUM PER SANDWICH (14): 4.562 MG
SODIUM PER (½-INCH) SLICE (64): .998 MG

1½ cups warmed (105°F to 115°F) no-sodium bottled distilled water (trace)
 ½ cup Sourdough Starter (page 118) (2.259 mg)
 1 level tablespoon powdered buttermilk (33.6 mg)
 1 tablespoon apple cider vinegar (.15 mg)
 1 tablespoon extra virgin olive oil (trace)
 2 teaspoons Sure-Jell Ever-Fresh* (3.328 mg)

*Diabetics may exchange the Sure-Jell (12 g of sugars) with 3 level tablespoons minced orange zest.

⅛ teaspoon Don's Flavor Enhancer (page 177) (.108 mg)
5½ cups white, unbleached, or best for bread machine flour
     (13.8 mg)
  1 level tablespoon white granulated sugar or Splenda (.126 mg)
  2 tablespoons vital wheat gluten (4.5 mg)
  1 level tablespoon finely minced garlic† (.476 mg)
  1 tablespoon bread machine yeast (6 mg)

Place ingredients in bread pan in order listed. Set machine for Dough cycle.

When ready, roll out onto a lightly floured breadboard. Cut the dough ball in half. Work with one at a time. Roll each half using your hands to make log. Lay the log into your two-trough French bread pan. Do the same with the other half. (You can extend this recipe by forming three equal size loafs and using your triple trough baguette pan.)

Cover with a very light cloth or lightly greased wax paper and set in a warm place to rise for 45 minutes to an hour.

Preheat the oven to 375°F when you are almost ready to proceed. Bake for 20 to 25 minutes or until golden brown.

Cool on a rack.

Nutrient Values per Sandwich (14):
Calories: 219.3. Protein: 6.885 g. Carbohydrate: 43.3 g. Dietary Fiber: 1.647 g. Total Sugars: 1.462 g. Total Fat: 1.579 g. Saturated Fat: .236 g. Monounsaturated Fat: .789 g. Polyunsaturated Fat: .304 g. Cholesterol: .32 mg. Calcium: 14.7 mg. Iron: 2.661 mg. Potassium: 85.9 mg. Sodium: 4.562 mg. Vitamin K: .473 mcg. Folate: 104.5 mcg.

Nutrient Values per (½-inch) Slice:
Calories: 48. Protein: 1.506 g. Carbohydrate: 9.476 g. Dietary Fiber: .36 g. Total Sugars: .32 g. Total Fat: .345 g. Saturated Fat: .052 g. Monounsaturated Fat: .173 g. Polyunsaturated Fat: .067 g. Cholesterol: .07 mg. Calcium: 3.208 mg. Iron: .582 mg. Potassium: 18.8 mg. Sodium: .998 mg. Vitamin K: .103 mcg. Folate: 22.8 mcg.

❖ SOURDOUGH STARTER ❖

DIABETIC ADAPTABLE

Use this recipe to make your own Sourdough Starter. Let stand near an open window (on cool days) for about 7 days. Refrigerate. Take out every two weeks, stir or pour off "black" liquid and stir. Once a month, to keep your starter alive, add ¼ cup white flour and ¼ cup no-sodium bottled water. (Chlorinated water will kill sourdough.)

MAKES 2 CUPS   SODIUM PER RECIPE: 9.04 MG
SODIUM PER ½ CUP: 2.26 MG

†Or 1 teaspoon garlic powder (.728 mg).

2 cups no-sodium bottled water (trace)
2 cups white, unbleached flour (5 mg)
2 teaspoons active dry yeast (3.996 mg)
1 teaspoon white granulated sugar or Splenda (trace)

In a medium-size bowl (such as Tupperware), stir the above ingredients together and let the bowl stand, uncovered, near an open window for about 5 to 7 days. Stir once a day. Refrigerate with a loose lid when it's done. After using for bread making, replace the sourdough you've used with equal measurements of water and flour. If you use a cup of sourdough, replace with a cup of flour and a cup of water. Pour out any black liquid that forms while storing. Check this once a week. Stir in the lightly dark liquid that forms if it hasn't turned black.

Nutrient Values per ½ Cup:
Calories: 237.5. Protein: 7.221 g. Carbohydrate: 49.5 g. Dietary Fiber: 2.107 g. Total Sugars: 1.039 g. Total Fat: .704 g. Saturated Fat: .109 g. Monounsaturated Fat: .106 g. Polyunsaturated Fat: .258 g. Cholesterol: 0 mg. Calcium: 10.7 mg. Iron: 3.232 mg. Potassium: 106.9 mg. Sodium: 2.26 mg. Vitamin K: 0 mcg. Folate: 143 mcg.

❈ DON'S TASTY BURGER BUNS ❈

BREAD MACHINE KNEAD, HAND SHAPED, OVEN BAKED

I created this bun just for Scott's Heluva Good Cheese Venison Burger (page 95). But it's worked so well that I now use it for other burgers, too, especially anything off the barbecue. You can add some beaten egg white to the bun tops and then sprinkle sesame seeds on them if you like. Let the buns rise, then back as instructed.

MAKES 18 BUNS SODIUM PER RECIPE: 422.2 MG
SODIUM PER BUN: 23.4 MG

1¾ cups warmed Knudsen or other lower-sodium buttermilk
     warmed to about 100°F. (227.5 mg)
  1 tablespoon apple cider vinegar (.15 mg)
  1 tablespoon olive oil (trace)
  2 large egg whites (109.6 mg)
  1 egg yolk (7.138 mg)
  5 cups white, unbleached, or best for bread machine flour
     (12.5 mg)
1½ teaspoons Sure-Jell Ever-Fresh* (2.496 mg)

*Diabetics may exchange the Sure-Jell (12 g of sugars) with 3 level tablespoons minced orange zest.

1 tablespoon vital wheat gluten (2.25 mg)
1 tablespoon white granulated sugar (.126 mg)
1 tablespoon bread machine yeast (6 mg)
1 egg white for glazing (54.8)
2 tablespoons sesame seeds (1.98)

Place the ingredients except egg white for glazing and sesame seeds in the bread machine in the order listed or according to your manufacturer's instructions. Always set bread machine yeast on a dry area before starting the machine. Set the machine for the Dough cycle.

When the dough is ready, roll it out onto a lightly floured breadboard. Cut it in half. Press down with your hands until the dough is about ¾ inch thick. You may gently use a rolling pin, also.) Make round or rectangular cuts for the buns of your choice.

If you are using sesame seeds, brush the beaten egg glazing on top of each bun. Sprinkle with the sesame seeds.

Set the buns on lightly greased baking sheets (use olive oil in a spray can). Cover with a very light cloth or wax paper and set in a warm place.

Let the dough rise for about 45 minutes to an hour.

Preheat the oven to 375°F when you are ready to proceed. Bake for about 12 to 18 minutes or until the buns are golden brown.

Cool on a rack.

Nutrient Values per Bun:
Calories: 153. Protein: 5.635 g. Carbohydrate: 28.4 g. Dietary Fiber: 1.196 g. Total Sugars: 1.208 g. Total Fat: 2.388 g. Saturated Fat: .608 g. Monounsaturated Fat: .896 g. Polyunsaturated Fat: .463 g. Cholesterol: 14.2 mg. Calcium: 45 mg. Iron: 5.243 mg. Potassium: 64.8 mg. Sodium: 23.4 mg. Vitamin K: .467 mcg. Folate: 71.6 mcg.

❖ WHOLE-WHEAT FLOUR TORTILLAS ❖

MAKES 12 FLOUR TORTILLAS   SODIUM PER RECIPE: 30.9 MG
SODIUM PER TORTILLA: 2.572 MG

2 cups unbleached bread flour (5 mg)
2 cups whole-wheat pastry flour (12 mg)
1 tablespoon Featherweight Baking Powder (13.5 mg)
2 teaspoons Ener-g Baking Soda (trace)
½ cup plus 1 tablespoon extra virgin olive oil (trace)
1½ cups plus 1 tablespoon warmed no-sodium bottled water or orange juice (trace)
1 teaspoon grated lemon zest (.12 mg)
1 tablespoon apple cider vinegar (.15 mg)
1 teaspoon white granulated sugar or Splenda (trace)
1 teaspoon fresh lime juice (.05 mg)

Combine the flour and baking powder in a medium-size mixing bowl. Add the olive oil, using a wooden spoon or fork. Slowly add the zest, vinegar, sugar, lime juice, water or orange juice, mixing together while doing this. When the dough cleans the side of the bowl, stop adding the liquid. Too much water can make a tortilla tough.

Knead the dough about five turns only. Form a small ball and cover it with plastic wrap or a cloth. Let it sit for about 30 minutes to 2 hours in a warm place. You can roll this ball into a log, if you like. After the dough has sat, cut the ball or log into twelve pieces and roll each piece in your hands to form a ball. On a lightly floured or greased pan, set the balls apart from each other and cover. Let sit for about a half hour in a warm place.

Let sit for ½ hour (warm place lightly floured). Bring the balls to a breadboard. Press a ball of dough over your forefinger to create a hole. Set the ball on the breadboard, hole side down, and, using a rolling pin, roll out the dough. To make a circle, roll it once, then turn the dough 90 degrees, then roll again, continuing doing that until the dough is thin. These balls should make a 10- to 12-inch disk. You can roll one out, cook, then roll again while the first is cooking, or you can roll out all the disks and set them aside, one on top of the other with wax paper between them.

Heat an ungreased pan on the stove top to medium heat. When a splash of water bounces on the pan, you are ready to cook the disks. I prefer to cook while rolling.

Cook the tortillas for about 20 to 30 seconds on each side. Turn the disk when you see bubbles begin to pop up. As each tortillas is cooked, set it on a paper or cloth towel or put them on top of each other again with wax paper between them. Serve hot or soon. You can store the tortillas overnight in Ziploc bags but no longer (because of the absence of salt). You may freeze these for up to 3 months, however, and thaw them later either by setting out in the microwave.

Nutrient Values per Tortilla:
Calories: 236.1. Protein: 4.898 g. Carbohydrate: 31.5 g. Dietary Fiber: 3.049 g. Total Sugars: .347 g. Total Fat: 10.7 g. Saturated Fat: 1.465 g. Monounsaturated Fat: 7.527 g. Polyunsaturated Fat: 1.094 g. Cholesterol: 0 mg. Calcium: 82.7 mg. Iron: 1.892 mg. Potassium: 231.5 mg. Sodium: 2.572 mg. Vitamin K: 4.961 mcg. Folate: 40.9 mcg.

❧ TUSCAN BREAD ❧

BREAD MACHINE PREPARATION
DIABETIC ADAPTABLE

When I traveled to France to film, then down to Italy, I went from a French baguette for a meal to Italian Tuscan Bread. There didn't seem to be any difference, except possibly that the French overcooked theirs and the Italians may have been undercooking some of theirs. The shape was different, too, but also the same. In Italy you could find Tuscan bread in round loaves, standard loaves, and just like the baguettes. This bread is not your basic Wonder Bread. But if you like baguettes and Italian bread for salads and some sandwiches, this recipe will work for you. I think it's delicious.

MAKES 1 *BAGUETTE*   SODIUM PER SERVING: 21.6 MG
SODIUM PER SLICE (16 SLICES):* 1.35 MG

¾ cup warmed no-sodium bottled water (105°F to 115°F) (trace)
1 teaspoon apple cider vinegar (.05 mg)
1 teaspoon white granulated sugar or Splenda (.042 mg)
2¼ cups white bread machine flour (5.625 mg)
¼ cup whole-wheat flour (1.5 mg)
1 teaspoon onion powder (1.134 mg)
1 tablespoon vital wheat gluten† (2.25 mg)
1 teaspoon Sure-Jell Ever-Fresh‡ (1.6444 mg)
1 tablespoon bread machine yeast (6 mg)

Place the ingredients in the bread machine pan in the order listed or according to your manufacturer's instructions. Keep the yeast dry. Set the machine on Dough.

When the dough is ready, roll out onto a lightly floured breadboard.

Flatten the dough into an oblong shape. Roll or fold the dough loosely (you don't want to overhandle it) into a baguette. This should be about 18 inches long. (If you don't have an 18-inch-long pan or baking sheet, then slice the dough in half and make two 9-inch baguettes. Bake for

---

*You can slice the bread into twenty to twenty-eight thinner slices.

You may also make a round loaf out of this. Or you may slice it into three or four sandwich buns for a great Italian Mock Sausage (page 86, *No-Salt, Lowest-Sodium Cookbook*) or other sandwich.

†Leave the gluten out of this recipe, if you prefer.

‡Diabetics exchange the Sure-Jell (12 g sugars) with 3 level tablespoons minced orange zest.

only 35 minutes if you do.) Transfer seam side down to a lightly floured baguette pan (or a baking sheet (but a baguette pan works better). You can use cornmeal as the pan's lubricant also.

Cover the baguette with a light cloth or wax paper and set in a warm place to rise. It will double in size in about an hour.

Preheat the oven to 375°F when you are ready to proceed.

Bake the bread for 45 to 60 minutes on the middle rack of the oven, or until the crust is quite brown and the bread sounds hollow when tapped on top.

Remove from the oven and cool on a rack. Stores well in a Ziploc bag for up to 2 days or in the freezer for up to a month.

Nutrient Values per Slice:
Calories: 79.7. Protein: 2.733 g. Carbohydrate: 16.3 g. Dietary Fiber: .868 g. Total Sugars: 1.01 g. Total Fat: .251 g. Saturated Fat: .038 g. Monounsaturated Fat: .039 g. Polyunsaturated Fat: .088 g. Cholesterol: 0 mg. Calcium: 4.252 mg. Iron: 1.018 mg. Potassium: 43 mg. Sodium: 1.35 mg. Vitamin K: 0 mcg. Folate: 45.7 mcg.

❂ DON'S WHITE SANDWICH BREAD ❂

BREAD MACHINE RECIPE
DIABETIC ADAPTABLE

The crust of this bread is the best I've eaten in a long time. Give it a try. Most white breads get their flavors from the salt. This one gets flavor from a bit of whole-wheat flour, onion, and the powdered buttermilk.

MAKES 1 LOAF   SODIUM PER RECIPE: 51.7 MG
SODIUM PER SLICE (16): 3.229 MG

¾ **cup plus 2 tablespoons no-sodium bottled water heated to**
   105°F to 115°F (trace)
2½ **cups white, unbleached, best for bread machine flour**
   (6.25 mg)
½ **cup whole-wheat flour or whole-wheat pastry flour (3 mg)**
1 **tablespoon apple cider vinegar (.30 mg)**
1 **tablespoon extra virgin olive oil (trace)**
1 **tablespoon vital wheat gluten (2.25 mg)**
1 **tablespoon dry buttermilk powder (33.6 mg)**
1 **teaspoon Sure-Jell Ever-Fresh* (1.664 mg)**
1 **tablespoon white granulated sugar or Splenda (.126 mg)**

*Or Fruit-Fresh. Diabetics, use 2 level tablespoons of grated orange zest instead (use garlic press for help).

¼ **large onion, diced (1.125 mg)**
2¼ **teaspoons bread machine yeast (3.5 mg)**

Place all the ingredients in the bread machine pan and set machine for white bread, medium crust, 2-pound loaf. Check it halfway through the kneading process to make sure your flour has the proper water amount. If it's too sticky, add more flour, up to 2 tablespoons. If it hasn't come together as a ball, add water, 1 tablespoon at a time, but no more than 2 tablespoons.

Nutrient Values per Slice:
Calories: 101.3. Protein: 3.225 g. Carbohydrate: 19.4 g. Dietary Fiber: 1.119 g. Total Sugars: 1.03 g. Total Fat: 1.16 g. Saturated Fat: .174 g. Monounsaturated Fat: .666 g. Polyunsaturated Fat: .183 g. Cholesterol: .28 mg. Calcium: 9.828 mg. Iron: 1.14 mg. Potassium: 55.9 mg. Sodium: 3.229 mg. Vitamin K: .46 mcg. Folate: 42.6 mcg.

❖ PARKER HOUSE ROLLS ❖

DIABETIC ADAPTABLE

When I was young, I called these "tri-tops" because of the three-way split of each roll. Fresh out of the oven for Sunday dinners, they were my mother's favorite to make. When they first appeared in markets commercially, she disdained their texture and flavor. Here's her best, without the salt, but with enough of the right stuff to make them practically just like hers.

**MAKES 18 ROLLS   SODIUM PER RECIPE: 17 MG
SODIUM PER ROLL: .945 MG**

THE BREAD
1 **cup less 3 tablespoons no-sodium bottled water, warmed to
     105°F to 115°F (trace)**
1 **tablespoon honey (.84 mg)**
1 **tablespoon white wine vinegar (15 mg)**
2 **tablespoons extra virgin olive oil (trace)**
3 **cups white, unbleached, or best for bread flour (7.5 mg)**
1 **tablespoon vital wheat gluten (2.25 mg)**
1 **tablespoon white granulated sugar or Splenda (.126 mg)**
1 **teaspoon Sure-Jell Ever-Fresh* (.99 mg)**

*Diabetics may exchange the Sure-Jell (12 g sugars) with 3 level tablespoons minced orange zest.

1 teaspoon onion powder (1.134 mg)
2¼ teaspoons bread machine yeast (3.5 mg)

Place the ingredients into the bread machine pan in the order listed, or according to your manufacturer's instructions. Always set bread machine yeast on a dry area before starting the machine. Set the machine on Dough and let it run through a cycle.

When the dough is ready, roll out onto a lightly floured breadboard. Break away what will become fifty-four 1-inch balls of dough. Place three balls into each of the cups of a lightly greased and floured standard-size (18 count) muffin pan or into lightly greased heavy muffin cups that you can then bake in a 15 × 11-inch baking dish.

Cover with lightly greased wax paper and let rise in a warm place for about 45 minutes.

Preheat the oven to 375°F when you are ready to proceed.

Bake for 18 to 22 minutes or until golden brown.

The rolls freeze well in Ziploc bags. Defrost on a countertop or covered with wax paper in the microwave using the defrost setting.

Serve warm.

Nutrient Values per Roll:
Calories: 99.7. Protein: 2.636 g. Carbohydrate: 18.1 g. Dietary Fiber: .653 g. Total Sugars: 1.849 g. Total Fat: 1.73 g. Saturated Fat: .237 g. Monounsaturated Fat: 1.134 g. Polyunsaturated Fat: .213 g. Cholesterol: 0 mg. Calcium: 3.874 mg. Iron: 1.045 mg. Potassium: 31.8 mg. Sodium: .945 mg. Vitamin K: .735 mcg. Folate: 41.4 mcg.

❖ DUTCH CRUNCH BREAD ❖

BREAD MACHINE KNEAD—HAND SHAPE—OVEN BAKE
DIABETIC ADAPTABLE

One of my favorite sandwich breads in the past and now. Easy to make, this one will impress your friends as well. Freeze for up to 3 months or serve right out of the oven.

MAKES 12 BUNS OR 2 LOAVES   SODIUM PER RECIPE: 59.3 MG
SODIUM PER BUN: 4.943 MG

BREAD DOUGH INGREDIENTS
1¾ cups warmed (90°F to 100°F) distilled or sodium-free water (trace)
   3 tablespoons extra virgin olive oil (trace)
   2 tablespoons non-fat milk, slightly warmed (15.9 mg)
   1 teaspoon vanilla (.378 mg)
   1 tablespoon cider vinegar (.15 mg)

1 teaspoon onion powder (1.134 mg)
1 tablespoon Sure-Jell Ever-Fresh (4.992 mg)
2 teaspoons white granulated sugar (.084 mg)
1 tablespoon bread machine yeast (6 mg)
5 cups best for bread machine white flour (12.5 mg)

THE DUTCH CRUNCH TOPPING

4 teaspoons sugar (.168 mg)
3 tablespoons yeast (.18 mg)
¾ cup white rice flour* (trace)
2 teaspoons extra virgin olive oil (trace)
⅔ cups distilled or bottle no-sodium water, warmed (trace)

BREAD DOUGH INSTRUCTIONS

Place dough ingredients into bread machine in order listed. Set for dough.

Forty minutes before dough is ready to roll out of machine, prepare the topping.

In a medium to large mixing bowl stir together all the ingredients and cover and sit (35 to 40 minutes). Stir well before applying to pre-cooked dough.

When dough is ready, knead slightly on a lightly floured board and shape into 12 sandwich (elongated) buns, two or three logs for baguette pans.

Place buns in baguette pans. Spread room-temperature topping over each bun or loaf generously and evenly. (It cannot be colder than the dough.) Spread down sides of dough as well. Let rise uncovered in a warm place (room temperature) until they double or more in size.

Preheat oven to 375°F. Bake on middle rack at temperature until deep golden, about 18 to 25 minutes.[†]

Nutrient Values per Bun:
Calories: 289.7 g. Protein: 7.605 g. Carbohydrate: 52.7 g. Dietary Fiber: 2.493 g. Total Sugars: 3.079 g. Total Fat: 4.959 g. Saturated Fat: .702 g. Monounsaturated Fat: 3.228 g. Polyunsaturated Fat: .6 g. Cholesterol: .051 mg. Calcium: 15.3 mg. Iron: 3.146 mg. Potassium: 150.9 mg. Sodium: 4.943 mg. Vitamin K: 2.022 mcg. Folate: 174.6 mcg.

*We used Bob's Red Mill White Rice Flour for our tests.
[†]May shape into 3 baguettes and cut into sandwich rolls after cooking.

SALADS

❖ ❖ ❖ ❖ ❖ ❖ ❖ ❖

THE HISTORY OF SALADS

It is from *Herba Salta*, Latin for "salted herbs," that we get the word "salad." Literally translated, it means lots of herbs seasoned with lots of salt.

The salads and dressings in this book don't use salt, but they do use herbs, spices, and fresh vegetables. Gone for us are the popular commercial dressings, the most popular of which are Ranch-style dressing (the most highly rated) and Italian, Creamy Italian, Thousand Island, French, and Caesar. In America, no restaurant has to serve any more than these to be known as a successful salad establishment.

Dressings and sauces for salad date back as far as five thousand years. The Chinese are known to have used soy sauce for at least those five thousand years. Babylonians used oil and vinegar as long as two thousand years ago. And Worcestershire has been around since Caesar. (No, the Caesar Salad was not invented by Julius, but instead by Caesar Cardini, who invented it in Tijuana, Mexico, in 1924.)

Our biggest enemy for our own survival is salt. Were we Romans we'd all be in trouble. The Romans, it turns out, preferred their herbs and leaves or grass heavily covered with salt.

France, a country that today seems to disdain mayonnaise, first brought it to life about two hundred years ago.

Salad history is more colorful, it seems, than soup history. Maybe it was the clientele. Salads were favorites for all of Europe's monarchs. Giant salad bowls were whisked together by royal salad chefs, combining well over thirty ingredients. These included everything from rose petals and nasturtiums to marigolds and violets. King Henry IV loved a tossed salad of new potatoes, which were boiled and diced. (Was this the first potato salad?) He would add sardines and that messy stuff from France—mayonnaise with herbs, referred to as herb dressing.

It was well known that Mary Queen of Scots liked her ingredients boiled, including her celery roots, diced of course. She also liked mustard dressing and mixed in truffles, hard-boiled egg slices, chervil, and lettuce.

Everyone got into the salad act, though. Just as we have. During the twentieth century, we saw Americans develop a plethora of dressings using just oil, vinegar, and spices as well as lemon juice to make up a huge variety of dressings, sauces, and other toppings. Salads had become not only popular as a side dish, but as a main course.

Part of the fascinating history of salads is that commercial dressings didn't become available until the beginning of the twentieth century. Before that, home chefs had to create their own, starting from scratch, and because of variations in ingredients, results were also extremely varied. Gradually, restaurants began packaging and selling their consistently good special dressings to delighted customers, and the salad dressings' industry was born. Many of the major brands of dressings and sauces available today were introduced as early as the 1920s.

Want to know where some of the top popular brands came from, or how they got started?

In 1912 New York deli owner Richard Hellman marketed his blue-ribbon mayonnaise in wooden containers. In response to strong consumer demand, Mr. Hellmann began to market the mayonnaise in glass jars.

In 1925 Kraft entered the salad business with the purchase of several regional mayonnaise manufacturers including Milani Company. This brought Kraft into the dressing business with French dressing its first flavor. For a great history of individual salads by name, visit: http://whatscookingamerica.net/History/SaladHistory.htm

❖ ASIAN CHICKEN SALAD ❖

ENTRÉE
DIABETIC ADAPTABLE

Here's a salad that's also a great meal. Complete this dinner serving with a French roll from our recipe on page 112.

Serve cold.

LET'S MAKE THE DRESSING FIRST

2 tablespoons rice vinegar (unseasoned) (.3 mg)

2 tablespoons extra virgin olive oil (trace)

1 tablespoon white gram sugar or Splenda (.378 mg)

1 tablespoon sesame oil (trace)

1 teaspoon mustard powder (trace)

1 tablespoon finely grated fresh, peeled ginger (.78 mg)

1 teaspoon dried red pepper flakes (.54 mg)

PUTTING THE SALAD TOGETHER

20 snow pea pods (2.72 mg)

½ seedless cucumber (3.01 mg)

6 green onions (14.4 mg)

2 cups shredded cooked white chicken meat* (92.3 mg)

2 cups shredded Napa cabbage (98.8 mg)

½ cup chopped fresh cilantro (12.4 mg)

Whisk together all the dressing ingredients. Set aside.

Cut snow peas into diagonal bite-size pieces. Chop the cucumber into small pieces. Finely chop green onions; include some of the green part.

Toss all the ingredients in a large bowl with the dressing until they are well mixed. Serve.

Nutrient Values per Serving:
Calories: 196.7. Protein: 10.2 g. Carbohydrate: 15.5 g. Dietary Fiber: 1.977 g. Total Sugars: 9.356 g. Total Fat: 11.1 g. Saturated Fat: 1.591 g. Monounsaturated Fat: 6.55 g. Polyunsaturated Fat: 2.264 g. Cholesterol: 20.6 mg. Calcium: 79.2 mg. Iron: 1.59 mg. Potassium: 391.6 mg. Sodium: 56.4 mg. Vitamin K: 10.8 mcg. Folate: 57 mcg.

❖ ASPARAGUS SALAD ❖

ENTRÉE
DIABETIC ADAPTABLE

Stop me if I've told you this one before. Asparagus crops are the most peculiar-looking of all crops. Single stalks down a long, furrowed row. But after you taste this salad, you may appreciate that labor that goes into each stalk. This is a good one. Try it on a summer day.

*Approximately ½ pound, edible portion only.

THE SALAD FIXINGS
1   teaspoon olive oil (trace)
1   pound asparagus spears, washed and chopped into ½-inch pieces (20 mg)
1   ear of white corn, kernels removed from the cob (21.4 mg)
½   red bell pepper, chopped (to equal 1 cup) (2.98 mg)
½   red onion, chopped (to equal 1 cup) (4.8 mg)

THE VINAIGRETTE
1   tablespoon olive oil (trace)
1   tablespoon white wine vinegar (.15 mg)
½   teaspoon dry mustard (trace)
1   teaspoon white granulated sugar or Splenda (.042 mg)
White pepper to taste (trace)

Wash the asparagus and break the spears from white end where it breaks naturally, before chopping.

Place the olive oil in a fry pan and heat at medium level. Sauté the asparagus and corn together in the oil over medium heat until their color brightens, about 1 minute.

Add the red pepper and onion and sauté an additional minute. Remove from the heat and place the mixture in a colander to cool. The vegetables will be crisp.

Prepare the vinaigrette by mixing the 1 tablespoon olive oil with the white wine vinegar, dry mustard, and sugar. Whisk together and pour over the vegetables when they are cool. Sprinkle with the white pepper and serve chilled. It may be made ahead of time and stored in the refrigerator without dressing for up to 4 hours. Toss with dressing before serving.

Nutrient Values per Serving:
Calories: 124.5. Protein: 4.289 g. Carbohydrate: 18.5 g. Dietary Fiber: 4.53 g. Total Sugars: 1.039 g. Total Fat: 5.331 g. Saturated Fat: .752 g. Monounsaturated Fat: 3.497 g. Polyunsaturated Fat: .754 g. Cholesterol: 0 mg. Calcium: 33.9 mg. Iron: 1.37 mg. Potassium: 503.4 mg. Sodium: 9.356 mg. Vitamin K: 43 mcg. Folate: 160.2 mcg.

◧ BROCCOLI SALAD ◧

SIDE SALAD
DIABETIC ADAPTABLE

George Senior may not have liked broccoli, but we love it. And it's terrifically healthy for us. Try this and you'll know why. Use any sour cream you prefer, the nonfat, light, or regular.

SERVES 4 SODIUM PER RECIPE: 104.8 MG
SODIUM PER SERVING: 26.2 MG

4 tablespoons sour cream (nonfat, light, or regular) (25.4 mg)
1 tablespoon apple cider vinegar (.15 mg)
1 tablespoon white granulated sugar or Splenda (.126 mg)
1 large broccoli crown (71.3 mg)*
½ red onion (3.3 mg)
¼ cup (or more) golden raisins (4.35 mg)
   White pepper to taste (trace)

Mix together the sour cream, vinegar, and sugar.

Clean and chop the broccoli (use the peeled stems). You should have 3 to 4 cups chopped broccoli. Finely chop the red onion.

Mix all the ingredients with the dressing. Serve chilled or immediately after making.

Nutrient Values per Serving:
Calories: 94.7. Protein: 2.972 g. Carbohydrate: 16.9 g. Dietary Fiber: 2.837 g. Total Sugars: 3.118 g. Total Fat: 2.832 g. Saturated Fat: 1.622 g. Monounsaturated Fat: .75 g. Polyunsaturated Fat: .233 g. Cholesterol: 5.28 mg. Calcium: 56.2 mg. Iron: .835 mg. Potassium: 346.4 mg. Sodium: 26.2 mg. Vitamin K: 136 mcg. Folate: 53.7 mcg.

MAUREEN'S OWN EASY CAESAR SALAD
◧ WITH CROUTONS ◧

ENTRÉE

My wife Maureen, as you can tell from this book, is a great chef. There are never any arguments when she says she knows how to create a tasty dish. When I asked her to do a Caesar salad for this book, believing to myself only

---

*If your crown makes 4 cups chopped broccoli, add 23.7 mg to recipe total or 6 mg per serving. The figure given in the ingredients is for 3 cups.

that such a salad would be impossible to replicate, she leaped at the opportunity. Well, she did it. It has no grated Parmesan, like the real thing, but it's just as tasty if not a lot more. You'll make this one more than once.

By the way, this makes a complete meal for me.

SERVES 4   SODIUM PER RECIPE: 268.4 MG
SODIUM PER SERVING: 67.1 MG

3   **tablespoons olive oil (trace)**
3   **cloves garlic, chopped or minced (1.53 mg)**
1   **head romaine lettuce, chilled, torn into bite-size pieces, (about 4 cups) (17.9 mg)**
3   **tablespoons freshly squeezed lemon juice (.45 mg)**
1½ **cups freshly grated low-sodium Swiss cheese* (239.9 mg)**
    Dash of white or black pepper† (.044 mg)
3   **cups Don's Salad Croutons (¾-inch cubes) (page 114) (8.837 mg)**

In a small bowl blend the olive oil and garlic with a handheld blender or your food processor. In a larger bowl place the lettuce and toss with the oil mixture to coat the lettuce. Pour the lemon juice over the lettuce, add the low-sodium Swiss cheese, and toss again until everything is well coated.

To each serving, add pepper to taste and sprinkle the croutons over. Serve.

Nutritient Values per Serving:
Calories: 442.3. Protein: 20.1 g. Carbohydrate: 35.4 g. Dietary Fiber: 3.59 g. Total Sugars: 1.248 g. Total Fat: 25.2 g. Saturated Fat: 8.906 g. Monounsaturated Fat: 13 g. Polyunsaturated Fat: 1.952 g. Cholesterol: 34.1 mg. Calcium: 470.7 mg. Iron: 2.914 mg. Potassium: 396.4 mg. Sodium: 67.1 mg. Vitamin K: 6.946 mcg. Folate: 141.8 mcg.

*Data from average figures form the USDA for low-sodium Swiss cheeses available as of this writing. Check FDA labels of the cheese you buy and adjust the sodium level accordingly.
†Dash equals .044 mg sodium.

❧ CALIFORNIA CHICKEN SALAD ❧

ENTRÉE
DIABETIC ADAPTABLE*

*This makes a satisfying summer entrée when served
chilled. Serve with a no-salt dinner roll.*

SERVES 4   SODIUM PER RECIPE: 332 MG
SODIUM PER SERVING: 83 MG

CHICKEN
2   4-ounce chicken half breasts (153.4 mg)
½ teaspoon ground tarragon (.496 mg)
½ teaspoon onion powder (.567 mg)
1   cup no-sodium bottled water (trace)

THE DRESSING
3   tablespoons light sour cream (19.1 mg)
¾ teaspoon dried dill weed (1.56 mg)
1   tablespoon fresh lemon juice (.15 mg)
1   teaspoon white granulated sugar or Splenda (.042 mg)
⅛ teaspoon white pepper (.015 mg)

THE SALAD
2   baked chicken half breasts
½ cup chopped celery (52.2 mg)
1   cup red seedless grapes* (3.2 mg)
½ cup chopped unsalted pecans, lightly toasted (.56 mg)
4   cups or 1 fresh bag mixed salad greens, chilled (55.9 mg)
4   lemon wedges

Preheat the oven to 350°F.

Clean the chicken and sprinkle it with the tarragon and onion powder.
Add 1 cup water, cover with foil, and bake for about 40 minutes. When
done, let cool.

When the chicken is cool, shred it. Prepare the salad dressing and set
aside.

Combine the chicken with the celery and grapes. Gently mix the salad
dressing with the chicken.

*Diabetics may exchange the grapes for ½ cup unsalted caramelized walnut quarters,
or just leave the grapes out. (Caramelize using Splenda.) Walnuts have sugars in them—
½ cup has about 6 carbohydrates and 1.3 sugars. Adds 1 mg sodium.

Just before serving, mix in the pecans. Serve on a bed of the chilled salad greens with the lemon slice/wedge for added flavor.

Nutrient Values per Serving:
Calories: 258.4. Protein: 17.5 g. Carbohydrate: 18.7 g. Dietary Fiber: 3.174 g. Total Sugars: 1.585 g. Total Fat: 13.9 g. Saturated Fat: 2.639 g. Monounsaturated Fat: 6.68 g. Polyunsaturated Fat: 3.67 g. Cholesterol: 38.9 mg. Calcium: 103.6 mg. Iron: 2.032 mg. Potassium: 623.3 mg. Sodium: 83 mg. Vitamin K: 2.055 mcg. Folate: 79.8 mcg.

❈ CRANBERRIES, NUTS, AND RICE SALAD ❈

ENTRÉE OR SIDE SALAD
NOT DIABETIC ADAPTABLE

When I was a child I loved cranberries. Years later I discovered dried cranberries. They make great additions to puddings, breads, and salads. Add some brown rice, a few pecans, a great dressing, and you've got a terrific entrée or a side salad for yourself and your guests.

SERVES 6   SODIUM PER RECIPE: 141.6 MG
SODIUM PER SERVING: 23.6 MG

THE SALAD
1   cup uncooked brown or white rice (makes 2 cups cooked) 7.6 mg)
2   cups no-sodium bottled water (trace)
½   cup unsalted pecans, lightly toasted (.55 mg)
2   bunches green onions, chopped (24 mg)
2   medium stalks celery, chopped (69.6 mg)
½   cup chopped or minced Italian parsley* (16.8 mg)
½   cup dried cranberries (cranberry raisins) (trace)

THE DRESSING
¼   cup extra virgin olive oil (trace)
¼   cup fresh or bottled lemon juice (.61 mg)†
1   tablespoon Grandma's unsulfured molasses‡ (5 mg)
1   teaspoon garlic powder (.728 mg)
2½   teaspoons ground cumin (8.82 mg)
⅛   teaspoon white pepper (.015 mg)

*If Italian parsley is not available in your area, then use regular parsley. (Italian parsley has more "punch.")
†Bottled lemon juice is higher in sodium than fresh—¼ cup bottled = 12.8 mg sodium.
‡Check each brand's FDA label for the sodium count. Some are too high to use.

Cook the rice according to package instructions or put 1 cup of rice into a medium saucepan along with 2 cups no-sodium bottled water and bring to a boil. Cover, reduce the heat, and let simmer for about 40 minutes (or until tender). When done, transfer the rice to a large bowl and let cool.

While the rice is cooking, toast the pecans at 350°F for 10 to 15 minutes or until the oils appear and the nuts are crunchy. Set aside. A toaster oven works great.

While rice is cooling, in a small bowl whisk together the dressing. Set aside.

Mix the vegetables and cranberries into the cooled rice and then add the dressing. Add the pecans just before serving and toss again. It's delicious. Serve warm or cold.

Nutrient Values per Serving:
Calories: 322. Protein: 4.692 g. Carbohydrate: 41.1 g. Dietary Fiber: 3.947 g. Total Sugars: 2.464 g. Total Fat: 2.085 g. Saturated Fat: 2.085 g. Monounsaturated Fat: 10.9 g. Polyunsaturated Fat: 3.309 g. Cholesterol: 0 mg. Calcium: 73.3 mg. Iron: 2.716 mg. Potassium: 445 mg. Sodium: 23.6 mg. Vitamin K: 33 mcg. Folate: 37.7 mcg.

❈ CREAMY CHICKEN SALAD ❈

ENTRÉE SALAD
DIABETICS—CONTAINS LEMON JUICE

When Maureen returned from attending a friend's wedding in a small mining town along the Mother Lode of California she was excited about a lunch salad she'd had in a restaurant that was housed in an old mining camp's general store. So, as she's done so many times, she spent a few days in the kitchen (and the market) putting together as close a version of that salad as she could. I think you'll like this one a lot.

SERVES 4   SODIUM PER RECIPE: 365.6 MG
SODIUM PER SERVING: 91.4 MG

THE SALAD
2 boneless, skinless chicken half breasts (cut into bite-size pieces) (153.4 mg)
4 cups no-sodium bottled water (trace)
1 teaspoon onion powder (1.134 mg)
3 tablespoons lemon juice (about 1 lemon) (.45 mg)
1 cob of corn (21.4 mg)
1 15-ounce can no-salt-added Eden Organic Pinto Beans* (52.5 mg)

*You may obtain no-salt-added Eden Organic Pinto Beans from www.healthyheart-market.com; it's also available in some markets.

2 **small tomatoes (16.4 mg)**
1 **bunch green onions (14.4 mg)**
1 **small head iceberg lettuce (or enough to serve four)**
   (29.2 mg)

THE DRESSING
½ **cup light sour cream† (73.2 mg)**
1 **tablespoon lemon juice (.15 mg)**
1 **teaspoon cumin (3.528 mg)**

GARNISH
   No-salt tortilla chips for garnish
4 **lemon wedges for garnish**

Clean the chicken and cut into bite-size pieces.

Fill a 2-quart pan with 4 cups of water and the onion powder. Bring it to a full boil, then add chicken. Turn down the heat and simmer for 3 to 4 minutes or until the chicken is cooked through. Drain thoroughly and cool in a colander or strainer. When cool, transfer to a small bowl. Pour 2 tablespoons of lemon juice on the chicken and place in the refrigerator.

Heat the corn. Microwave for 1 minute or cook in boiling water for about 15 seconds.

While the chicken is in the refrigerator, drain and rinse the beans, seed and chop the tomatoes. Chop the onions, cut the corn kernels off the cob. Wash the lettuce and tear it into bite-size pieces.

Place the lettuce in a large bowl and crisp in the refrigerator.

Mix the dressing thoroughly with a whisk until smooth. Pour the dressing over the chicken and the other salad ingredients except the lettuce and mix thoroughly.

Place the lettuce on individual plates and top with the dressed mixture.

Garnish each serving with no-salt tortilla chips (trace) and a lemon wedge (trace). Serve chilled.

Nutrient Values per Serving:
Calories: 264.3. Protein: 23.2 g. Carbohydrate: 32 g. Dietary Fiber: 8.566 g. Total Sugars: 1.984 g. Total Fat: 5.343 g. Saturated Fat: 2.673 g. Monounsaturated Fat: .41 g. Polyunsaturated Fat: .544 g. Cholesterol: 49.7 mg. Calcium: 98.8 mg. Iron: 1.938 mg. Potassium: 942.4 mg. Sodium: 91.4 mg. Vitamin K: 2.73 mcg. Folate: 88.3 mcg.

†Data based on Kraft's Breakstone's Reduced-Fat Sour Cream.

CREAMY COLESLAW
❖ WITH TANGY DRESSING ❖

SIDE SALAD
DIABETIC ADAPTABLE*

As a kid I never liked coleslaw. But our tastes grow as we do and our experiments with foods, recipes, and of course our search for good nutrient values in what we eat often lead us back to foods we rejected as youngsters. This coleslaw was Maureen's way of introducing me to this valuable side salad. Full of nutrients and a nice tangy dressing, it's perfect for many meals.

SERVES 4 SODIUM PER RECIPE: 152.4 MG
SODIUM PER SERVING: 38.1 MG

THE SALAD FIXINGS
½ medium head green cabbage (about 2 to 3 cups chopped) (81.7 mg)
2 medium carrots (42.7 mg)

THE DRESSING
1 teaspoon dry wasabi horseradish (equals ½ teaspoon prepared (.5 mg)
1 teaspoon white granulated sugar or Splenda (.042 mg)
3 tablespoons light sour cream* (27.4 mg)
1 tablespoon white balsamic vinegar or white wine or apple cider vinegar (.15 mg)

Thinly slice the cabbage, then finely chop. Rinse thoroughly and set aside in a bowl.

Clean, peel, and shred the carrots. Place in the bowl with the cabbage.

Make the wasabi by mixing the dry wasabi with an equal amount of no sodium bottled water. Let sit 5 minutes while you mix the next three ingredients in a small bowl.

Whisk the sugar, sour cream, and vinegar together, then add the wasabi.

Pour over the cabbage and carrots and mix thoroughly. Chill. Serve when ready in small dishes or on the side.

*Data Based on Kraft's Breakstone's Reduced Fat Sour Cream. Other brands are similar.

Nutrient Values per Serving:
Calories: 64.8. Protein: 2.509 g. Carbohydrate: 11.5 g. Dietary Fiber: 3.568 g. Total Sugars: 1.783 g. Total Fat: 1.766 g. Saturated Fat: .93 g. Monounsaturated Fat: .03 g. Polyunsaturated Fat: .162 g. Cholesterol: 5.812 mg. Calcium: 82.3 mg. Iron: .871 mg. Potassium: 413 mg. Sodium: 38.1 mg. Vitamin K: 166.1 mcg. Folate: 53.1 mcg.

❖ CURRIED CHICKEN SALAD ❖

ENTRÉE SALAD
DIABETIC ADAPTABLE*

If you like curry you'll love this salad. It's a complete entrée, so serve with your favorite bread. This is one of Maureen's special creations.

SERVES 4   SODIUM PER RECIPE: 298.4 MG
SODIUM PER SERVING: 74.6 MG

LET'S DO THE DRESSING FIRST
1 teaspoon honey* (.28 mg)
½ cup light sour cream† (73.2 mg)
2 teaspoons curry (2.08 mg)
½ teaspoon ground ginger (.288 mg)

Combine the ingredients and stir until smooth. Set aside in the refrigerator.

LET'S PREPARE THE SALAD SECOND
2 boneless, skinless chicken half breasts (about ½ pound) (153.4 mg)
½ cup no-sodium bottled water
    Dash of onion powder (trace)
    Dash of garlic powder (trace)
½ cup chopped green onions (8 mg)
½ cup chopped celery (52.2 mg)
1 Gala or Fuji apple, cored and chopped‡ (0 mg)
⅓ cup unpacked seedless golden raisins (5.794 mg)
¼ cup unsalted almonds, sliced or chopped§ (.345 mg)

*Replace the honey with ½ teaspoon of Splenda.
†Data based on Kraft's Breakstone's Reduced-Fat Sour Cream. Check the FDA label of your brand and apply any differences.
‡FDA rates all apples at 0 sodium level.
§Cashews may also be substitute for the almonds. Among other stores, Trader Joe's carries unsalted cashews.

4 large leaves fresh iceberg lettuce (2.88 mg)
A few chopped unsalted peanuts or cashews for garnish

Preheat the oven to 350°F.

Wash the chicken and put it into a small casserole dish with ½ cup no-sodium bottled water. Sprinkle lightly with a dash of onion powder and garlic powder. Cover with aluminum foil and bake for approximately 25 minutes or until completely cooked. Cool for a few minutes when done.

Cut the chicken into bite-size pieces.

Chop the green onions, celery, and apple into small pieces and mix together in a medium-size bowl. Add the raisins and almonds. Add the chicken. Pour the dressing over the salad and stir, covering all. Chill; serve on bed of large lettuce leaves.

Garnish with a few chopped unsalted peanuts or cashews.

Nutrient Values per Serving:
Calories: 248.3. Protein: 18 g. Carbohydrate: 25.2 g. Dietary Fiber: 4.001 g. Total Sugars: 3.805 g. Total Fat: 9.467 g. Saturated Fat: 2.987 g. Monounsaturated Fat: 3.156 g. Polyunsaturated Fat: 1.385 g. Cholesterol: 49.7 mg. Calcium: 111.3 mg. Iron: 1.761 mg. Potassium: 541.5 mg. Sodium: 74.6 mg. Vitamin K: 1.8 mcg. Folate: 25.6 mcg.

FRESH MOZZARELLA, TOMATO,
❖ AND BASIL SALAD ❖

DIABETIC ADAPTABLE

The title says it. If you don't have all the ingredients listed in the recipe, make it without them. They just give it a little more texture and color. Of course, make this dish with all three ingredients in the title, and you'll really enjoy this mealtime salad. The mozzarella is usually available in a water-packed package in your deli section. It lists some salt, but mostly that's in the water and we don't use the water.

SERVES 4   SODIUM PER RECIPE: 103.6 MG
SODIUM PER SERVING: 25.9 MG

THE SALAD
1 **bunch fresh basil (16 medium to large leaves) (.3 mg)**
4 **small tomatoes, seeded and chopped or sliced (32.8 mg)**
1 **medium cucumber, peeled, seeded, and chopped (4.02 mg)**
1 **small red onion or other mild onion, chopped (2.1 mg)**
2 **cups sliced fresh mushrooms (5.6 mg)**

8 leaves green leaf lettuce (red, butter, or other mild lettuce) (40.3 mg)

8 ounces fresh mozzarella* bocconcini (baw-kawn-CHEE-nee) divided into 4 portions (18.1 mg)

THE DRESSING

3 tablespoons extra virgin olive oil (trace)

3 tablespoons red wine vinegar (.45 mg)

½ teaspoon dry mustard powder (trace)

1 teaspoon white granulated sugar or Splenda (.042 mg)

⅛ teaspoon cracked black pepper (trace)

Prepare the basil for the salad. Wash the basil leaves, then stack them on top of each other, and roll tightly. Slice the leaves from side to side, making thin strips. Reserve a few leaves for garnish.

Except for the green leaf lettuce and mozzarella, combine all the salad ingredients in a small to medium salad bowl.

Whisk together the dressing ingredients and pour over the salad. Toss lightly and let the ingredients marinate while you prepare the lettuce and mozzarella.

Wash lettuce and chop four leaves. Keep the other four whole. Lay one leaf on each plate and top with one-fourth chopped lettuce, and then add one-quarter of the marinated vegetables per serving. Top with one quarter of the bocconcini (mozzarella) and garnish with extra basil leaves.

Add pepper and serve immediately.

Nutrient Values per Serving:
Calories: 236.6. Protein: 11.6 g. Carbohydrate: 15.1 g. Dietary Fiber: 4.296 g. Total Sugars: 1.039 g. Total Fat: 15.9 g. Saturated Fat: 4.58 g. Monounsaturated Fat: 8.939 g. Polyunsaturated Fat: 1.42 g. Cholesterol: 15.3 mg. Calcium: 303.8 mg. Iron: 2.719 mg. Potassium: 777.5 mg. Sodium: 25.9 mg. Vitamin K: 246 mcg. Folate: 88.2 mcg.

❧ FRUIT SALAD ❧

MAY NOT BE DIABETIC ACCEPTABLE

Each season has its special fruits. I find that I like mine served without dressing. However, if you like a dressing on your fruit you can use one or both special dressings I created just for fruit salads. They are listed with their page numbers at the end of this "recipe."

*See "mozzarella" in Glossary for specifics.

Cut the following (leave the berries whole) into bite-size pieces, place in a bowl, and enjoy! Bananas are available any time of the year, but remember to add them just before serving to prevent browning. Also, canned pineapple seems to go with every season, but fresh is lovely when it's available in the summertime.

Summer
    Berries
    Melons
    Nectarines
    Peaches
    Plums
    Grapes

Fall
Nuts are particularly good with fall fruits and vegetables such as celery and jicama. Also, dried fruits such as cranberries can be added as well.
    Apples
    Pears
    Persimmon
    Kiwi

Winter
Mild red onion or any sweet variety seems to go well with citrus and can be combined with winter pears and nuts for a delicious treat. Often you'll still see fall fruits available in the markets during the winter, and they combine nicely with citrus, too.
    Oranges
    Mandarins

Spring
Strawberries, strawberries, what a treat! Bananas always work with strawberries. Cherries are difficult to work with in a salad because of the pits.

Dressings
    Sour Cream and Honey Dressing (page 168)
    Spicy Orange Dressing (page 168)

❖ GERMAN POTATO SALAD ❖

DIABETIC ACCEPTABLE

This is closer yet to my favorite potato salad. Add more onions, some garlic, or chop up some sweet B&G Bread and butter chips from Healthy Heart Market. The crispy overcooked finely chopped pork rib gives you that "bacon" appearance and "chew," although not the bacon fat or sodium level.

**SERVES 4   SODIUM PER RECIPE: 93.2 MG
SODIUM PER SERVING: 23.3 MG**

2 **ounces lean, well-cooked pork country rib, finely diced to simulate chopped bacon (38 mg)**
6 **medium red potatoes (43.9 mg)**
1 **tablespoon olive oil (trace)**
½ **teaspoon balsamic vinegar (trace)**
¼ **large red onion (1.125 mg)**
4 **large mushrooms (cap or shiitake) (.36 mg)**
4 **green onions, diced (9.6 mg)**
   Pepper to taste

Great for leftover pork ribs. If using fresh meat then cook just one country rib, well done. (We're trying to simulate bacon here.)

Wash and lightly scrub the potatoes. Boil in no-salt-added water for about 35 to 40 minutes or until a fork just pierces them. Set aside. (You can make them the day before and chill them overnight or you can keep them warm and make a warm potato salad.) If you decide to set the potatoes aside for a same-day serve, let them cool for about a half hour.

When the potatoes are ready, quarter them and place them in a medium to large salad bowl. Sprinkle on the olive oil and balsamic vinegar and stir gently with a wooden spoon.

Finely dice the large red onion and add it to the potatoes.

Dice the mushrooms and add them to the salad bowl.

Dice the green onions (up into the green stems about 2 inches) and add them to the mix with the well-cooked pork rib. Stir gently, tossing lightly.

Add pepper to taste.

Nutrient Values per Serving:
Calories: 176.3. Protein: 6.974 g. Carbohydrate: 35 g. Dietary Fiber: 3.535 g. Total Sugars: 0 g. Total Fat: 1.408 g. Saturated Fat: .46 g. Monounsaturated Fat: .539 g. Polyunsaturated Fat: .227 g. Cholesterol: 9.072 mg. Calcium: 28.8 mg. Iron: 2.228 mg. Potassium: 1110 mg. Sodium: 23.3 mg. Vitamin K: 1.652 mcg. Folate: 36.3 mcg.

Guacamole Chicken Salad

◈ with Avocado Dressing ◈

A Full Entrée Serving
Diabetics See Note at End*

I can remember a childhood event when my mother found herself with a huge bag of avocados one of the neighbors delivered to her. Avocados grow prolifically in southern California and we often had one too many around the house. On this particular occasion I was watching her make an avocado dish for guests, who were to arrive soon. She had peeled too many of them and sighed quite heavily, fearing she would have to discard the unused fruit. I gladly jumped in to save her and ate every one of them. She warned me that I wasn't going to feel good if "you keep that up." Why are mothers always right?

SERVES 4   SODIUM PER RECIPE: 436 MG
SODIUM PER SERVING: 109 MG

THE DRESSING
½ firm ripe California avocado, peeled and pitted (10.4 mg)
¼ cup light sour cream† (36 mg)
¼ cup fresh lime juice (.6 mg)
½ teaspoon Grandma's (see "chili powder" in Glossary) or other non-salted chili powder
1 teaspoon chopped/minced jalapeño‡ (.017 mg)
1 clove garlic, chopped (.51 mg)
¼ teaspoon black or white pepper (.231 mg)

THE SALAD FIXINGS
½ pound (uncooked) white chicken breast meat (153.4 mg)
4 cups chopped Napa cabbage,§ (197.6 mg)
½ cup chopped‖ green onions, (8 mg)
½ cup chopped fresh cilantro (12.4 mg)

---

*Sugar grams are mostly in the sour cream. Carbohydrates come mostly from the tomato and the dressing's sour cream.
†Data based on Kraft's Breakstone's, Reduced Fat Sour Cream
‡Caution: When preparing hot peppers such as jalapeños, make sure to wear rubber gloves and wash your hands thoroughly afterward. If you cut a jalapeño and then touch your eyes, you will appreciate this word of caution.
§Romaine lettuce may be substituted for the cabbage.
‖Or sweet white, like Walla Walla or Maui onions.

1 teaspoon chopped fresh jalapeño (.017 mg)
1 large tomato, peeled, seeded, and chopped (16.4 mg)

MAKING THE DRESSING

Place the ingredients into a food processor or blender and puree until smooth.

MAKING THE SALAD

Prepare the chicken by poaching, baking, or barbecuing, and then shred it. You should have about 2 cups.

In a medium bowl, mix the chopped vegetables together; add the shredded chicken and dressing and toss until everything is covered. Refrigerate and serve chilled.

Nutrient Values per Serving:
Calories: 157.9. Protein: 16.8 g. Carbohydrate: 9.295 g. Dietary Fiber: 2.931 g. Total Sugars: .992 g. Total Fat: 6.752 g. Saturated Fat: 1.982 g. Monounsaturated Fat: 2.655 g. Polyunsaturated Fat: .762 g. Cholesterol: 42 mg. Calcium: 132.1 mg. Iron: 1.844 mg. Potassium: 699.2 mg. Sodium: 109 mg. Vitamin K: 2.73 mcg. Folate: 86.6 mcg.

❧ JULY FOURTH POTATO SALAD ❧

DIABETIC ADAPTABLE*

July Fourth—picnics, flag-waving, sparklers, and rockets! Take this potato salad along to serve with your July Fourth picnic. Keep it chilled. It will be a highlight—and all without salt. If you have any no salt-added sweet or dill relish† on hand, add about ¼ cup and mix it into the salad.

SERVES 6 TO 8   SODIUM PER RECIPE: 284.4 MG/284.6
SODIUM PER SERVING (6) 47.4 MG
SODIUM PER SERVING (8): 35.6 MG

5 medium to large red potatoes (30 mg)
2 tablespoons thinly sliced green onions (1.944 mg)
2 tablespoons chopped fresh parsley‡ (4.256 mg)
⅓ cup light or regular sour cream(40.6 mg)
⅓ cup low-fat plain yogurt (57.3 mg)

*Most of the sugar grams are in the honey mustard and sugar. Use Splenda and exchange the honey mustard with dry mustard powder to taste to lower the sugars to near zero.
†www.healthyheartmarket.com has no-salt-added pickle relish. They also have no-salt pickles; you can make your own relish with that.
‡Place the fresh parsley in a food processor fitted with the steel blade. Process for about 30 to 40 seconds to get the right texture for fresh parsley flakes.

½ **teaspoon dried dill weed or to taste (1.04 mg)**
1 **tablespoon plus 1 teaspoon honey mustard* (20 mg)**
1½ **tablespoons red wine vinegar (.225 mg)**
1 **teaspoon white granulated sugar or Splenda (.042 mg)**
⅛ **teaspoon Don's Flavor Enhancer (page 177) (.108 mg)**
½ **teaspoon white or black pepper (.06 mg)**
¾ **teaspoon celery seed (2.4 mg)**
2 **large eggs, hard-boiled, chopped (126 mg)**
1 **teaspoon paprika (about) or to taste (.714)**

Wash the potatoes and quarter. Don't peel them. Boil in sodium-free bottled water until they are tender. Don't overcook them.

While the potatoes cook, combine all the other ingredients except the eggs and paprika in a medium mixing bowl.

Drain the potatoes and cool. When cool, cut them into bite-size pieces (about 1-inch cubes). Place the potatoes in a large mixing bowl. Add the mixture of the other ingredients a little at a time, stirring the potatoes until they are coated.

Sprinkle with chopped eggs and a little paprika; cover and refrigerate for at least 4 hours before serving.

Nutrient Values per Serving (6):
Calories: 74.7. Protein: 4.989 g. Carbohydrate: 17.9 g. Dietary Fiber: 1.678 g. Total Sugars: 2.86 g. Total Fat: 4.698 g. Saturated Fat: 2.357 g. Monounsaturated Fat: 1.519 g. Polyunsaturated Fat: .38 g. Cholesterol: 77.3 mg. Calcium: 66.8 mg. Iron: 1.268 mg. Potassium: 480.9 mg. Sodium: 47.4 mg. Vitamin K: 9.384 mcg. Folate: 29.4 mcg.

Nutrient Values per Serving (8):
Calories: 56. Protein: 3.742 g. Carbohydrate: 13.5 g. Dietary Fiber: 1.258 g. Total Sugars: 2.145 g. Total Fat: 3.523 g. Saturated Fat: 1.768 g. Monounsaturated Fat: 1.139 g. Polyunsaturated Fat: .285 g. Cholesterol: 58 mg. Calcium: 50.1 mg. Iron: .951 mg. Potassium: 360.7 mg. Sodium: 35.6 mg. Vitamin K: 7.038 mcg. Folate: 22.1 mcg.

❈ MAUREEN'S FRESH GREEN BEAN SALAD ❈

DIABETIC ADAPTABLE*

Maureen was the first to introduce me to "fresh raw vegetables," slightly steamed. Until then my practice had been to boil, broil, bake, or barbecue them. But about thirty years ago she opened a new door with a new steamer. Here's a great example of what you can do with fresh vegetables, one that lightly cooks them, holds their nutritional value, and tastes terrific.

*The sugars are mostly in the walnuts.

PREPARE THE VINAIGRETTE
1½ tablespoons extra virgin olive oil (trace)
1½ tablespoons apple cider vinegar (.225 mg)

Whisk together the ingredients well. Set aside.

PREPARE THE SALAD
4 cups fresh green beans (26.4 mg)
1 cup unsalted walnut halves (2 mg)
2 tablespoons chopped fresh mint leaves (3.42 mg)
1 cup grated low-sodium Swiss cheese† (159.9 mg)

Steam the green beans in boiling no-sodium bottled water to even for approximate 3 to 4 minutes or until the beans turn bright green and are tender. Drain and immediately rinse with cold water. Place in a bowl to cool.

While the beans cool, lightly toast the walnut halves at 350°F in the toaster oven (or in the regular oven, although we recommend a toaster oven for this type of light toasting). Toast for 5 to 10 minutes and watch carefully. Don't let them burn!

When the walnuts and beans have cooled, mix them together with the chopped mint and grated cheese. Whisk the vinaigrette quickly and pour it over the salad, mixing gently. Chill for at least 30 minutes and serve.

Nutrient Values per Serving:
Calories: 348.4. Protein: 15.1 g. Carbohydrate: 13 g. Dietary Fiber: 3.849 g. Total Sugars: .652 g. Total Fat: 28.4 g. Saturated Fat: 6.831 g. Monounsaturated Fat: 7.596 g. Polyunsaturated Fat: 12.6 g. Cholesterol: 22.8 mg. Calcium: 357.9 mg. Iron: 2.461 mg. Potassium: 429 mg. Sodium: 48 mg. Vitamin K: 2.481 mcg. Folate: 69.9 mcg.

†Data supplied by FDA is a general average of all low-sodium Swiss cheese on the market. Check your local brand and adjust accordingly. (*see* low-sodium Swiss in glossary)

Maureen's Salmon Salad
with Raspberry Vinaigrette

Entrée
Diabetic Adaptable

We love fresh wild salmon around our house, and we understand the salmon "loves" our hearts. It's one of the best foods we can eat. But how to prepare and how to serve? That's the question many ask us. Here's our answer for a delicious salmon salad. One for which you'll receive raves.

SERVES 4   SODIUM PER RECIPE: 230.8 MG
SODIUM PER SERVING: 57.7 MG

THE DRESSING AND SALAD
3 tablespoons raspberry vinegar (.45 mg)
3 tablespoons extra virgin olive oil (trace)
1 teaspoon white granulated sugar or Splenda (.042 mg)
⅓ cup fresh raspberries, chopped (trace)
½ cup finely chopped celery (52.2 mg)
½ cup finely chopped red onion (2.4 mg)

Whisk together first three ingredients. Add the second three ingredients and mix thoroughly. Pour over the prepared salmon and chill covered in the refrigerator for at least an hour.

POACHING THE SALMON
1 pound wild salmon fillets* (156.4 mg)
   3 to 4 cups cold no-sodium bottled water plus more if needed
   to cover (trace)
1 teaspoon dried dill (2.08 mg)
2 tablespoons chopped celery (include leaves) (13.1 mg)
1 tablespoon chopped parsley (2.128 mg)
¼ cup thinly sliced onion (.862 mg)
¼ lemon, thinly sliced (1.12 mg)

Remove any bones in the fillets. We use needle-nose pliers to pull the smaller bones out.

Using a deep pan large enough to accommodate the fillets, combine

---

*Atlantic salmon, prevalent in many markets, is not a good salmon for this recipe and should generally be avoided in any of our recipes. Our salmon recipes are based on using Pacific Wild Salmon.

the cold no-sodium bottled water with all the other ingredients. Put the salmon into the water, making sure the salmon is covered. Turn on the heat and bring the cooking liquid to a boil, uncovered. When the liquid boils, turn the heat down and simmer for 5 minutes. Turn the heat off after 5 minutes and let stand for 10 minutes. The salmon should be perfectly cooked, depending on its thickness. Check the thickest part for doneness. Remove the fish from the cooking liquid and cool. Remove the skin and any missed bones. When cool, place the salmon in a small container, cover with the chilled dressing mixture, and affix the lid. Chill in the refrigerator until ready to serve.

SERVING THE SALMON

Arrange leaves of butter lettuce or other soft green lettuce on each plate and divide the salmon into four servings. Pour any extra dressing over each. Serve with a wedge of lemon for those who like lemon with their fish. Delicious!

Nutrient Values per Serving:
Calories: 241.4. Protein: 19.1 g. Carbohydrate: 7.137 g. Dietary Fiber: 1.788 g. Total Sugars: 1.039 g. Total Fat: 15.3 g. Saturated Fat: 2.461 g. Monounsaturated Fat: 9.296 g. Polyunsaturated Fat: 2.611 g. Cholesterol: 38.2 mg. Calcium: 55.3 mg. Iron: 1.026 mg. Potassium: 511.9 mg. Sodium: 57.7 mg. Vitamin K: 12.9 mcg. Folate: 23 mcg.

MIXED GREENS
WITH LOW-SODIUM SWISS AND WALNUTS
❧ WITH RASPBERRY VINAIGRETTE ❧

DIABETIC ADAPTABLE

Here's an easy-to-make, delicious salad treat. It's perfect for a summer patio dinner or serve it with your favorite barbecue meal. It's also a great salad for winter evenings while curled up by the fireplace. Always a favorite.

SERVES 4   SODIUM PER RECIPE: 188.4 MG
SODIUM PER SERVING: 47.1 MG

THE VINAIGRETTE

- 3 **tablespoons raspberry vinegar (.45 mg)**
- 2 **tablespoons extra virgin olive oil (trace)**
- 1 **tablespoon white granulated sugar or Splenda (.126 mg)**
- ½ **teaspoon dry mustard (trace)**

THE SALAD

1 **6-ounce (or equivalent) package Mixed Salad Greens***
    (55.9 mg)
1 **cup red seedless grapes (3.2 mg)**
½ **cup unsalted walnuts, toasted until oily (1 mg)**
4 **ounces grated low-sodium Swiss† (127.9 mg)**

Whisk together the four ingredients for the vinaigrette.

In a medium salad bowl, mix the last four ingredients and top with the dressing. Toss and serve. Delicious!

Nutrient Values per Serving:
Calories: 277.4. Protein: 10.4 g. Carbohydrate: 15.2 g. Dietary Fiber: 2.013 g. Total Sugars: 3.445 g. Total Fat: 20.9 g. Saturated Fat: 5.449 g. Monounsaturated Fat: 7.443 g. Polyunsaturated Fat: 6.885 g. Cholesterol: 18.2 mg. Calcium: 277.4 mg. Iron: 1.456 mg. Potassium: 372.2 mg. Sodium: 47.1 mg. Vitamin K: 3.308 mcg. Folate: 78.9 mcg.

❖ MUSHROOM SALAD ❖

DIABETIC ACCEPTABLE

When mushrooms are on sale, this is a great salad to make. It's great when they aren't, too, especially when serving guests.

SERVES 4   SODIUM PER RECIPE: 41.2 MG
SODIUM PER SERVING: 10.3 MG

2 **pounds fresh mushrooms (about 10 cups) (28 mg)**
½ **cup finely chopped onion (2.4 mg)**
    3 to 4 cloves garlic, finely chopped (2.04 mg)
¼ **cup chopped parsley (8.4 mg)**
1 **tablespoon extra virgin olive oil (trace)**
1 **tablespoon white wine vinegar or white balsamic vinegar**
    (.15 mg)
1 **lemon, quartered, juice use only (.117 mg)**

Clean and slice the mushrooms. Place them in a large salad bowl.

Add the onion, garlic the parsley, and toss with the oil and wine or

---

*Check the FDA label for the salad greens you buy. They may vary in nutrient values.
†Ask your deli clerk for a chunk of low-sodium Swiss cheese. If it only comes sliced, then roll a slice like a cigar, fold it over, and grate it. Other brands range from 3.2 mg per ounce to 45 mg per ounce. Adjust the recipe accordingly. We use Alpine Lace, which is a national brand.

vinegar. Serve with the quartered lemon for the juice to be added if desired.

Nutrient Values per Serving:
Calories: 58.4. Protein: 5.62 g. Carbohydrate: 10.6 g. Dietary Fiber: 2.658 g. Total Sugars: 0 g. Total Fat: .654 g. Saturated Fat: .093 g. Monounsaturated Fat: .026 g. Polyunsaturated Fat: .268 g. Cholesterol: 0 mg. Calcium: 23.8 mg. Iron: 2.171 mg. Potassium: 719.1 mg. Sodium: 10.3 mg. Vitamin K: 20.7 mcg. Folate: 31 mcg.

❖ MUSKETEER SALAD ❖

ENTRÉE
DIABETIC ADAPTABLE

If you're not familiar with the Musketeers then visit our No-Salt, Lowest-Sodium Baking Book (page 87). The Musketeers are our grandchildren, and they have grown a bit since the baking book—and increased in numbers. Now, they understand and like soups, salads, and other foods. When Maureen and I had them to our summer retreat along the coast for a visit, she asked them what they'd like in a salad. So, they piled into the kitchen and helped her with this one. During the creation of this salad, the children suggested when asked that the tomatoes be "put on the side." That brought a few smiles, but now, everyone likes it. It's for adults, too.

SERVES 4   SODIUM PER RECIPE: 223.6 MG
SODIUM PER SERVING: 55.9 MG

THE SALAD FIXINGS
2 **cups dry pasta (bow tie or fusilli) (16 mg)**
½ **cup shredded carrot (19.2 mg)**
½ **cup chopped zucchini (1.86 mg)**
1 **cup frozen unsalted peas* (7.25 mg)**
1 **cup corn kernels from fresh cob (23.1 mg)**

THE DRESSING
1 **tablespoon extra virgin olive oil (trace)**
2 **tablespoons apple cider vinegar (.3 mg)**
1 **teaspoon white granulated sugar or Splenda (.042 mg)**
½ **teaspoon dry mustard (trace)**

*We made it a second time and used Eden Organic No-Salt Added Black Beans instead of the peas. The result was delicious.

Boil pasta (.3 mg) (.042 mg) according to package direction. Drain and set aside.

Place the corn and unsalted frozen peas in a microwave-safe bowl with 2 tablespoons low-sodium water. Microwave for one minute or until the vegetables brighten but are barely cooked. Remove and drain any excess moisture. If you don't have a microwave, simply heat the corn and peas in one cup of boiling water on the stovetop for 15 to 20 seconds. They will cook rapidly. Drain.

Make the dressing by whisking the four ingredients together.

Transfer the salad ingredients to a medium bowl and pour the dressing over the salad, mixing thoroughly.

FOR SERVING
1 **cup cherry tomatoes (16.2 mg)**
½ **lemon, cut into 4 wedges (.47 mg)**

Add the cherry tomatoes and refrigerate the salad. Put a lemon wedge on each plate and serve the salad well chilled.

Nutrient Values per Serving:
Calories: 222.6. Protein: 8.739 g. Carbohydrate: 38.3 g. Dietary Fiber: 6.742 g. Total Sugars: 1.039 g. Total Fat: 5.154 g. Saturated Fat: .781 g. Monounsaturated Fat: 2.94 g. Polyunsaturated Fat: .946 g. Cholesterol: 18 mg. Calcium: 35.5 mg. Iron: 2.637 mg. Potassium: 510.3 mg. Sodium: 55.9 mg. Vitamin K: 15.6 mcg. Folate: 122.4 mcg.

ORGANIC BEAN SALAD
❖ WITH BELL PEPPER ❖

DIABETIC ACCEPTABLE

Pete Eiden at www.healthyheartmarket.com introduced us to Eden Organic beans about five years ago. Since then we've created many salads, soups, and entrées with these products. Eden has produced some delicious, high-quality beans and they are worth a try. We think you'll enjoy this salad as a good example.

SERVES 4   SODIUM PER RECIPE: 113.6 MG
SODIUM PER SERVING: 28.4 MG

THE DRESSING
1 **tablespoon fresh squeezed lime juice (.15 mg)**
2 **tablespoons extra virgin olive oil (trace)**
2 **tablespoons red wine vinegar (.3 mg)**

½ teaspoon dry mustard powder (trace)
¼ teaspoon cumin (.882 mg)
¼ teaspoon ground coriander (.157 mg)
½ teaspoon dried tarragon (.496 mg)
½ teaspoon dried basil (.288 mg)
3 tablespoons honey or 2 tablespoons white granulated sugar
   or 1½ tablespoons Splenda (.252 mg)
⅛ teaspoon white pepper (trace)

THE SALAD
2 15-ounce cans Eden Organic Kidney, Garbanzo, or Black
   Beans* (52.5 mg)
1½ cups chopped mixed green, red, and yellow peppers
   (4.47 mg)
½ cup chopped red onion (2.4 mg)
½ cup chopped celery (1 stalk) (34. 8 mg)
½ cup chopped fresh parsley (16.8 mg)

MAKING THE DRESSING
Mix together all the ingredients, whisking until well blended. Prepare this a day ahead of time and store in a sealed container in your refrigerator. Shake well before using.

MAKING THE SALAD
Drain the liquid from the beans and rinse with water. Put the beans into a medium bowl.

Add the remaining salad ingredients to the bowl with the beans and toss. Add the dressing and serve. Stores well.

Nutrient Values per Serving:
Calories: 203.8. Protein: 6.472 g. Carbohydrate: 29.4 g. Dietary Fiber: 7.326 g. Total Sugars: 6.237 g. Total Fat: 7.112 g. Saturated Fat: .966 g. Monounsaturated Fat: 5.085 g. Polyunsaturated Fat: .697 g. Cholesterol: 0 mg. Calcium: 33 mg. Iron: 1.151 mg. Potassium: 535.8 mg. Sodium: 28.4 mg. Vitamin K: 45.4 mcg. Folate: 31.6 mcg.

*Or mix either kidney and black or kidney and garbanzo equally.

❖ SHRIMP SALAD WITH RICE ❖

ENTRÉE
DIABETIC ACCEPTABLE

Yes, shrimp. You can enjoy this tasty dish and keep your sodium low. We used six medium, fresh, and raw shrimp as a serving size. You can make it smaller if you like and lower the sodium even more. As for cholesterol, a serving of six medium shrimp is equal to 3 ounces of wild salmon. A single egg yolk has 233 mg of cholesterol. This is an exciting and delicious salad, so give it a try. We think you'll want to have it again.

SERVES 4   SODIUM PER RECIPE: 308.4 MG
SODIUM PER SERVING: 77.1 MG

1 cup long-grain or basmati rice (9.25 mg)
2 cups no-sodium bottled water (trace)
3 thin slices lemon (.42 mg)
½ cup plus 2 tablespoons finely minced celery (65.2 mg)
24 medium raw shrimp, shelled and deveined (213.1 mg)
1 tablespoon olive oil (trace)
3 tablespoons fresh lime juice (.45 mg) plus 4 lime wedges
   for garnish
2 cloves garlic, minced (1.02 mg)
¼ cup minced fresh parsley (8.4 mg)
½ cup minced green onion (approximately 1 bunch)
   (8 mg)
½ cup finely minced red onion (2.4 mg)
¼ teaspoon white pepper (.03 mg)

Cook the rice according to directions. Should make 2 cups cooked rice.

Using a small pan, bring 1½ to 2 cups bottled water to a boil with 3 slices of lemon and 2 tablespoons chopped celery. Simmer the shrimp until they turn bright pink and are cooked through, about 1 to 2 minutes. Remove from the heat; drain and cool in a small bowl.

When the shrimp are cool, stir in the tablespoon of oil, lime juice, and garlic.

Place the cooked rice in another bowl and add the parsley and the minced vegetables.

Sprinkle with the white pepper and mix gently.

Add the shrimp with any juice that has collected in the bowl and mix thoroughly. Chill and serve with an additional lime wedge.

Nutrient Values per Serving:
Calories: 260. Protein: 11.5 g. Carbohydrate: 43 g. Dietary Fiber: 1.967 g.
Total Sugars: 0 g. Total Fat: 4.452 g. Saturated Fat: .684 g. Monounsaturated Fat: 2.701 g.
Polyunsaturated Fat: .658 g. Cholesterol: 54.7 mg. Calcium: 62.8 mg. Iron: 3.492 mg.
Potassium: 285.9 mg. Sodium: 77.1 mg. Vitamin K: 25 mcg. Folate: 132.2 mcg.

SHRIMP SALAD
WITH SNOW PEAS
❖ AND UNSALTED WALNUTS ❖

DIABETIC ADAPTABLE*

This recipe may be broken up into four to six side salads when you have guests. Just add a few more shrimp, a little more rice, and voilà!

SERVES 2   SODIUM PER RECIPE: 115.8 MG
SODIUM PER SERVING: 57.9 MG

THE SALAD FIXINGS
12 medium shrimp, shelled and deveined (106.6 mg)
½ cup uncooked long-grain rice (4.625 mg)
7 whole unsalted walnuts, quartered* (.284 mg)
1 teaspoon white granulated sugar or Splenda (.042 mg)
2 cups no-sodium bottled water (trace)
20 snow peas, trimmed (2.72 mg)
¼ cup crushed pineapple (canned) (1.23 mg)

THE DRESSING
2 tablespoons white wine vinegar (.3 mg)
1 tablespoon sesame oil (trace)
1 teaspoon white granulated sugar or Splenda (.042 mg)

Set the shrimp aside in the refrigerator, covered until needed.

Cook the rice according to directions or use a steamer.

Prepare the walnuts by roasting in a toaster oven at 350°F for approximately 8 minutes or until they are crisp and turn slightly browner. Sprinkle with 1 teaspoon of sugar.

Bring 1 cup of the water to a boil in a nonstick skillet; simmer the shrimp for 1 to 2 minutes until they turn pink and are cooked through. Drain and set aside in a bowl to cool.

---

*Sugars are in the pineapple and in the walnuts. You may leave either or both out. If you leave both out, flavor-enhance with just a bit more sesame oil.

Bring the remaining cup of water to a boil in pan and simmer the snow peas for 1 minute until they brighten and are still crisp yet tender.

Drain and transfer the snow peas to the shrimp bowl and add the pineapple.

Mix the dressing. Stir it into the shrimp bowl. Add the rice and chill. Serve topped with walnuts.

Nutrient Values per Serving:
Calories: 357.6. Protein: 12.9 g. Carbohydrate: 48.9 g. Dietary Fiber: 2.452 g. Total Sugars: 2.264 g. Total Fat: 12.5 g. Saturated Fat: 1.618 g. Monounsaturated Fat: 3.533 g. Polyunsaturated Fat: 6.551 g. Cholesterol: 54.7 mg. Calcium: 63.4 mg. Iron: 2.488 mg. Potassium: 312.2 mg. Sodium: 57.9 mg. Vitamin K: .691 mcg. Folate: 29 mcg.

SOUTHWESTERN CORN
❂ AND BEAN SALAD ❂

SIDE SALAD
DIABETIC ADAPTABLE

I think Maureen grew up with a kitchen knife in one hand and a recipe in the other. This one is certainly a salad you'll enjoy and only she can remember the recipe—until now. It's chock full of vitamins, flavor, and easy to assemble. Enjoy!

SERVES 8   SODIUM PER RECIPE: 148.8 MG
SODIUM PER SERVING: 18.6 MG

THE DRESSING
4 tablespoons white balsamic vinegar (.6 mg)
2 tablespoons extra virgin olive oil (trace)
2 teaspoons Grandma's or other unsalted chili powder (trace)
⅛ teaspoon black pepper (.115 mg)
½ teaspoon Splenda

Whisk the ingredients together in a small bowl and set aside.

THE SALAD FIXINGS
3 cups corn kernels firm, fresh cobs (69.3 mg)
1 cup chopped red bell pepper (2.98 mg)
1 large cucumber or zucchini, peeled and chopped (5.6 mg)
¾ cup chopped green onions (including some green) (12 mg)
1 15-ounce can Eden Organic Kidney or Black Beans, drained and rinsed (52.5 mg)

2 tablespoons chopped parsley (4.256 mg)
¼ cup lemon juice (.61 mg)

Place the corn kernels in a microwave-safe bowl and microwave for 2 minutes. You may cook in small amount of boiling water for 30 seconds if you don't have a microwave. Drain and cool. The kernels should be barely cooked.

Place parsley and all the vegetables in a large salad bowl along with the drained and rinsed beans.

Stir in the lemon juice and chill.

Mix in the dressing and toss until all is covered.

Refrigerate to chill.

To serve, mound the salad in small bowls.

You may store the salad in an airtight container in the refrigerator overnight or for a day if you want to prepare ahead of time.

Nutrient Values per Serving:
Calories: 142.1. Protein: 5.984 g. Carbohydrate: 23.4 g. Dietary Fiber: 6.908 g. Total Sugars: 0 g. Total Fat: 4.338 g. Saturated Fat: .593 g. Monounsaturated Fat: 2.703 g. Polyunsaturated Fat: .675 g. Cholesterol: 0 mg. Calcium: 17.3 mg. Iron: .727 mg. Potassium: 486.2 mg. Sodium: 18.6 mg. Vitamin K: 7.072 mcg. Folate: 44.2 mcg.

❖ SPICY CHICKEN APPLE SALAD ❖

DIABETIC ADAPTABLE*

Refreshing crisp celery and diced fresh apples make this salad an exciting afternoon entrée. Don't be surprised by the mix of cinnamon and nutmeg. You'll like it!

SERVES 4   SODIUM PER RECIPE: 261.2 MG
SODIUM PER SERVING: 65.3 MG

2 cups diced cooked white chicken meat (2 cooked boneless, skinless half breasts)† (153.4 mg)
⅛ teaspoon ground white pepper (trace)
½ cup chopped fresh celery (about 3 large stalks) (52.2 mg)
1 fresh apple, diced (trace)
1 tablespoon fresh lemon juice (.15 mg)
¼ cup packed golden raisins (4.95 mg)
4 tablespoons light sour cream (50 mg)
¼ teaspoon ground nutmeg (trace)

*Most of the sugars are in the sour cream and raisins.
†This salad can also be made without the chicken as a delicious faux Waldorf salad. Use ½ cup broken walnuts (trace sodium) instead of the chicken pieces.

1½ tablespoons white granulated sugar or Splenda (.189 mg)
¼ teaspoon ground cinnamon (.149 mg)
    Iceberg or romaine lettuce

Sprinkle the chicken with white pepper. In a large bowl mix together the chicken and celery. Mix the apple with the lemon juice to prevent discoloration. Add the apple and raisins to the chicken and celery. Set aside.

In a smaller bowl, combine the light sour cream, nutmeg, sugar, and cinnamon. Fold into the chicken mixture. Keep refrigerated until serving time. Serve on a bed of fresh, crisp iceberg or romaine lettuce.

Nutrient Values per Serving:
Calories: 156.8. Protein: 15.9 g. Carbohydrate: 20.3 g. Dietary Fiber: 1.74 g. Total Sugars: 5.678 g. Total Fat: 1.98 g. Saturated Fat: 1.023 g. Monounsaturated Fat: .194 g. Polyunsaturated Fat: .227 g. Cholesterol: 50.9 mg. Calcium: 22.9 mg. Iron: .805 mg. Potassium: 316.1 mg. Sodium: 65.3 mg. Vitamin K: 1.8 mcg. Folate: 8.546 mcg.

▓ SPINACH, MUSHROOM AND BEET SALAD ▓

DIABETIC ADAPTABLE*

SERVES 4   SODIUM PER RECIPE: 310.6 MG
SODIUM PER SERVING: 77.4 MG

THE SALAD
2 beets (127.9 mg)
1 6-ounce package baby spinach† (134.6 mg)
2 medium carrots, grated (42.7 mg)
6 mushrooms, sliced (4.32 mg)

Preheat the oven to 350°F. To prepare the beets, wash, trim root and stem; do not peel. Bake in a small pan with ½ cup no-sodium bottled water, covered with foil, at for approximately 45 to 50 minutes, depending on the size. When a fork easily penetrates beets, they're done. Cool. Peel, slice, and dice. Set aside.

THE VINAIGRETTE
2 tablespoons olive oil (trace)
3 tablespoons white (not dark) balsamic vinegar (.45 mg)
1 clove garlic (.51 mg)
1 tablespoon white granulated sugar or Splenda (.126 mg)

*Splenda is a substitute for sugar. Cooks just like sugar.
†Or equivalent from a bunch of fresh spinach.

Blend all four ingredients. Set aside.

On individual salad plates assemble the spinach greens. Put a nest of grated carrots in the center. Arrange the sliced mushrooms around the perimeter and the beets in the center.

Lovely presentation.

When ready to serve, drizzle over the dressing, and serve.

Nutrient Values per Serving:
Calories: 121.4. Protein: 3.023 g. Carbohydrate: 13.7 g. Dietary Fiber: 3.553 g. Total Sugars: 3.118 g. Total Fat: 7.12 g. Saturated Fat: .968 g. Monounsaturated Fat: 4.997 g. Polyunsaturated Fat: .717 g. Cholesterol: 0 mg. Calcium: 60.4 mg. Iron: 2.024 mg. Potassium: 583.7 mg. Sodium: 77.4 mg. Vitamin K: 176.5 mcg. Folate: 134.9 mcg.

❖ SUSHI SALAD ❖

ENTRÉE OR SIDE SALAD
DIABETIC ADAPTABLE

We lived in a small community in northern California for thirty-two years. Once a year the local Japanese citizens, who had been there long before we arrived, held an annual bazaar where they served all the popular Japanese dishes of the day including of course, sushi. Maureen bases her sushi salad on what she has enjoyed at the bazaar. This is quite good and easy to make.

SERVES 4 AS AN ENTRÉE   SERVES 8 AS A SIDE SALAD
SODIUM PER RECIPE: 173.7 MG
SODIUM PER SERVING (ENTRÉE): 43.4 MG
SODIUM PER SERVING (SIDE SALAD): 21.7 MG

THE SALAD BASE
2 **cups uncooked white rice* (3.9 mg)**
1 **cup chopped celery (about 2 stalks) (104.4 mg)**
1 **cup chopped cucumber (2.66 mg)**
1 **cup grated carrots (38.5 mg)**
¼ **cup chopped cilantro (6.21 mg)**
8 **lettuce leaves**
¼ **cup chopped unsalted dry-roasted cashews† (5.48 mg)**

*Long grain, short grain, basmati all work.
†Garnish with unsalted cashews. Nutrient Values per Tablespoon: 1.3 mg Sodium; 4 g Total Fat; 49.4 Calories)

THE DRESSING

2 tablespoons sesame oil (trace)
2 tablespoons honey‡ (1.68 mg)
4 tablespoons unseasoned rice vinegar (.6 mg)
1 tablespoon no-sodium bottled water (trace)

WASABI TOPPING

½ avocado (10.1 mg)
   Juice of ½ lemon (.235 mg)
1 teaspoon prepared wasabi§ (1 mg)

Prepare 2 cups uncooked rice according to directions. When cooked place in bowl and cool.

When the rice is cool, whisk together the dressing until blended. Add to the cooked rice and chill.

When chilled, add the vegetables and cilantro to the rice and mix thoroughly.

Prepare the wasabi topping by mashing the avocado with the lemon juice and wasabi.

Serve the chilled rice salad on a lettuce leaf topped with wasabi and a few chopped cashews.

Nutrient Values per Serving as an Entrée (4):
Calories: 557.5. Protein: 9.063 g. Carbohydrate: 96.9 g. Dietary Fiber: 4.571 g. Total Sugars: 8.4 g. Total Fat: 15.3 g. Saturated Fat: 2.55 g. Monounsaturated Fat: 7.647 g. Polyunsaturated Fat: 4.213 g. Cholesterol: 0 mg. Calcium: 43.3 mg. Iron: 5.516 mg. Potassium: 549.3 mg. Sodium: 43.4 mg. Vitamin K: 15.7 mcg. Folate: 266.4 mcg.

Nutrient Values per Serving as a Side Salad (8):
Calories: 278.8 g. Protein: 4.531 g. Carbohydrate: 48.4 g. Dietary Fiber: 2.286 g. Total Sugars: 4.2 g. Total Fat: 7.672 g. Saturated Fat: 1.275 g. Monounsaturated Fat: 3.824 g. Polyunsaturated Fat: 2.107 g. Cholesterol: 0 mg. Calcium: 21.7 mg. Iron: 2.758 mg. Potassium: 274.6 mg. Sodium: 21.7 mg. Vitamin K: 7.853 mcg. Folate: 133.2 mcg.

‡You may replace honey with Splenda. Use 2 teaspoons of Splenda, taste test, then add more as needed.
§Purchase wasabi powder and prepare with water according to directions.

❧ TACO SALAD ❧

A COMPLETE MEAL
DIABETIC ADAPTABLE*

We received an e-mail from a man in Texas asking if we had any Mexican recipes. Well, we did, but mostly tacos, in a shell, the kind you picked up in your hands and ate. Later, we developed an enchilada that was perfect for low-sodium lifestyles and now we have this taco chip salad. It's a complete meal for lunch or dinner. Delicious. Try it; we think you'll really enjoy it. By the way, prepare the corn first. (See salad ingredients below.)

SERVES 4   SODIUM PER RECIPE: 412 MG
SODIUM PER SERVING: 103 MG

FIRST
2 **medium ears of fresh corn (27 mg)**

Remove the kernels from the cob with a sharp knife. Place the kernels in a microwave-safe bowl and microwave 2 minutes. Also may be cooked in boiling water for 2 minutes.

LET'S DO THE DRESSING
¼ **cup fresh lime juice (.615 mg)†**
½ **cup chopped fresh cilantro (12.4 mg)**
2 **teaspoons white granulated sugar or Splenda* (.084 mg)**
¼ **teaspoon white pepper (.03 mg)**
¼ **cup plus 1 tablespoon olive oil (trace)**

Blend the ingredients together with a handheld blender or a food processor. You can use a whisk if you chop the cilantro finely. Set aside.

LET'S PUT TOGETHER THE SALAD
2 **teaspoons olive oil (trace)**
2 **cups chopped onions (4.8 mg)**
2 **cloves garlic, chopped (1.02 mg)**
2 **teaspoons unsalted chili powder (trace)**
2 **teaspoons ground cumin (7.056 mg)**

---

*Most of the sugar in this recipe is from the sugar. Using Splenda gets rid of nearly 95 percent of sugars.
†¼ cup bottled lime juice has 9.4 mg sodium.

2 boneless, skinless chicken half breasts, cut into bite-size
   pieces (138.5 mg)
1 8-ounce can no-salt-added tomato sauce (73.2 mg)
1 tablespoon plus 1 teaspoon fresh lemon juice (.188 mg)
¼ cup no-sodium bottled water (trace)
¼ teaspoon black pepper (.231 mg)

In a 12-inch heavy skillet over moderate heat, sauté the onions and garlic in the oil, until softened. Add the unsalted chili powder and cumin, stirring occasionally—about 5 minutes. Add the chicken and continue cooking, stirring often until the chicken is thoroughly cooked—about 5 minutes.

Add the no-salt-added tomato sauce, lemon juice, water, and pepper to the chicken and cook, stirring, until slightly thickened, about 3 more minutes. Remove from the heat.

AND NOW, THE SALAD
1 California avocado, firm and ripe (20.8 mg)
1 head iceberg or other green leaf lettuce, torn into pieces
   (8 cups) (48.5 mg)
2 large tomatoes, seeded, peeled, and chopped (32.8 mg)
2 ears of fresh corn on the cob (27 mg)
1 cup chopped red onion or sweet white onion or green onion
   (4.8 mg)
¼ pound coarsely grated low-sodium Cheddar‡ (40 mg)
4 servings of no-salt-added tortilla chips (trace)

Peel and pit the avocado, then cut into ½-inch pieces. Spread the lettuce over the bottom of a shallow salad bowl or make individual servings on separate dishes. Spoon the mixture evenly over the lettuce. Then layer on top of that the tomatoes, corn, onion, and low sodium Cheddar cheese. Drizzle the dressing over the salad. Toss lightly. Finish with the avocado and tortilla chips. Arrange avocado on top of the salad and the chips around the side for a lovely presentation.

Nutrient Values per Serving:
Calories: 561.3. Protein: 28 g. Carbohydrate: 56.7 g. Dietary Fiber: 11 g. Total Sugars: 2.079 g. Total Fat: 34.7 g. Saturated Fat: 9.633 g. Monounsaturated Fat: 17 g. Polyunsaturated Fat: 3.003 g. Cholesterol: 30.9 mg. Calcium: 85.3 mg. Iron: 3.802 mg. Potassium: 1517 mg. Sodium: 103 mg. Vitamin K: 15 mcg. Folate: 161.3 mcg.

‡Nutritional value figured on Heluva Good Low-Sodium Cheese. See www.heluvagood.com

❖ THAI SALAD ❖

DIABETIC ADAPTABLE

Thai food is generally hard to duplicate since most Thai recipes use a high-sodium fish sauce called nam plah. I have two friends who live in Bangkok who often send me recipes from Thailand that they believe can be adapted. One friend, Picha Srisansansee, sent me an entire CD full of recipes once, yet only two were adaptable when it came to keeping the integrity of the recipe. Maureen, who attended a friend's bridal shower, created this salad. A Thai salad was served and she loved it. However, she had to alter it a bit for us. Now, I can send a recipe back to Picha with, of course, our compliments.

SERVES 4   SODIUM PER RECIPE: 212.8 MG
SODIUM PER SERVING: 53.2 MG

THE SALAD MAKINGS
1   teaspoon ground ginger (.576 mg)
1   teaspoon onion powder (1.134 mg)
2   boneless, skinless chicken half breasts (153.8 mg)
1   red onion, thinly sliced (4.5 mg)
1   red bell pepper, thinly sliced (approximately 2 cups) (3.28 mg)
1   cup cilantro, chopped (24.8 mg)
½   medium head iceberg lettuce, cut into bite-size pieces and set aside (24.3 mg)

In a fry-pan, bring enough water to cover the chicken to a boil, add ginger and onion powder to the water, then insert chicken and simmer for 8 to 10 minutes or until chicken is cooked through. Remove chicken, discard water and ginger. Cool chicken, then cut into bite-size pieces and chill while preparing salad mix and dressing.

Assemble the salad by combining the red pepper, red onion, and cilantro in a medium to large salad bowl.

THE DRESSING
2   tablespoons no-sodium bottled water (trace)
1   tablespoon peanut or expeller pressed canola oil (trace)
3 to 4 tablespoons unseasoned rice vinegar (.6 mg)
1   tablespoon white granulated sugar (.126 mg)

Make dressing by whisking the above dressing ingredients together. Then place chilled chicken into salad mix, and toss with dressing. Place lettuce on four serving plates and top with salad.

Nutrient Values per Serving:
Calories: 148.6. Protein: 15.4 g. Carbohydrate: 12.6 g. Dietary Fiber: 2.848 g. Total Sugars: 3.118 g. Total Fat: 4.46 g. Saturated Fat: .699 g. Monounsaturated Fat: 2.714 g. Polyunsaturated Fat: .593 g. Cholesterol: 34.2 mg. Calcium: 41.5 mg. Iron: 1.396 mg. Potassium: 473.1 mg. Sodium: 53.2 mg. Vitamin K: 2.404 mcg. Folate: 64.4 mcg.

SUMMER CUCUMBER

❖ TOMATO SALAD ❖

SIDE SALAD

This is probably the easiest salad in this book to make and one of the best summer salads for brightening your day and your health. It's chock full of fresh cucumbers, tomatoes, and red onions.

SERVES 4   SODIUM PER RECIPE: 54 MG

SODIUM PER SERVING: 13.5 MG

THE FIXINGS
1 cucumber (about 2 cups chopped) (6.02 mg)
4 medium tomatoes (about 2 cups chopped) (44.3 mg)
1 small red onion (about 1 cup chopped (3.3 mg)

THE DRESSING
1 tablespoon extra virgin olive oil (trace)
2 tablespoons white balsamic vinegar or white wine or apple cider vinegar (.3 mg)
½ teaspoon white granulated sugar or Splenda (.021)
½ teaspoon dry mustard (trace)
   White pepper to taste (optional)

Place all the salad ingredients in a bowl.

Prepare the dressing by whisking all dressing ingredients together until well combined.

Pour the dressing over the salad, toss with a spoon, and chill before serving. Stores in well-sealed container in refrigerator for up to 3 days.

Nutrient Values per Serving:
Calories: 79.5. Protein: 1.915 g. Carbohydrate: 11.1 g. Dietary Fiber: 2.45 g. Total Sugars: .52 g. Total Fat: 3.96 g. Saturated Fat: .55 g. Monounsaturated Fat: 2.576 g. Polyunsaturated Fat: .519 g. Cholesterol: 0 mg. Calcium: 23 mg. Iron: .875 mg. Potassium: 432.8 mg. Sodium: 13.5 mg. Vitamin K: 23.9 mcg. Folate: 33.5 mcg.

SPECIAL SALAD DRESSINGS

❈ ❈ ❈ ❈ ❈ ❈ ❈ ❈

❈ MAUREEN'S CREAMY CHEESE DRESSING ❈

DIABETIC ACCEPTABLE

Have you missed your favorite bleu cheese dressing or one of those other "creamy" dressings that come in a fancy bottle? Miss no more. This isn't blue cheese but it's a nice replacement. Maureen created this for us when I started to pine for blue cheese. Hmmmm, good.

MAKES 9 TABLESPOONS   SODIUM PER RECIPE: 105.3 MG
SODIUM PER TABLESPOON: 11.7 MG

2 **tablespoons light sour cream* (18.3 mg)**
2 **tablespoons buttermilk (16.3 mg)**
1 **tablespoon white wine vinegar (.15 mg)**
2 **ounces low-sodium Swiss cheese† (23 mg)**
½ **teaspoon onion powder (.567 mg)**
½ **teaspoon garlic powder (.364 mg)**

Using your hand blender or other food processor, combine all the ingredients and process until smooth. Serve cold.

Nutrient Values per Tablespoon:
Calories: 27. Protein: 2.096 g. Carbohydrate: .668 g. Dietary Fiber: .025 g. Total Sugars: .345 g. Total Fat: 1.819 g. Saturated Fat: 1.193 g. Monounsaturated Fat: 0 g. Polyunsaturated Fat: .001 g. Cholesterol: 6.514 mg. Calcium: 15.7 mg. Iron: .496 mg. Potassium: 11.7 mg. Sodium: 11.7 mg. Vitamin K: 0 mcg. Folate: .197 mcg.

*Data figured from Kraft's Breakstone's Reduced-Fat Sour Cream.
†See "low-sodium Swiss" in Glossary.

Maureen's Creamy
❖ Avocado Dressing ❖

We didn't want to call this Green Goddess, but it's a great replacement for that higher-sodium dressing. Commercial Green Goddess dressing has 162.5 milligrams of sodium per tablespoon and 7.4 g of fat. Compare that to this dressing and you'll enjoy this even more.

MAKES 6 TABLESPOONS   SODIUM PER RECIPE: 23.4 MG
SODIUM PER TABLESPOON: 3.895 MG

¼ **California avocado (5.19 mg)**
1 **tablespoon light sour cream* (9.145 mg)**
1 **tablespoon buttermilk† (7.8 mg)**
1 **teaspoon onion powder (1.134 mg)**
2 **teaspoons fresh lemon juice (.01 mg)**

Using a Braun hand blender or other handheld model, puree until smooth. Serve cold. (See "handheld mixer" in Glossary.)

Nutrient Values per Tablespoon:
Calories: 18.8. Protein: .4 g. Carbohydrate: 1.192 g. Dietary Fiber: .382 g. Total Sugars: .255 g. Total Fat: 1.613 g. Saturated Fat: .414 g. Monounsaturated Fat: .809 g. Polyunsaturated Fat: .149 g. Cholesterol: 1.542 mg. Calcium: 9.219 mg. Iron: .439 mg. Potassium: 56.5 mg. Sodium: 3.895 mg. Vitamin K: 0 mcg. Folate: 5.555 mcg.

❖ Don's Italian Dressing ❖

Commercial salad dressings are a big no-no in our low sodium world. So, we have to make up our own. Here's one I've kept a secret for a long time. Easy to put together, you can "rebalance" it for your own taste buds. Use more olive oil or less, more vinegar or less. In other words, make it to taste. I think you'll like it.

MAKES 12 TABLESPOONS   SODIUM PER RECIPE: 3.49 MG
SODIUM PER TABLESPOON: .291 MG

3 **tablespoons extra virgin olive oil (trace)**
4½ **tablespoons red wine vinegar (.675 mg)**
1 **teaspoon fresh-squeezed lemon juice (.15 mg)**

---

*Figured on Kraft's Breakstone's Reduced Fat Sour Cream.
†Data figured on Knudsen Reduced Fat 1 percent Buttermilk.

3 cloves garlic, minced, or 1 level teaspoon Oregon Flavor Rack
   Garlic Lover's Garlic (1.5 mg)
¼ teaspoon dried basil (.119 mg)
¼ teaspoon dill (.52 mg)
¼ teaspoon oregano (trace)

Shake vigorously. You may adapt this to your own taste by increasing or
decreasing any of the ingredients.

Nutrient Values per Tablespoon:
Calories: 32.4. Protein: .071 g. Carbohydrate: .759 g. Dietary Fiber: .065 g. Total Sugars:
0 g. Total Fat: 3.39 g. Saturated Fat: .457 g. Monounsaturated Fat: 2.492 g.
Polyunsaturated Fat: .288 g. Cholesterol: 0 mg. Calcium: 3.761 mg. Iron: .104 mg.
Potassium: 13.1 mg. Sodium: .291 mg. Vitamin K: 1.654 mcg. Folate: .351 mcg.

❊ GINGER SALAD DRESSING ❊

DIABETIC ADAPTABLE

Ginger has always been a favorite at our house. Of
course that includes gingerbread cookies, gingersnaps,
and using ginger while barbecuing some meats. Ginger is
also great for salads, helping to punch up the flavors of
various greens and vegetables used in salads. Give this
one a try. We think you'll really like it.

MAKES 1½ CUPS   SODIUM PER RECIPE: 9.624 MG
SODIUM PER TABLESPOON: .401 MG

¼ cup minced onion (1.2 mg)
¼ cup extra virgin olive oil (trace)
3 tablespoons unseasoned rice vinegar (.45 mg)
1 tablespoon no-sodium bottled water (trace)
1 tablespoon minced fresh ginger (.78 mg)
1 tablespoon minced celery (6.525 mg)
2 teaspoons white granulated sugar or Splenda (trace)
1 teaspoon fresh lemon juice (.05 mg)
1 clove garlic, minced (.51 mg)
⅛ teaspoon white pepper (trace)

Combine all the ingredients in a hand blender set at high speed for about
30 to 40 seconds or until the ginger is throroughly pureed.

Nutrient Values per Tablespoon:
Calories: 22.6. Protein: .036 g. Carbohydrate: .721 g. Dietary Fiber: .047 g. Total Sugars:
.347 g. Total Fat: 2.256 g. Saturated Fat: .305 g. Monounsaturated Fat: 1.659 g.
Polyunsaturated Fat: .191 g. Cholesterol: 0 mg. Calcium: .893 mg. Iron: .03 mg.
Potassium: 7.201 mg. Sodium: .401 mg. Vitamin K: 1.173 mcg. Folate: .464 mcg.

❖ SPICY ORANGE DRESSING ❖

MAKES 5 TABLESPOONS   SODIUM PER RECIPE: 2.426 MG
SODIUM PER TABLESPOON: .485 MG

¼ **cup fresh-squeezed orange juice (.62 mg)**
½ **teaspoon cumin (1.764 mg)**
1½ **tablespoons olive oil (trace)**
1 **teaspoon white granulated sugar or Splenda (.042 mg)**

Mix the ingredients thoroughly. This is particularly good with fall and win-ter fruits. If you like cilantro, just add 2 tablespoons chopped fresh cilantro and mix in with the fruit.

Nutrient Values per Tablespoon:
Calories: 45.4. Protein: .124 g. Carbohydrate: 2.222 g. Dietary Fiber: .047 g. Total Sugars: .832 g. Total Fat: 4.122 g. Saturated Fat: .553 g. Monounsaturated Fat: 3.019 g. Polyunsaturated Fat: .352 g. Cholesterol: 0 mg. Calcium: 3.328 mg. Iron: .18 mg. Potassium: 28.6 mg. Sodium: .485 mg. Vitamin K: 1.997 mcg. Folate: 3.741 mcg.

❖ SOUR CREAM AND HONEY DRESSING ❖

This is a nice sweet dressing for a fruit salad mix. Serve cold. Great salad dressing for summer picnics.

MAKES 5 TABLESPOONS   SODIUM PER RECIPE: 28.4 MG
SODIUM PER TABLESPOON: 5.685 MG

3 **tablespoons light sour cream (27.4 mg)**
1 **tablespoon honey (.84 mg)**
1 **tablespoon fresh lemon juice (.15 mg)**

Mix thoroughly and test for sweetness. Pour over fruit right before serving.

Nutrient Values per Tablespoon:
Calories: 27.7. Protein: .443 g. Carbohydrate: 4.324 g. Dietary Fiber: .03 g. Total Sugars: 3.955 g. Total Fat: 1.116 g. Saturated Fat: .707 g. Monounsaturated Fat: 0 g. Polyunsaturated Fat: 0 g. Cholesterol: 4.65 mg. Calcium: 15.4 mg. Iron: .024 mg. Potassium: 25.4 mg. Sodium: 5.685 mg. Vitamin K: 0 mcg. Folate: .474 mcg.

❧ OLD FASHION RUSSIAN DRESSING ❧

DIABETIC ADAPTABLE

Remember when salad used to consist of a wedge of iceberg lettuce with Russian or French dressing drizzled on the top? They still sell the bottled dressing and it brings with it a little nostalgia. Here's our version and it's terrific as well as very low in sodium. In fact, Maureen tasted the high-sodium bottled version and preferred ours.

**MAKES 5 TABLESPOONS—SERVES 2   SODIUM PER RECIPE: 10.4 MG
SODIUM PER TABLESPOON: 2.078 MG**

- **2 tablespoons white wine vinegar (.30 mg)**
- **1 tablespoon extra virgin olive oil (trace)**
- **2 teaspoon no-salt-added tomato paste (9.525 mg)**
- **2 teaspoons honey (.554 mg)**
- **¼ teaspoon balsamic vinegar (trace)**
- **⅛ teaspoon dry mustard (trace)**

Blend with a small whisk. Serve.

Nutrient Values per Tablespoon:
Calories: 35.2. Protein: .1 g. Carbohydrate: 3.078 g. Dietary Fiber: .094 g. Total Sugars: 2.218 g. Total Fat: 2.727 g. Saturated Fat: .369 g. Monounsaturated Fat: 1.999 g. Polyunsaturated Fat: .237 g. Cholesterol: 0 mg. Calcium: 1.423 mg. Iron: .104 mg. Potassium: 28.2 mg. Sodium: 2.078 mg. Vitamin K: 1.323 mcg. Folate: .532 mcg.

DON'S RASPBERRY
❧ SANDWICH VINAIGRETTE ❧

I used this in veggie sandwiches to help punch up the flavors.

SERVES 1   SODIUM PER RECIPE: .15 MG

- **1 tablespoon raspberry vinegar (.15 mg)**
- **½ tablespoon olive oil (trace)**
- **Pinch Splenda or sugar (trace)**

Nutrient Values per Recipe:
Calories: 61.8. Protein: 0g. Carbohydrate: .885 g. Dietary Fiber: 0 g. Total Sugars: 0 g. Total Fat: 6.75 g. Saturated Fat: .911 g. Monounsaturated Fat: 4.975 g. Polyunsaturated Fat: .567 g. Cholesterol: 0 mg. Calcium: .9 mg. Iron: .116 mg. Potassium: 15 mg. Sodium: .15 mg. Vitamin K: 3.308 mcg. Folate: 0 mcg.

SPICE AND HERB MIXES

HOW TO USE SPICES/HERBS

The biggest question for new users of spices and herbs is how, when, and why? This is a quick guide for you. After you get used to using these, and the spices and herbs in our recipes, you'll find yourself experimenting and becoming an expert. Use with barbecues, broiling, boiling, baking, basting, marinades, or just to flavor what's on your plate.

A General Outlook

Basil—Add ⅓ to ½ teaspoon of dried basil or three times that amount of fresh, chopped basil to each 2 cups of green vegetables.

Curry Powder—Add 1 tablespoon to 2 pounds of lamb; 1 tablespoon to 2 pounds ground beef or more to taste.

Dill Weed—Add ¼ to ½ teaspoon fresh dried dill weed to fish or vegetables for seasoning. Add to a mix of light sour cream and yogurt to make a mayonnaise substitute.

Nutmeg—Add a dash of nutmeg to mixed vegetables or spinach or up to ¼ teaspoon to ground beef, turkey, or chicken.

Paprika—Add to chicken, beef, or white vegetables or to potato salads and some salad dressings.

Parsley—Add 1 tablespoon to each pound of ground beef or ¼ teaspoon for vegetables, meat, and fish or more to taste.

Tarragon—Add ¼ teaspoon to 1 pound of fish or ⅓ teaspoon to 1 pound of fowl.

Unsalted Chili Powder—Add 1 tablespoon per pound of ground beef or 2 to 3 pounds of pot roast (Crock-Pot or stove top).

White Pepper—Add to vegetables and other dishes to taste.

A Specific Outlook

Basic Seasoning Without Salt and Salt Substitutes

Spices and herbs can be used directly on meats and vegetables as shown below. This extensive list may help you become an expert sooner than you thought possible.

Meat, Fish, and Poultry

Beef—Marjoram, fresh mushrooms, nutmeg, onion, garlic, pepper, sage, thyme, coriander, bay leaf (soups), dry mustard powder (stews, barbecue), green pepper, dill weed, lavender, and rosemary.

Chicken—Green pepper, lemon juice, marjoram, mushrooms, paprika, parsley, poultry seasoning, sage, thyme, coriander, cardamom, savory, lavender, and pepper.

Fish—Bay leaf, curry powder, dry mustard powder, green pepper, lemon juice, marjoram, mushrooms, and paprika.

Lamb—Curry powder, garlic, mint, mint jelly, pineapple, rosemary, cloves, a touch of ginger, and pepper.

Veal—Marjoram, oregano, bay leaf, curry powder, ginger, apricot, and pepper.

Vegetables

Asparagus—Garlic, lemon juice, and vinegar.

Corn—White pepper, green pepper, pimento, and fresh cilantro.

Cucumbers—Dill weed, chives, and vinegar.

Green Beans—Lemon juice, marjoram, dill weed, nutmeg, pepper, and oregano.

Greens—Garlic, shallots, onion, pepper, and vinegar.

Peas—Mint, white pepper, parsley, garlic, and onion.

Potatoes—Rosemary, white pepper, parsley, onion, green pepper, chives, and pimento.

Rice—Onion, saffron, green pepper, chives, and pimento.

Squash—Onion, nutmeg, ginger, mace, cinnamon, and brown sugar.

Tomatoes—Fresh basil, oregano, marjoram, and onion.

❦ BEEF RUB ❦

This spice mix is the taste kick you want for prime rib, steaks, lamb, and other red meats when barbecuing, baking, or broiling. Rub the mix into meat before cooking.

**MAKES 1 TABLESPOON   SODIUM PER RECIPE: 5.061 MG
SODIUM PER TEASPOON: 1.687 MG**

1 teaspoon garlic powder (.728 mg)
1 teaspoon onion powder (1.134 mg)
1 teaspoon celery seed or celery powder (3.2 mg)
½ teaspoon dried mustard powder (optional)

Mix together. You may double or triple this recipe, depending upon your needs or whether you'd like to store for future use. Fresh spices and herbs keep in airtight containers for about 3 months.

Nutrient Values per Teaspoon:
Calories: 8.141. Protein: .348 g. Carbohydrate: 1.519 g. Dietary Fiber: .211 g. Total Sugars: 0 g. Total Fat: .183 g. Saturated Fat: .017 g. Monounsaturated Fat: .107 g. Polyunsaturated Fat: .031 g. Cholesterol: 0 mg. Calcium: 15.1 mg. Iron: .343 mg. Potassium: 26.2 mg. Sodium: 1.687 mg. Vitamin K: 0 mcg. Folate: 1.247 mcg.

❦ DON'S CAJUN SPICE MIX ❦

Use with catfish, trout, or bass when broiling or barbecuing. Can also be mixed in with ground beef for a hot Cajun-style hamburger or taco. If you want it "cooler," then cut the cayenne in half. If you want it hotter, then add a bit more paprika and cayenne pepper.

**MAKES 9 TABLESPOONS   SODIUM PER RECIPE: 18.6 MG
SODIUM PER TABLESPOON: 2.072 MG**

2 tablespoons paprika (4.692 mg)
2¼ tablespoons garlic powder (5.46 mg)
1 tablespoon white pepper (.355 mg)
1 tablespoon onion powder (3.51 mg)

1   **tablespoon cayenne pepper (1.59 mg)**
1   **tablespoon dried or ground oregano (.675 mg)**
1   **tablespoon dried thyme (2.365 mg)**

Mix all ingredients together in a dry bowl. Store in an airtight bottle for up to 3 months.

Nutrient Values per Tablespoon:
Calories: 21.7. Protein: .943 g. Carbohydrate: 4.636 g. Dietary Fiber: 1.35 g. Total Sugars: 0 g. Total Fat: .429 g. Saturated Fat: .087 g. Monounsaturated Fat: .048 g. Polyunsaturated Fat: .226 g. Cholesterol: 0 mg. Calcium: 27.1 mg. Iron: 1.414 mg. Potassium: 93.1 mg. Sodium: 2.072 mg. Vitamin K: 0 mcg. Folate: 6.253 mcg.

✥ DON'S SALT-FREE CHILI POWDER ✥

I created this salt-free chili powder recipe after learning that commercial salt-free chili powder was difficult to find in some areas of the MegaHeart world. There are a few like Grandma's, a national brand from Grandma's Spanish Pepper Company, Lenexa, Texas, but it's nice to be able to make up your own, too. It's a good replacement for the chili powder called for in any of our recipes.

MAKES 4 TABLESPOONS   SODIUM PER RECIPE: 11.1 MG
SODIUM PER TEASPOON: .924 MG

⅓   **teaspoon cayenne pepper (.135 mg)**
2½ **tablespoons paprika (5.865 mg)**
1   **teaspoon ground cumin (3.528 mg)**
1   **teaspoon ground turmeric (.836 mg)**
1   **teaspoon garlic powder (.728 mg)**

Combine all the ingredients and thoroughly mix together (shaking in a container).

Nutrient Values per Teaspoon:
Calories: 6.354. Protein: .301 g. Carbohydrate: 1.189 g. Dietary Fiber: .391 g. Total Sugars: 0 g. Total Fat: .251 g. Saturated Fat: .04 g. Monounsaturated Fat: .046 g. Polyunsaturated Fat: .133 g. Cholesterol: 0 mg. Calcium: 4.751 mg. Iron: .541 mg. Potassium: 44.8 mg. Sodium: .924 mg. Vitamin K: 0 mcg. Folate: 1.657 mcg.

◈ DON'S HERBES DE PROVENCE SPICE MIX ◈

My wife brought home a small bag of spices from Provence, France. We tried them and they were out of this world. It was a mix that we found we could use on beef, chicken, turkey, soups, and just about anything that had meat or potatoes in it. This is what we have come up with as a substitute for that mix.

MAKES 14.6 TEASPOONS   SODIUM PER RECIPE: 18.3 MG
SODIUM PER TEASPOON: .418 MG

- 4 tablespoons ground or fresh thyme (9.46 mg)
- 4 tablespoons ground summer savory (4.224 mg)
- 1 tablespoon lavender (trace)
- 1 tablespoon dried or ground basil (1.53 mg)
- 2 teaspoons dried sage (.154 mg)
- 1 tablespoon ground or dried rosemary (1.65 mg)
- 3 tablespoons dried marjoram (2.618 mg)
- ½ teaspoon savory (trace)

Mix the ingredients together; shake well. Store in a tightly sealed container. Use with meats and potatoes and with soups and stews.

Nutrient Values per Teaspoon:
Calories: 2.89. Protein: .09 g. Carbohydrate: .681 g. Dietary Fiber: .431 g. Total Sugars: 0 g. Total Fat: .075 g. Saturated Fat: .032 g. Monounsaturated Fat: .006 g. Polyunsaturated Fat: .011 g. Cholesterol: 0 mg. Calcium: 20.4 mg. Iron: .744 mg. Potassium: 12.6 mg. Sodium: .418 mg. Vitamin K: 0 mcg. Folate: 1.783 mcg.

◈ DON'S ITALIAN SEASONING ◈

This mix is pleasant to the taste. Wet the tip of a finger after mixing this and pick up some of the mix. Put it to your tongue for a taste. I think you'll find it's just right for anything Italian from salad dressings to meat and pasta dishes.

MAKES 17 TABLESPOONS   SODIUM PER RECIPE: 28 MG
SODIUM PER TEASPOON: .539 MG

- 2 tablespoons dried rosemary (3.3 mg)
- 2 tablespoons dried or 2 tablespoons ground basil (3.06 mg)
- 2 tablespoons dried marjoram (2.618 mg)
- 2 tablespoons dried or 1½ tablespoons ground oregano (1.35 mg)

2 tablespoons dried coriander leaf (7.596 mg)
2 tablespoons ground thyme (4.732 mg)
2 tablespoons ground sage (.44 mg)
2 tablespoons savory (2.112 mg)
1 tablespoon lavender* (trace)

Combine all the ingredients in the bowl or container of your food processor fitted with the steel blade and process for about 20 to 30 seconds only.

Place into a tight container (possibly an older spice jar or container) and store in a cool dry place. Date it. Store all your spices no more than 3 to 4 months.

Nutrient Values per Teaspoon:
Calories: 3.219. Protein: .125 g. Carbohydrate: .715 g. Dietary Fiber: .45 g. Total Sugars: 0 g. Total Fat: .09 g. Saturated Fat: .031 g. Monounsaturated Fat: .011 g. Polyunsaturated Fat: .026 g. Cholesterol: 0 mg. Calcium: 20.7 mg. Iron: .623 mg. Potassium: 21.5 mg. Sodium: .539 mg. Vitamin K: 0 mcg. Folate: 2.698 mcg.

◧ DON'S POULTRY SEASONING ◧

Ever wonder how those restaurants that serve chicken always seem to make it tasty, even when they don't fry it? Here's a good way for you to compete. Just rub this into any fowl including wild game, and then bake or barbecue and you'll love it.

MAKES 1 SERVING   SODIUM PER SERVING: 2.58 MG

¾ **teaspoon ground cardamom (.27 mg)**
¼ **teaspoon ground cinnamon (.149 mg)**
⅛ **teaspoon ground cloves (.638 mg)**
½ **teaspoon ground fennel (.88 mg)**
½ **teaspoon garlic powder (.364 mg)**
¼ **teaspoon ground red or cayenne pepper (.135 mg)**
¼ **teaspoon fresh ground ginger† (.144 mg)**

Combine all the ingredients in an airtight container. Shake well for a few minutes or until well mixed.

If using later, store in a cool dry place in a sealed container or in a small spice bottle left over from other uses. Like all spices, store only for 3 to 4 months.

Rub the chicken, turkey, or other fowl, including game birds, prior to

---

*Available in natural food sections or stores or in your garden. Optional, but offers a fine European spice flavor. Nutrients unknown but not suspected to alter figures.
†You may substitute 2 teaspoons grated crystallized ginger.

barbecuing or baking. There's enough spice here for up to three pounds of meat. You can double each ingredient to make more.

May also use as a rub for lamb or as a seasoning for mixed vegetables.

Nutrient Values per Serving:
Calories: 18. 1. Protein: .688 g. Carbohydrate: 3.761 g. Dietary Fiber: 1.537 g. Total Sugars: 0 g. Total Fat: .435 g. Saturated Fat: .058 g. Monounsaturated Fat: .136 g. Polyunsaturated Fat: .094 g. Cholesterol: 0 mg. Calcium: 28.8 mg. Iron: .762 mg. Potassium: 70 mg. Sodium: 2.58 mg. Vitamin K: 0 mcg. Folate: 1.091 mcg.

❈ DON'S FLAVOR ENHANCER ❈

When we say "salt substitute," we aren't speaking of salt, but a substitute for flavor. Salt substitutes that don't use or contain salt will not help out as a leavening agent or a preservative. My flavor enhancer replaces salt in many recipes as a "kicker" when a mix of spices is needed. It works well with soups, Italian dishes, barbecued meats, and it even works in some bread recipes. This recipe is for a big batch that you can put into a large shaker or store in a Mason jar. You can also adapt this to your own tastes. Keep testing while putting it together. Like most of my spice mixes, I suggest buying larger containers of ingredient spices from a discount grocery store like Smart and Final, Costco, or a fine restaurant supplier. It's less expensive in the long run. Always store in a tight container and in a dark, cool place. Remember, too, real salt has 2,350 mg of sodium per teaspoon while this flavor enhancer has only 2.76 mg of sodium per teaspoon.

MAKES 13½ TEASPOONS   SODIUM PER RECIPE: 37.7 MG
SODIUM PER TEASPOON: 2.793 MG

5 **tablespoons unsalted onion powder (17.5 mg)**
3½ **tablespoons unsalted garlic powder (7.644 mg)**
1 **tablespoon paprika (2.346 mg)**
2 **tablespoons dry mustard powder (0 mg)**
1 **tablespoon ground thyme (2.365 mg)**
1 **teaspoon white pepper (.12 mg)**
2 **teaspoons celery seed (6.4 mg)**
¼ **teaspoon ground cloves (1.276 mg)**

Mix all the ingredients together, shake well, store what you aren't going to use soon in a tight container in a cool, dark place. Taste before storing. If you want one of the flavors above to be increased then add ¼ teaspoon at a time and shake well before testing again.

If you want to kick this up even more, add some lemon zest, pureed to a powder in a food processor. Also, powder some dill weed and add that if you're using this on vegetables.

Nutrient Values per Teaspoon:
Calories: 23.8. Protein: 1.011 g. Carbohydrate: 4.416 g. Dietary Fiber: .672 g. Total Sugars: 0 g. Total Fat: .485 g. Saturated Fat: .081 g. Monounsaturated Fat: .194 g. Polyunsaturated Fat: .169 g. Cholesterol: 0 mg. Calcium: 25.6 mg. Iron: .851 mg. Potassium: 70.8 mg. Sodium: 2.793 mg. Vitamin K: 0 mcg. Folate: 5.538 mcg.

❈ FLAVOR KICKER ❈

DIABETIC ACCEPTABLE

I like to play with spices. You may find yourself getting into this, too, and creating your own favorite mixes. (I'd like to use my coffee grinder to mince spices.) Here's another flavor booster that you can use instead of salt. It works well.

MAKES 6½ TABLESPOONS   SODIUM PER RECIPE: 21.5 MG
SODIUM PER TEASPOON: 1.104 MG

1 **tablespoon celery seed or powder (10.4 mg)**
1½ **tablespoons onion powder (5.265 mg)**
2 **teaspoons cream of tartar (3.12 mg)**
1½ **teaspoons garlic powder (1.092 mg)**
2 **teaspoons dried minced, orange zest* (.12 mg)**
1½ **teaspoons Splenda (trace)**
½ **teaspoon white pepper (.06 mg)**
½ **teaspoon dried thyme (.385 mg)**
¼ **teaspoon minced, dried lemon zest (.03 mg)**
¼ **teaspoon cayenne pepper (.135 mg)**
¼ **teaspoon lavender (trace)**
1 **teaspoon black pepper (.924 mg)**

Place all the ingredients in your blender.

Process until the mixture is fine.

Put the mixture into a convenient empty spice jar or an old, you-should-have-discarded-it-a-long-time ago salt shaker.

Store in a tightly sealed small jar in a cool, dark place for up to 3 months.

Nutrient Values per Teaspoon:
Calories: 5.391. Protein: .175 g. Carbohydrate: 1.09 g. Dietary Fiber: .178 g. Total Sugars: 0 g. Total Fat: .103 g. Saturated Fat: .012 g. Monounsaturated Fat: .056 g. Polyunsaturated Fat: .019 g. Cholesterol: 0 mg. Calcium: 9.613 mg. Iron: .268 mg. Potassium: 65.2 mg. Sodium: 1.104 mg. Vitamin K: 0 mcg. Folate: 1.072 mcg.

*You can let your orange peel sit out for about a week to dry or dry it in your oven for about an hour or two at very low temperature.

◈◈ Cardamom Rub (Poultry Seasoning) ◈◈

Both domestic and wild game birds can often use a little flavoring help. Rub this mix into chicken, turkey, or wild game birds before barbecuing, broiling, or baking. Lift the skin if you're leaving it on, and push some of it between the meat and skin. Put some into the bird's cavity as well.

SERVES 1   SODIUM PER SERVING: 2.58 MG

¾ **teaspoon ground cardamom (.27 mg)**
¼ **teaspoon ground cinnamon (.149 mg)**
⅛ **teaspoon ground cloves (.638 mg)**
½ **teaspoon ground fennel (.88 mg)**
½ **teaspoon garlic powder (.364 mg)**
¼ **teaspoon ground red or cayenne pepper (.135 mg)**
¼ **teaspoon ground ginger* (.144 mg)**

Combine all the ingredients in a container. Cover and shake thoroughly until well mixed. If you are going to use this later, store in a sealed container or a small spice bottle left over from other uses.

Rub chicken, turkey, or other fowl including game birds prior to barbecuing or baking. There's enough spice here for up to 3 pounds of meat.

May also use as a rub for lamb or as a seasoning for mixed vegetables.

Nutrient Values per Serving:
Calories: 18.1. Protein: .688 g. Carbohydrate: 3.761 g. Dietary Fiber: 1.537 g. Total Sugars: 0 g. Total Fat: .435 g. Saturated Fat: .058 g. Monounsaturated Fat: .136 g. Polyunsaturated Fat: .094 g. Cholesterol: 0 mg. Calcium: 28.8 mg. Iron: .762 mg. Potassium: 70 mg. Sodium: 2.58 mg. Vitamin K: 0 mcg. Folate: 1.091 mcg.

◈◈ French Provence Rub ◈◈

This is a lighter flavored French rub than Don's own Herbes de Provence Spice Mix, which is based on a spice/herb mix Maureen found while traveling in France. Use this on red meats.

MAKES 7 TABLESPOONS   SODIUM PER RECIPE: 15.3 MG
SODIUM PER TEASPOON: .73 MG

4 **tablespoons thyme (9.46 mg)**
4 **tablespoons summer savory (4.224 mg)**

*Substitute up to 2 teaspoons of grated gingerroot for ¼ teaspoon ground ginger or use 2 teaspoons grated crystallized ginger.

2 tablespoons lavender* (trace)
1 tablespoon rosemary (1.65 mg)

Grind together in your blender or in a coffee bean grinder.

Store in an airtight jar in a cool dark place. Good for up to 3 months if you're using fresh spices.

Nutrient Values per Teaspoon:
Calories: 5.06. Protein: .139 g. Carbohydrate: 1.2 g. Dietary Fiber: .753 g. Total Sugars: 0 g. Total Fat: .134 g. Saturated Fat: .061 g. Monounsaturated Fat: .009 g. Polyunsaturated Fat: .013 g. Cholesterol: 0 mg. Calcium: 35.4 mg. Iron: 1.376 mg. Potassium: 17 mg. Sodium: .73 mg. Vitamin K: 0 mcg. Folate: 2.727 mcg.

◈ DON'S SOUTHWEST SEASONING ◈

MAKES 9 TABLESPOONS   SODIUM PER RECIPE: 27.3 MG
SODIUM PER TABLESPOON: 3.028 MG

4 tablespoons minced dried onion (4.2 mg)
1½ teaspoons garlic powder (2.184 mg)
1 teaspoon cayenne pepper (.54 mg)
2 tablespoons Grandma's† or other no-salt chili powder (trace)
2 tablespoons ground cumin seed (20.1 mg)
¾ teaspoon oregano (.338 mg)

Mix the ingredients and store in a covered container. Use 5½ teaspoons with every pound of meat in tacos or chili.

Nutrient Values per Tablespoon:
Calories: 23.5. Protein: .631 g. Carbohydrate: 4.646 g. Dietary Fiber: .545 g. Total Sugars: 0 g. Total Fat: .695 g. Saturated Fat: .033 g. Monounsaturated Fat: .195 g. Polyunsaturated Fat: .075 g. Cholesterol: 0 mg. Calcium: 21.1 mg. Iron: 1.016 mg. Potassium: 76.3 mg. Sodium: 3.028 mg. Vitamin K: 0 mcg. Folate: 4.395 mcg.

◈ DON'S CURRY MIX ◈

Why not make a batch and store in an old spice bottle?
Simply increase the measurements to 2 tablespoons each.
If curry and cloves are too much bite for you, cut those in
half.

*Lavender can be found in many natural food stores or possibly in your own garden. If growing your own, let the flowers dry before using them.
†We often call for Grandma's Chili Powder in our recipes that use chili powder. Grandma's is a national brand, however we recognize it's not always available everywhere. You can also get two salt-free chili powder brands from www.healthyheartmarket.com. Ask for Wayzata or Frontier chili powder.

1 **teaspoon dried thyme (.766 mg)**
1 **teaspoon cloves (5.099 mg)**
1 **teaspoon dried crushed marjoram (.462 mg)**
1 **teaspoon coriander (1.266 mg)**
1 **teaspoon curry (1.04 mg)**

If too thick for salt shaker, mix together and crush or grind to a fine "dust." Can be used without crushing by "pinching" onto meats. Can be used for flavoring fowl after cooking or while cooking. Add along with pepper if you want. This herb mix is truly delicious.

Nutrient Values per Teaspoon:
Calories: 4.827. Protein: .161 g. Carbohydrate: .939 g. Dietary Fiber: .579 g. Total Sugars: 0 g. Total Fat: .233 g. Saturated Fat: .044 g. Monounsaturated Fat: .08 g. Polyunsaturated Fat: .055 g. Cholesterol: 0 mg. Calcium: 14.9 mg. Iron: .659 mg. Potassium: 19.5 mg. Sodium: 1.601 mg. Vitamin K: 0 mcg. Folate: 2.103 mcg.

GLOSSARY

Acorn Squash: Oval-shaped winter squash. Ribbed and dark green with some orange at the "bottom" and in the stem area. Usually halve them to bake, but cutting is difficult since the shell is hard. Bake and eat from the shell or puree for pies and soups, or dice unbaked and use for soups, depending on instructions.

Al Dente: Firm to the bite, usually referring to vegetables or pasta.

Anaheim Chili: One of the most common fresh chilies available in the United States. It is long, narrow, green, and usually mild.

Ancho Chili: A dried poblano chili with a deep reddish brown color. This chili is usually 3 to 4 inches long. Also known as the sweetest of dried chilies.

Arborio Rice: Short, fat, starchy rice best known for its use in Italian cooking. A prime ingredient for risotto.

Artichoke: One of Maureen's favorite vegetables. It is the bud of a large plant of the thistle family. It has tough petal-shaped leaves. When cooked, you break off the leaves one by one, dip in butter or sauce, and draw the base of the leaf through your teeth scraping off the pulp and discarding the rest of the leaf. You really have to like these to eat them. (Don calls them "transporters of high fat.") The bottom center of this "bulb" is called the "heart," and this is what the artichoke aficionados like the best. Succulent, it can be eaten without the butter or other dipping sauce. Used in soups, stews, and salads and side dishes. As an aside: The Jerusalem artichoke is not a true artichoke but a tuber resembling a gingerroot.

Barley: Barley is one of the oldest ingredients we use for soups and stews. It dates clear back to the Stone Age. Barley is used for making beer and whiskey, soups, cereals, and Scotch broth. It's turned into barley flour or meal and used for breads. There was once barley water. There are varieties of barley but we use mostly pearl barley, which has the bran removed; it has been polished and steamed. Pearl barley comes in coarse, medium, and fine sizes.

Basil: Member of the mint family. Fresh basil is preferred in our recipes over dried basil. Often described as a mix of licorice and cloves, it's a big Mediterranean cooking ingredients. Most well known for Italian pesto. Also has varieties: opal, lemon, anise, clove, and cinnamon basil. The opal has purple coloring. Others are green leaves but their names come from their fragrance and flavors. Dried basil, like most herbs that are dried, does not taste the same or have the same fragrance.

Basmati Rice: Don's favorite rice, basmati, is a long-grain, nutty-flavored rice originally grown in the Himalayan foothills in India. It steams very well.

Baste: To brush food with a basting liquid, marinade, or barbecue sauce; also can use melted unsalted butter, a special mix, meat drippings, or stock. Basting keeps baked or roasted foods moist.

Bell Pepper: The best known of American sweet peppers, they come in orange, red, green, yellow, purple, and brown. They belong to the *Capsicum* family, like the chili pepper, but the bell pepper is mild, sweet-flavored, and crisp. Used in salads, soups, and sandwiches. It's also used in cooking or eaten raw, always with seeds and stems removed.

Bernard Cream of Mushroom Soup and Gravy Base: Another soup base high in potassium chloride. (*See* Herb-Ox, Home Again, and Redi-Base in this Glossary.) We tested it and used it with one soup in this book. It's tasty, but the potassium may prove a problem for some. Ingredients include flour, potassium chloride, whey protein concentrate, natural flavors, dextrose, chicken fat, partially hydrogenated soybean and cottonseed oils (trans fats), guar gum, dehydrated mushrooms, parsley flakes, and turmeric.

Bisque: Thick soup, with either pureed vegetables, poultry, or fish as main ingredient.

Bite-Size: Some recipes may call for a bite-size piece, such as slicing a snow pea into a "bite-size" piece. This generally means about

1 inch in length or for some ingredients, like cheese or apples, etc., a half-inch cube.

Blanch: Usually a way to make peeling some vegetables and fruits easier. Also good for heightening the color of vegetables. **To peel:** insert food into boiling water briefly, then into cold water. This firms the flesh and loosens the skin of tomatoes and peaches, for instance, and either sets the color or flavor (or both) for vegetables; food is often blanched before freezing.

Blend: Generally mixing two or more ingredients together with a spoon, whisk, or electric blender until smooth.

Boil/Boiling: Heating a liquid until it bubbles and breaks at the surface. Boiling temp is 212°F for water at sea level. (Altitude affects boiling temperatures.) A rolling boil is one that can't be slowed by stirring.

Bone Marrow: A fatty substance with incredible flavor, used for soups, stews, and the Italian dish osso bucco, which is veal shank. Osso bucco is served with small forks so the diner can dig the marrow from the bones and spread it on some fresh French or sourdough bread. It is best when obtained from veal shank or soup bones of younger beef. The only similar substitute is suet, although suet doesn't have the same texture and the flavor isn't as pronounced.

Borscht Soup: (recipe on page 8) A Russian/Polish dish made with fresh beets. As can be served hot or cold but it should be garnished with a dollop of light sour cream.

Bouillabaisse: Another French word and French-origin stew. From Provence, France. A seafood stew usually made with a variety of fish, shellfish, tomatoes, wine, olive oil, herbs, saffron, and of course, the ubiquitous garlic.

Bouillon: A strained broth made by cooking any vegetable, meat, seafood, or poultry in water. The broth is the liquid we strain off after cooking the above in very hot water. Some substitutes for this include Herb-Ox granules, Home Again, Redi-Base, and Bernard, each of which is listed in this Glossary, but not used in this cookbook. Used for soups and sauces.

Braise: To cook with low to moderate heat with a small amount of liquid in a covered pan.

Bread Enhancer: Bread enhancers are combinations of active ingredients that working together help unsalted breads to rise and aerate, serving as a leavening agent. These work only with yeast breads. Enhancers typically include a citric acid, sugar, and gluten. Don's Flavor Enhancer (page 177) combination is already included as separate ingredients in the bread recipes in this book. To make your own, combine 1 tablespoon of citric acid or use Sure-Jell Ever-Fresh or the product Fruit-Fresh with 1 tablespoon of vital wheat gluten and 2 teaspoons white granulated sugar or Splenda. Use this mixture for every 3 cups of white flour you have in a recipe other than in this book. You may substitute orange or lemon zest in the same measurements as the citric acid products mentioned above. The zest will add the flavor of the fruit you are using.

Broth: A liquid derived from simmering meats, bones, and/or vegetables in liquid.

Brown: To sear an ingredient with a small amount of fat until browned on all sides. Used to seal in juices and enhance the appearance.

Bruschette/Bruschetta: Traditionally, this is toasted bread rubbed with garlic and olive oil. Today, you'll find bruschetta more often topped with tomatoes, herbs, mushrooms, and other ingredients like cheese, mushrooms, basil, etc. Generally spelled bruschette, you'll also find bruschetta.

Butterfly: To split food such as meat, fish, shellfish, down the center, not quite cutting all the way through. Two halves are opened for cooking and serving.

Butter Head Lettuce: The most well-known varieties are Bibb and Boston, which are sometimes referred to as Limestone lettuce. Delicate flavor and plant. Must handle gently, wash carefully. Exquisite taste—juicy and succulent.

Buttermilk: Low-sodium buttermilk brands that might be available in your area include Knudsen (130 mg), A&P (125 mg), Borden (130 mg), Borden Skim-Line (150 mg), Crowley (130 mg), Darigold Trim (130 mg), and Weight Watchers (140 mg).

Cabbage: Varietal plant with many different shapes, sizes, and thickness. Usually thick heads with wax-like leaves. We use Napa variety (also known as Chinese) cabbage for some of our salads and soups. Choose a fresh cabbage with crisp leaves, firmly packed. Refrigerate in a Ziploc bag.

Calzone: A baked or fried Italian turnover made of pizza dough and filled with vegetables, meat, or cheese or a combination of either.

Canola Oil: Extracted from rape seeds, this oil comes from yellow flowers that grow on high richly green grass. Rape seed oil was the first term used for this, but because of the name, it was changed to canola oil by the Canadian seed-oil industry. Low in saturated fat, with a cholesterol-cutting monounsaturated fat that in second only to olive oil, it contains Omega-3 fatty acids (polyunsaturated fat). Bland flavor.

Caramelize: This cooking technique is applied to frying, sautéing, and topping. If you are topping a dish with sugar and then melting the sugar with high heat, you are "caramelizing" the whole dish. This is the technique used to make crème brûlée (*see* Glossary page 191). You may also caramelize onions, and a few other vegetables, by including the sugar in the fry pan when sautéing them.

Caraway Seed: Used to flavor breads, soups, stews, cakes, meats, cheeses, and vegetables. Aromatic, caraway smells at times like anise. Nutty, they should be stored in a cool, dark place. They lose their fragrance and benefit after about 6 months storage time.

Cardamom: Native to India, this spice is a member of the ginger family. Can be purchased as ground cardamom, the type we use in this book. This is not as flavorful, but it is more readily available. If you can get fresh pods, then remove the seeds, and using a mortar and pestle, grind them down. You can then grind the rest of the pod. You don't need much cardamom for any recipe.

Cauliflower: We use cauliflower for some soups and a salad or two. Not liked by everyone, this cruciferous vegetable is high in vitamin C and is a good source of iron. It can be eaten raw or cooked. It can also be cut up and placed in a "party" assortment of raw vegetables with a no-salt, low-sodium dip. Comprised of a bunch of florets in clusters at the end of a stalk. It comes in three colors, although we use only the white. You can also find it in purple and green. The purple turns green when cooked. Choose a fresh hard cauliflower with nice fresh crisp leaves.

Cayenne: Bright red, very hot chili pepper. Used to make cayenne pepper flakes or cayenne ground pepper. We use it in some of our spice mixes and in some soups and stews.

Celery: A popular vegetable that might seem high in sodium, but is usable since we don't really exceed any limits with the amount we generally use. We use the stalks and leaves in soups and salads.

Chard: Related to the beet, this vegetable is used for its leaves and stalks. High in iron and vitamins A and C. Somewhat high in sodium, but usable.

Cheddar Cheese: While making Cheddar cheese, the firm curd is finely chopped or "cheddered" to drain the whey. It is then pressed into blocks or cylinders. A normal Cheddar wheel weighs 60 to 75 pounds. Nearly 90 percent of all cheese sold in the United States is classified as a Cheddar-type cheese. In this book, and in our others, we have recommended low-sodium Cheddar cheese from various companies. Unfortunately two primary suppliers have canceled this product, leaving only two others we know of at this time. You may have to get your yellow or white low-sodium Cheddar or Colby cheese via mail/shipping.

Chicken: Yes, you know what a chicken is. But did you know that many "fresh" chickens are dunked in gobs of salty brine or broth before going to market? Make sure you are buying a "fresh chicken" or "fresh chicken meat." If the package or wrapping doesn't tell you, ask your butcher. In many states all nutrients are supposed to be posted, and that includes if sodium mixtures have been added. Such chickens can jump your sodium intake from 18 mg an ounce to 400 mg an ounce.

Chickpeas: Also garbanzo beans. We use some canned Eden Organic Garbanzo Beans in this book but we also use fresh chickpeas/garbanzos. We use them in salads and soups and you can also make a good hummus with garbanzo beans. Works with couscous, too. If you purchase fresh chickpeas, then cook them according to package instructions but without the salt. You'll love the fresh flavor.

Chili: The spicy chili fruit is native to Mexico. There are many varieties, ranging from large to small, mild to hot. Most of the "heat" is in the seeds and veins and comes from the chemical compound capsaicin. Canned chilies are generally high in sodium because of the salt used in the cans. Fresh chilies are very low in sodium.

Chili Powder: We often call for Grandma's Chili Powder in our recipes that use chili powder. Grandma's is a national brand, however we recognize it's not always available everywhere. You can also get two salt-free chili powder brands from www.healthyheart-market.com. Ask for Wayzata or Frontier chili powder.

Chinese Cabbage: Also known as Napa, celery cabbage, wong bok, and Peking cabbage. Bok choy is a different variety but is also called Chinese white cabbage or white mustard cabbage. These varieties do not have the same waxy head that cabbage has but instead they have a crisp, mild flavor. Available year-round. Refrigerate in a Ziploc bag for up to 3 or 4 days. We use it raw or sauté it and also in one of our soup recipes. High in vitamin A and potassium.

Chives: This is a hardy herb (*Allium schoenoprasum*) of the lily family, with slender green, hollow stems. They have a wonderfully mild onion flavor, and are available year-round. A wonderful touch on salads and potatoes and in some soups. You cut chives to lengths you like with a scissors. Buy those with a uniform green color, no browning or wilting. Can store in Ziploc bags in your refrigerator for up to 7 days. These are pretty high in potassium and calcium, but since few are actually eaten, the potassium doesn't present much of a problem. Used in soups, stews, and as a garnish with potatoes, salads, and other vegetables.

Chowder: Most often thought of as clam chowder, but is really any thick and chunky soup. The challenge in making clam chowder is finding fresh clams not packed in salt water. One fresh unsalted large clam has 11.2 mg sodium; 3 ounces of canned-in-water clams have 182 mg sodium. Manhattan chowder is made with tomatoes, New England–style is made with milk or cream.

Cilantro: The stems and leaves of the coriander plant, also known as Chinese parsley and coriander. Cilantro usually refers to the fresh leaves used as an herb, and coriander to the seed used as a spice. They are quite different in flavor and cannot be used as substitutes for one another. The roots are also eaten as a vegetable. Cilantro can be found sold in bunches in the fresh herb section of most markets year-round. It's one of those flavors you either like or you don't.

Citric Acid: *See* Bread Enhancers.

Cloves (ground): Cloves are dried flower buds that are picked before they open. Considered one of the most important spices in the world, half the production of cloves is used by Indonesia, where most of it is grown. They mix it with tobacco for smoking. The clove tree is a member of the myrtle family and is native to the Spice Islands of Indonesia (Moluccas). It's sold whole or ground. You can flavor beef, lamb, or port with whole cloves by sticking them into small holes you punch throughout the outer layer of meat before baking or barbecuing.

Colander: Round, deep utensil with drilled or mesh-like holes designed for draining liquid yet retaining residue for further use.

Coleslaw: A shredded or chopped salad of white or red (including Chinese/Napa) cabbage, mixed with our homemade mayonnaise, vinaigrette, or other dressing. You can make it more personal by including either chopped onion, celery, red or green bell pepper, carrots, or herbs. Traditional American coleslaws are made with a cream and vinegar sauce (along with other ingredients). Add some sugar for a sweet-and sour effect.

Collard: A Southern member of the cabbage family. Prepare as you would spinach. "Down South," they add bacon, but not with our low-sodium lifestyle.

Consommé: Consommés are really a clarified meat or fish broth. A consommé may be served hot or cold or used as a soup base—such as our broths, which are good enough to serve as a consommé. To make a thin consommé thicker and more flavorful, simply simmer until reduced to about half its volume.

Cooking Oil in Spray Cans: Aerosol cans with olive oil are recommended a few times in this book. These make a fine mist that brings out a minimum of oil, which can help keep the fat down in most recipes where it's used. Generally we use it when frying or sautéing. We also use a pump sprayer so that we can load it with extra virgin olive oil, our preferred choice. If you don't want to use a spray can or pump sprayer, then simply wipe your pan with a paper towel or cloth holding some extra virgin olive oil.

Coriander: One of Don's favorite spices. A spice made from the seeds of the coriander plant, whose leaves are the familiar cilantro of Asian and Mexican cooking. I use ground coriander since getting fresh coriander is very difficult in most cases. It's also used in pickling and for some drinks including wine. We use coriander in soups and in Don's Curry Mix (page 180). No promises but coriander is mentioned as an aphrodisiac in *The Tales of the Arabian Nights*.

Corn: On the cob or off, corn is delicious. We use frozen corn in a few soup recipes. Frozen corn is generally not salted so it is an asset for our low-sodium eating when we need it and generally it's available in most grocery stores.

Corn Bread: Don's corn bread is best when it's baked without salt or standard baking powder or baking soda. He's made one just to go along with the soups. You can find it on page 228, *No-Salt, Lowest-Sodium Cookbook*. Known as a quick bread, corn bread is made with very little flour. Don's corn bread is made with fine polenta (Golden Pheasant brand). You can add grated cheese, onions, chopped jalapeño, molasses, or brown sugar, and scallions. Bake in the oven but some like to bake it in a lightly greased fry pan or skillet. Known by Don's "banjo pickin'" friend in Nashville, Tennessee, as "hushpuppies."

Couscous: Also known as semolina. You can make porridge using couscous or use it as a salad dressing as we do. Sweeten it and mix with fruits for dessert. You can find unsalted couscous in most grocery stores.

Cream of Tartar: This may surprise you. Cream of tartar is a powdery acid that comes from deposits inside wine barrels. It is added to egg whites before beating to improve stability and to candy and frostings for a creamier consistency. It is also sometimes used as a leavener in some breads.

Crème Brûlée: This example of "caramelizing," used earlier, is a custard dish topped with sugar and then caramelized under a broiler or (if you're in a fancy restaurant) with a torch.

Crisphead Lettuce: Also known as iceberg. Great Lakes, Imperial (the valley in which Don's family grew this lettuce on their farm), Vanguard, and Western. Large and round, it's tightly packed. This is one of the best lettuce varieties for juiciness and the ability to not wilt. Choose lettuce that is heavy for its size and make sure there is no browning on the head. Works with nearly any salad except a Caesar salad.

Crock-Pot: Before the Crock-Pot there was the "slow-cooker," the "pressure cooker," and the stockpot that "mother used to do everything in." The Crock-Pot has been referred to as an electric casserole in some cookbooks. It provides a steady moist heat and was designed to cook food for 6- to 8-hour periods. Flavors blend nicely and cheaper cuts of meat usually come out tender. Sizes range from a quart to 6 quarts at this writing. Great for cooking dinner while you're at work.

Croustade: This is an edible container, which in this book, is for holding thick stews. Ours is a sourdough or French bread recipe you can find on page 110.

Croutons: A small cube of browned bread made so by sautéing or baking at a low temperature for a longer time. Used to garnish soups, salads, and other dishes, our crouton recipe is on page 114. You can season your croutons with herbs and spices, low-sodium cheese, and garlic, among other flavors.

Crumpet: Sometimes confused with English muffins, crumpets are toasted whole, not split like English muffins. They look a bit like English muffins since they are the same size, made in "crumpet rings," which we also use for our English muffin recipe (page 113, *No-Salt, Lowest-Sodium Baking Book*). *See* English Muffin.

Cube: To cut into small, approximately ½-inch cubes.

Cucumber: Pickles come from cucumbers. We have a great pickle recipe in our *No-Salt, Lowest-Sodium Cookbook*. Also, healthy-heartmarket.com sells B&G no-salt-added pickles that taste like the real thing. Cucumbers are also a great addition to salads and sandwiches, which is how we use them here. Long cylinder type vegetables, cucumbers are easy to grow in your yard or on your farm. Fresh cucumbers are best-tasting. Pick firm cucumbers (not soft). We like shiny colored skins. Can refrigerate after slicing for about 3 to 4 days. Whole cucumbers will store for up to a week to ten days.

Cumin: An aromatic spice sold in seed and ground form. Used in our soups, stews, sauces, spice mixes, it is best known for Asian, Mexican, and Middle Eastern cooking.

Curry: Refers to a vast number of spicy and hot gravy dishes from India.

Curry Powder: A ground blend of many spices, herbs, and seeds, often up to two dozen. Most favorite are chilies, cloves, pepper, saffron, paprika, turmeric and cumin, coriander, mace, and nutmeg. Have fun, make your own mix, and dub it your own curry powder.

Dash: Considered to be about $\frac{1}{16}$ teaspoon or at least less than $\frac{1}{8}$ teaspoon.

Deglaze: To add a moderate amount of liquid to a pan to dissolve or loosen cooked food particles, usually done while the pan is over the heat.

Dice: When we use the word we mean to cut food into small pieces about $\frac{1}{8}$- to $\frac{1}{4}$-inch cube.

Dill: An herb used in a variety of dishes and cuisines and in our homemade mayonnaise substitute, as well as some salads and in our spice mixes.

Dollop: An indeterminate measure of soft food, such as sour cream, which is spooned onto a dish or food. We like to think it's about a teaspoon full.

Dredge: To lightly coat foods with flour or a dry seasoning mixture such as Don's Herbes de Provence Spice Mix (page 175). Cornmeal or bread crumbs can also be used. Coating helps brown food when you are frying.

Drizzle: To pour a liquid in a fine stream over food.

Eggplant: Related to the tomato, which is a fruit. Most well known is the deep purple-colored eggplant but there are other colors.

Emulsify: To mix usually unmixable liquids. Emulsion is accomplished by adding one liquid to the other, a little at a time, while whisking vigorously or processing in a food processor or a blender until the unmixable liquids become one uniformly consistent liquid.

Endive: Used as a garnish mostly in salads, it can also be added to some soups for "punching up" the flavor. Generally bitter, there are Belgian endive, curled endive with curled, lacy leaves, and escarole, which is the mildest.

English Muffin: Like the crumpet, a round muffin (about 3 inches in diameter) baked using a yeast dough. These are generally baked on a griddle (which requires oil). Ours are baked in the oven, to help cut the "frying" fat and flavor. English muffins must be split in half with a fork. If you slice them, they won't give you the effect you want.

Enoki Mushroom: A fruity-tasting mushroom with long, thin stems and tiny white caps, it is delicate and should be handled with that in mind. High in vitamin D.

Evaporated Milk: Can be used as a substitute for cream, although the sodium level is nearly double. This canned milk has about 60 percent of the water removed. You can also mix with water to substitute for milk. The flavor is sweeter than either cream or milk.

Ever-Fresh from Sure Jell: Ever-Fresh is a fruit and produce protector that is essentially a combination of ascorbic acid and sugar. A teaspoon of Ever-Fresh has about 4 grams of sugar. You can replace this measure with a tablespoon of grated orange or lemon peel for the same effect. Or, if you have it available, you can use pure ascorbic acid in a proportion of one-half of what a recipe asks for. That is: if a recipe calls for one teaspoon Ever-Fresh, use ½ teaspoon ascorbic acid. (*See also* Fruit-Fresh.)

Fennel: A plant with celery-like stalks, a wide base, and delicate foliage. Fennel has a light, anise-like flavor and it's used in some spice mixes and soups in this book.

Fiber: We're told to eat "more fiber." So what is fiber? It's the part of plant foods we cannot digest.

Flour, Best for Bread: We often call for "best for bread" flour in our bread recipes. You may find flour in your store with package labels listing "Great for Breadmaking," "Bread Flour," "Best for Bread Machines," etc. Any label listing the flour as good for bread or breadmaking will work with our recipes. But do remember to use a flour that does indicate it is for making bread. All-purpose and other flours have a different level of gluten and often don't produce the bread you are expecting.

Focaccia: A round Italian (flat) bread brushed with olive oil and usually sprinkled with salt. In our baking book you sprinkle the bread with grated low-sodium Cheddar or garlic powder; top it with other herbs. Great as an addition to soups and stews and can be used to make sandwiches.

Food Processor: Electrical "gadget" used to puree or "break up" food items, or for blending/combining and other purposes. Most come with a variety of attachments and blades each designed for a different purpose.

Fruit-Fresh: Fruit-Fresh is a fruit and produce protector that is essentially a combination of ascorbic acid and sugar. A teaspoon of Fruit-Fresh has about 4 grams of sugar. You can replace this measure with a tablespoon of grated orange or lemon peel for the same effect. Or, if you have it available, you can use pure ascorbic acid in a proportion of one-half of what a recipe asks for. That is: If a recipe calls for one teaspoon Fruit-Fresh, use ½ teaspoon ascorbic acid. (*See also* Ever-Fresh from Sure-Jell.)

Fry Pan/Frying Pan: A thick-bottom pan used for shallow frying. We use heavy-duty stainless steel pans for even heat distribution.

Ginger/Gingerroot: Fresh ginger has a mild flavor. A young fresh ginger doesn't have to be peeled like a "mature ginger." It's easier to work, but difficult to find in stores. That's one reason Americans have turned to ground ginger. Ground ginger doesn't work well as a substitute in recipes calling for "fresh ginger," also known as gingerroot. We use ginger for soups in this book, but it's also good for cookies. Used generally in gingersnaps and gingerbread, it's also the core ingredient for ginger ale.

Gluten/Vital Wheat Gluten: Gluten is a natural protein with grain. Extracted from whole-wheat flour by washing with pure water, gluten is known as one of the secret ingredients of professional bakers. When combined with water, gluten retains the gas and steam from baking and gives bread its volume. In other words, it helps yeast dough increase the rise and improve the body. It is a necessity when making breads from whole-wheat, rye, or other low-protein flours and it helps some white flour products that are low in gluten. The recipes in this book call for as much gluten as any of the three flour products used in our testing need. You may learn after making your own bread that you need an additional tablespoon of gluten. With proper storage, gluten will stay fresh for up to a year in the refrigerator and longer in the freezer. You will look for "vital wheat gluten" in your local store or you can find it at www.bobsredmill .com.

Grating/Grate: Reducing some foods like cheese, and vegetables to fine particles by rubbing over a sharp, rough surface known as a "grater."

Grater: Usually handheld equipment that has sharp grooves or jagged edges of different sizes designed for the purpose of reducing food to a small size.

Handheld Mixer (Handblender): We recommend the Braun Handblender. At this writing, we use the 280-Watt version or model 550. Although we refer to it in the book as a "Hand Held" or hand-held, Braun calls it a Handblender. We use this instrument for soups, especially since you can mix the recipe in any bowl without the ingredients splashing out. The blender also comes with a puree device, a whisker, and a unique chopper that works very well with nuts and other vegetables. (Note: We recommend that you not use a standard double-blade beater for mixing the soup ingredients.)

Herb-Ox: The most popular and available of all the condensed (powder or granules) bullion-type soup bases. *(We have done our best to avoid using any of these powder/granule soup bases because their flavor is not very good, they leave an aftertaste, and the potassium chloride levels are high.)* This one is from Hormel Foods. They make a beef and a chicken bouillon. Ingredients include sweetener (sugar and/or dextrose), potassium chloride, onion powder, maltodestrin, monoammonium glutamate, gelatin, chicken fat (contains propylene glycol), TBHQ, and citric acid, extractive of turmeric, natural flavoring, parsley, disodium inosinate, and disodium guanylate.

Herbes of Provence (Herbes de Provence): A collection or mix of dried herbs. Don's version is listed in this book on page 175. Note: It contains lavender, which can be found in this Glossary. You can make up your own version and measurements according to your tastes. Works exceptionally well when baking beef, chicken, or fowl. Works on some salads and goes well with vegetables.

Herbs: Pronounced "erbs," these are generally well known. In this book we use chives, basil, bay leaf, coriander, marjoram, oregano, parsley, rosemary, sage, savory, tarragon and thyme. You can grow any of these in your yard if you live in a temperate zone. Fresh herbs are wonderful for soups, spice mixes, vegetables and meats.

Home Again (From American Natural and Specialty Brands): Another of the low-sodium powder stocks for soups. Like Herb-Ox and Redi-Base, this one is also high in potassium chloride. Sodium level is listed at 0 mg for 1 teaspoon (makes 1 cup liquid stock). Ingredients include: dextrose, beef fat, cottonseed oil, soybean oil, cornstarch, potassium chloride, onion powder, monopotassium glutamate, caramel color, beef extract, hydrolyzed soy protein (contains maltodextrin, calcium chloride), flavoring, oleoresin paprika.

Hummus: A Middle Eastern spread made from cooked and pureed chickpeas or garbanzo beans. It's usually seasoned with lemon juice, garlic, and oil and is often served with pita bread, salads, as a side dish, or for dipping.

Jicama: A bulbous root vegetable with a thick brown skin. The white flesh is crunchy and very tasty. Sweet and nutty, it's a great addition to salads. Contains vitamin C and potassium.

Julienne: To cut food into matchstick-thin strips.

Kidney Beans: We love these fresh, but we use Eden Organic Kidney Beans from www.healthyheartmarket.com a lot. Used in soups, stews, and salads in this book. If using fresh kidney beans, follow the cooking instructions on the package, but don't add any salt.

Knead: To work the dough with your hands by folding and pressing.

Lavender: The lavender plant is used often to make herb tea or herb mixes such as Don's Herbes de Provence Spice Mix (page 175). This plant is a relative of the mint plant, has violet flowers (which we dry), and a sweet flavor. It's available in specialty produce stores or natural food stores. The lavender growing in your yard may also be used.

Leaf Lettuce: These are the loose "heads" and not the tight heads. Leaves grow outward from a stalk into a loose bunch. These leaves are crispier and have more flavor than a tight head. Some cookbooks may refer to this type of lettuce as "loose leaf" or "Simpson." One of our favorites in this category is the red-edge or tipped leaves. Perishable. Store dry in Ziploc bags in your refrigerator's crisper drawer.

Leavening agent: Used mostly for breads, cakes, cookies, etc. Agents include yeast, baking soda, baking powder, egg whites. I use beaten egg whites for waffles, some cakes and cookies, and one or two bread recipes. Leavening agents help lighten the texture of flour-made items as well as expand their volume.

Leeks: If you haven't used leeks before, then please try one of our leek potato soups. Leeks have a great flavor when prepared correctly. Leeks appear to be giant scallions and are closely related to garlic and onions even though their flavor is much milder. Buy crisp leeks with bright green-colored leaves. Stay clear of spotted or wilted leaves. Smaller is better. Refrigerate in a Ziploc plastic bag. Wash thoroughly before using. Cook in soups; dice, chop, or slice for salads; or add to beef stews, etc.

Legumes: Refers to the seed pods that split along both sides after ripening. We consume beans, lentils, peanuts, peas, and soybeans out of the plethora of legumes available worldwide.

Lemon Juice: We call for "fresh" lemon juice in our soup and bread recipes sometimes. Fresh means squeezed from a fresh lemon. There are bottled and frozen lemon juice products but they don't resemble the real thing. The frozen is slightly passable but the bottled is not. Lemons are high in vitamin C content (one lemon represents about 70 percent of our daily minimum requirement), but after being squeezed the juice rapidly loses its vitamin C, even if stored in a refrigerator.

Lemon Grass or Lemongrass: You may see this listed either way in stores and in various cookbooks. It is a prevalent flavoring in Thai and Vietnamese cooking. The Lemongrass plant has long, thin, greenish leaves with a base that resembles a scallion. It gets its name from the citrus or "citral" that resembles that of a lemon. It is fragrant and generally available in larger supermarkets. Store in a Ziploc bag in your refrigerator. You may also see this referred to as citronella or *sereb*.

Lentils: These are a classic "pulse" seed. Always dried upon ripening, you'll have to prepare it according to the instructions on the package, unless we specify otherwise. We use the brown lentils, which is about all you're going to find in the United States. Other varieties are red or yellow, some with shells on the seeds others not. Store in Ziploc bags after opening the original package. Used in soups and salads.

Lettuce: We can't count the varieties of lettuce available throughout the world. No matter what time of year though, you can find your favorite lettuce for your favorite salad. Four classifications exist however. These include romaine (Don's personal favorite), butter head, leaf, and crisphead lettuce. Don claims there's a variety he calls "weedeater" lettuce. This of course is what we often find in packages in the produce chiller. The extensive variety, often a collection from the above classifications, tends to appear as though it came from the backyard. Lettuce has to be kept chilled. Once cleansed you should spin dry it in one of the popular spin driers and then store in a Ziploc plastic bag in your refrigerator. Almost all lettuce is high in calcium, vitamins A and C, and has nearly uncountable calories.

Low-Sodium Cheddar Cheese: The national manufacturers of low-sodium cheddar cheese varieties we are aware of at this writing include:

Heluvagood Cheese Company (www.heluvagood.com)
Rumiano Cheese Company (www.rumiano.com)
Bocconcini Mozzarella (*see* Mozzarella in this glossary)

Each of the above will sell their products to you on-line and ship quickly.

National manufacturers who once produced low sodium cheese products but have stopped at least for the time include:

Tillamook (Tillamook, Oregon)
Alpine Lace (Land 'O Lakes Company)

Low-Sodium Swiss: Alpine Lace was our Swiss of choice until recently. Established in 1977, Alpine Lace was purchased by Land 'O Lakes in 1997. Alpine Lace produced quality low-sodium Swiss cheese, recommended in our books and at Megaheart.com. However, while editing this book, Alpine Lace changed course. Like a few other food processors and producers have done in recent years, they dropped their low-sodium cheeses. They do have a "reduced sodium" Muenster that is good, but the sodium level is 85 mg per ounce. Alpine Lace also has a "reduced fat" Swiss that has 85 mg sodium per ounce.

Low-sodium Swiss is available from other companies, but mostly on a regional basis. We are listing our sodium per ounce in our recipes at the USDA listed level, which is 11.5 mg per ounce or 8.64 mg per ¾ ounce, which is generally a commercially pre-cut "slice." We remind you however, that producers will often vary from these numbers, so make sure to check the FDA labels on the packaging.

Marinate: To immerse food in a liquid to impart the flavor of the liquid to the food. To rub the food with a dry seasoning, and let stand for a period of time to enhance the flavor of the food.

Marjoram: Doesn't taste like mint, but it's a member of the mint family. Fresh marjoram tastes a bit like fresh oregano. We use dried marjoram in this book mostly, since it's a lot easier to find in stores than the fresh. Great for meats, soups, and stews and in spice/herb mixes.

Mash: To crush thoroughly into a pulpy paste.

Mayonnaise, Low-Sodium: Featherweight once produced soy-anaise, which was sufficient as a mayonnaise replacement. They dropped it a few years ago. At this writing, Hain makes an eggless mayo, but it's becoming difficult to find, which tells us that they are probably going to quit producing it. To the rescue! Healthy Heart Market (www.healthheartmarket.com) has a new sandwich spread product that works well as a sandwich spread and is low in sodium. It's called Ginger People Ginger Wasabi Sauce. It works with sandwiches and meats. It is not a mayonnaise replacement as much as it is an alternative. Sodium level for this product is 35 mg per ounce.

You can also use the homemade mayonnaise on page 306 in *The No-Salt Lowest-Sodium Cookbook.*

Mince: To cut or chop into very fine pieces, such as with raw garlic.

Mozzarella Balls, Low-Sodium: We call for mozzarella in water or mozzarella balls in a few of our recipes. The balls we ask for are small, about an inch in diameter. There is also a mozzarella ball that is the standard package you find in stores. Bocconcini, a national brand, produces both. The small balls are in salt water but are very low in sodium (just rinse off the cheese before using). The standard ½ pound ball is unsalted and very low in sodium. This is good for slicing. You can generally find it in most supermarkets and some specialty stores. It is manufactured variously but nationally, at this date, the popular brand is Bocconcini. (visit: http://www.ottomaneli.com/otto133.html) Regular mozzarella is too high in sodium.

Mulligan Stew: At the turn of the twentieth century, hobos roamed the land in search of work and food. When they gathered together, they collected the food each might have, threw it all into a pot, added water, heated and stirred, and had "mulligan stew" for dinner. Also known as Irish Stew. Our Irish soup maker Maureen, has her own version in this book.

Mulligatawny Soup: This generally means "pepper base" or "pepper water." Usually based on a rich meat like wild game or rabbit, it's seasoned with many spices, including a curry mix. Our Sporting Chef, Scott Leysath, has provided us with Rabbit Mulligatawny Soup. You can exchange the rabbit with chicken, he tells us. We checked, it won't alter the sodium levels at all. Make sure you get a salt-free chicken. You can buy Scott Leysath's *Wild Game Recipes* book at www.megaheart.com. Visit Megaheart's bookstore page.

Mushroom: If you are a mushroom expert and are able to pick wild mushrooms, I envy you. Fresh mushrooms are the very best for cooking and eating. But most of us can't do this so we have to stick to the store mushrooms. We use regular button mushrooms as well as portobello and shiitake mushrooms in this book. The shiitake is a wild mushroom sold in stores. Wild mushroom varieties good for soups, stews, and other dishes include the enoki, puffball, and wood ear. If you aren't an expert at picking wild mushrooms, then head for your grocery store. It can be dangerous to pick your own when you aren't experienced.

Napa Cabbage: *See* Chinese Cabbage.

Niçoise Salad: Don's first major coup in France was to eat a real "Niçoise salad" in Nice, France. He was at the Cannes Film Festival, which is right next door to Nice. Nice is the home of the Niçoise. Back then he could eat the olives, anchovies, and other high sodium ingredients. Niçoise can also include hard-boiled eggs, garlic, tomatoes, garden-fresh green beans, and a fine collection of herbs. Some may even add tuna.

Noodles: Shall we clear up the difference, or may we say confusion, between pasta and noodles? Spaghetti and macaroni are not "noodles." They are made exclusively with water and flour. Noodles contain water, flour, and eggs or just the yolk. Your store has an extensive variety of noodles. We use noodles in our soups and stews.

No-Sodium Bottled Water: Read the ingredients. Not all bottled water is without sodium. Kirkland bottled water from Costco, for instance, adds salt (sodium chloride). Others might add "flavorings," which amounts to sodium chloride. Still others may state "sodium chloride" added to enhance flavor. If the bottle doesn't state "no sodium" then purchase distilled water.

NSA: No Salt Added.

Olive Oil: There are various types of olive oil. Extra virgin, virgin, fino, and light. We use extra virgin exclusively and recommend that you do, too. Extra virgin is cold-pressed. It is the first pressing of the olives and contains only 1 percent acid. It is the tastiest or fruitiest of all the olive oils. It is consequently the most expensive. It is also the best to cook with. Olive oil is very low in saturated fat and high in monounsaturated fats. You can store Don's Italian Dressing, an olive oil salad dressing, in your refrigerator if it's necessary. It will become cloudy and too thick to pour but will clear up and be usable when it's returned to room temperature. See Don's Italian Dressing on page 166.

Pan-Fry: To cook over medium or higher heat in a pan in a small amount of fat.

Pine Nut: Known also as pignon, pignoli, piñon, and Indian nut. High in fat, these are from pine trees. Used in Italian pesto this pine cone nut grows best in China, Italy, and Mexico. It is now also grown in Arizona. Careful you don't use too many. The flavor can dominate over other foods. Make sure you buy the unsalted kind.

Pinto Bean: Pink bean with reddish brown lines or streaks. Like the Pinto horse, the word is Spanish and means "painted." Served in soups, stews, tacos, chili con carne, and it's the pinto bean that makes "refried beans." We often use Eden Organic Pinto Beans you can get at www.healthyheartmarket.com. If you use fresh pinto beans, follow the instructions on the package.

Poach: To cook gently with low heat in liquid, usually seasoned with vegetables, herbs, and stocks.

Porcini Mushroom: A flavorful brown mushroom that can range up to 10 inches in diameter. May be available fresh in the United States in some markets, but is usually found dry. Soak the dry mushrooms in hot water for about 20 to 30 minutes before using in recipes. Used in soups, stews, and some salads.

Portobello Mushrooms: An oversized mushroom. Also referred to as a white mushroom. Had you ever heard of Häagen-Daz Ice Cream before a marketing firm got hold of that small ice cream plant and gave it a Dutch-sounding name? Probably not. Well, the portobello is a victim of the same type of marketing. Growers couldn't sell these so they had to do something. They grow easily and plentifully. Enter yet another marketing firm and *voilà*! Something that was always plowed under, became the "in thing" with chefs, fancy restaurants, and now this cookbook. It is a tasty mushroom. A bit of a drama queen, the mushroom is usually presented in restaurants whole. We chop it up, although not into tiny pieces. Great for soups, stews, salads.

Potato Salad: Potatoes ad nauseum? Not if it's made well. This salad usually contains cooked, cubed potatoes that are mixed with hard-boiled eggs, mayonnaise, and seasonings. Many also add bacon. We can't have the mayo or bacon, so check out our version. It's an idea from a famous restaurant in Burbank, California.

Pot Roast: We have "pot roast" the noun, and "pot roast" the verb. One calls for action, the other defines the results. Usually braised, browned meat cooked with a little liquid. Add vegetables halfway through the cooking and you have what is known as Yankee Pot Roast. The best meats for pot roast include chuck and round. Chuck is juicier and a bit more tender because it's also much higher in saturated fats.

Provençal: We have one dish with this in the name. It means that the original came from Provence, an area in southern France. Most provençal dishes include tomatoes, garlic, olive oil, onions, and mushrooms. High-sodium ingredients often include olives and anchovies.

Pulse: Dried seed from legumes such as peas, beans, lentils. You'll find the word pulse used in many cookbooks and in newspaper and magazine recipes.

Puree: To make a pulp by mashing, straining, or processing food in a blender or food processor.

Radish: You can grow these in your yard and spend the rest of your summer handing them out to your neighbors. The radish is the root of a mustard plant family. Hot-tasting, it makes a great garnish on salads when thinly sliced. Wash well. Choose hard, red radishes with bright crispy leaves to ensure freshness.

Redi-Base: Not used in any recipes in this book. Another low-sodium soup/stock base. *Contains salt.* Most of their bases are pretty high in sodium for a very low-sodium diet. One, however, VLS Chicken-Flavored Base, is lower than the others at 35 mg per teaspoon (makes 8 fluid ounces). The other bases are 140 mg each. Ingredients for VLS include maltodextrin, modified food starch, chicken fat, onion powder, chicken flavor (contains yeast extract, *salt*, maltodextrin, dried whey, dried egg yolk, milk powder), de-hydrated chicken broth, potassium chloride, dehydrated carrot juice concentrate, natural flavors, garlic powder, disodium inosi-nate, disodium guanylate, and turmeric.

Reduce: To decrease the volume of a liquid by cooking over medium to high heat, uncovered. The water content of the liquid will evaporate, the liquid will thicken, and flavors will be more con-centrated and pronounced.

Rib: Single stalk of celery or a cut of meat such as short ribs, spareribs, each cut from the animal's rib section. *See* Celery.

Rice: We use basmati, long-grain rice, and short-grain rice in this book as well as white rice, which is sometimes referred to as "pol-ished rice."

Risotto: In our *No-Salt, Lowest-Sodium Cookbook* we have a Risotto Milanese from Milan, Italy. It's a recipe Don picked up in Milan, Italy, while filming there. Risotto is generally made by stirring a hot broth into a mixture of rice (Arborio) and chopped onions that have been sautéed in unsalted butter. When the broth has been ab-sorbed by the rice, more broth is added. When all the broth has been added and absorbed, you may then add your favorite ingredi-ents like chicken, homemade sausage, veggies, herbs, and some low-sodium cheese. In Italy, the risotto also had very fresh and well-scented saffron. Fresh bone marrow was also added to the risotto, which gave it a delicate meaty flavor.

Romaine Lettuce: Also known as Cos lettuce (from its origins on the Aegean island of Cos. The lettuce has crispy leaves with a slight bitter flavor. Don likes the crunchiness of it and says romaine is "juicy." In any case, it adds a nice touch to any salad and is the let-tuce to use when making a Caesar alad. See our Caesar salad on page 131.

Rosemary: A wild-growing plant anywhere in the world, this is one you can grow in your yard to obtain a really fresh, fragrant herb. It's a Mediterranean herb used extensively in Italian and

Greek cooking. Used here in Don's special spice mixes and our soups, stews, and salads. Fresh rosemary can also be added to bread for a very special flavor. Always best when fresh.

Round Beef: Used in our stews, this is the section of the hind leg extending from the rump to the ankle. Not very tender although the sirloin tip, known also as top sirloin or tri-tips or triangle can be oven-roasted or barbecued. If you see a chart of meat cuts at your butcher's you'll find four to six types of round. Essentially they are:

- *Rump*: a triangular cut from the upper part of the round. Also referred to as *rump steaks* or rump *roasts* or *standing rump roasts*. Used in stews in this book.
- *Top Round*: From the inside of the leg. Most tender of these tough cuts. Sometimes referred to as *butterball steak* or *London broil*. *London broil* cut works well for barbecue. May use in Crock-Pot stew, regular stew, or barbecue. Thinly slice after baking if baked in the oven.
- *Eye of the Round*: The least tender of the bunch. Requires slow, moist-heat cooking (like Crock-Pot). Sometimes called *round steaks* and sometimes mistaken for *tenderloin* because it appears to look like a tenderloin.
- *Bottom Round*: Cuts from this can make up *cube steaks* or the *bottom round roast*.
- *Heel of the Round*: Not used in this book except in ground beef, which is where most of this cut ends up.

Roux: A cooked mixture of fat and flour used for thickening sauces and soups.

Safflower Oil: Not used in this book. If you prefer safflower oil then exchange our recommended olive oil for this oil. Safflower oil is without flavor, and is expressed from safflower seeds. Contains more polyunsaturates than all other oils and has a high "smoke point," which means it's good for deep-fat frying. Used commercially for flavoring salad dressings since it doesn't solidify in the refrigerator. Lacks vitamin E found in other oils.

Saffron: Not used in this book although if you like it, you can add to some meat stews and some salads. Used mostly with risotto Milanese, paella, and bouillabaisse. It's also used to flavor many baked goods. The real stuff is very expensive. Imitations are available.

Sage: Another of our favorite herbs, used with poultry mostly. Also used in homemade sausage, stuffings, and with beans and pork dishes. Used extensively in some stews and soups in this book as well as in Don's Herbes de Provence Spice Mix (page 175).

Salad Spinner: Can't live without it if you're going to make a lot of salads. Uses centrifugal force to extract water from salad greens you have washed. Dries greens perfectly for storage in a Ziploc bag. We use the OXO spinner. We've tried all the leading brands and this seemed to be the most durable and effective. Check out www.megaheart.com and visit the Cabinet, which is located under the Kitchen button at the top of the home page.

Salt: There are a variety of "salts" out there. We most commonly know of *table salt*. It really doesn't matter which kind of salt you find, the basic sodium level remains at 2,350 mg per level teaspoon. The varieties include:

- Table Salt
- Iodized Salt
- Kosher Salt
- Sea Salt
- Celtic Salt
- Seasoned Salt (regular salt mixed with other flavors)
- Sour Sea Salt
- Pickling Salt
- Rock Salt

Salt Substitutes: A variety of efforts to replace salt with substitutes exists also. None cooks like salt. They only alter the flavor. However, there are a few brands of salt substitutes that include half salt. Watch out for these. We prefer to use Don's Flavor Enhancer (page 177).

BRANDS USING HERBS AND SPICES

- Mrs. Dash Seasonings
- Schilling Salt Free Seasonings
- Parsley Patch Seasonings

BRANDS USING POTASSIUM CHLORIDE

- No Salt—¼ teaspoon: 650 mg potassium/0 mg sodium
- Morton's Lite Salt—(contains some salt) ¼ teaspoon: 350 mg potassium/290 mg sodium

- Morton's Salt Substitute—¼ teaspoon: 610 mg potassium/0 mg sodium
- Cardia Salt Alternative (contains some salt)—¼ teaspoon: 180 mg potassium/270 mg sodium

Saucepan: We use All-Clad exclusively. This heavy stainless steel cookware gives even heating, consistent performance, and easy cleanup. Saucepans are round cooking utensils generally with a long handle and a well-fitting cover. Ours have straight sides although some have flared sides. Great for making soups, sauces, braising, and sautéing.

Sauté: To cook food quickly, generally in a little bit of oil in a fry pan, skillet, or saucepan.

Sauté Pan: Wide pan, straight or flared sides, slightly higher than a fry-pan. Long handle one side, loop handle opposite side. Stainless steel usually, but you can find them in cast iron, anodized aluminum, and even copper. Browns while cooking meats and other ingredients.

Savory: Ahh, what a very nice fragrant herb. Two varieties exist: summer and winter. Related to the mint group, savory has an aroma and flavor reminding one of a cross between thyme and mint. Great for salt substitute mixes and soups, stews, bean dishes. Used in this book in spice mixes, soups, and stews.

Scald: Plunging foods with skins into boiling water to loosen and split the skin for easier removal.

Scallion: Not a trouble-making child. This scallion, used in our soups, stews, and salads, is a member of the onion family. It's a "green onion" for many, which is how we often list it. It has a white base that is really an immature bulb, with long green, straight leaves. We use the green leaves often with julienned or thinly sliced for "chives," and the bulb for a unique flavor in our soups and salads. Best during spring and summer, these are available year-round.

Scant: Not quite up to full measure. A scant teaspoon would mean a bit less than a full teaspoon.

Sesame Oil: From the sesame seed, usually expressed. Great for salad dressings and some use it for sautéing. Asian sesame oil is dark with a strong flavor. A light sesame oil has a less penetrating flavor. Excellent for frying since it has a high smoke point.

Shallot: Herb from the lily family. Roots form small clusters of bulbs with a mild garlic flavor. You can find fresh shallots during the spring but for the rest of the year you may find only dried shallots. Available year-round. Use just as you would onions.

Shallots are used in soups, salads, sauces, etc., the shallot has a brown papery skin as opposed to the whitish skin of garlic, but combines the flavor of garlic with that of an onion. These are unique, so when a recipe calls for them it's best to use them instead of an onion. Shallots were first introduced to Europeans during the twelfth century. Crusaders brought them home as "valuable treasure" from the ancient Palestinian city of Ascalon.

Shiitake Mushroom: Also known as "golden oak." Dark brown, it sometimes has lighter or tan stripes or striations. Up to 10 inches across. (Competes with portobellos for size.) Has flavor resembling a steak. The stems are removed because of toughness, but you can use the stems for soup stock and the sauces for flavoring. Discard after cooking. Don't buy these if the caps are shriveled or broken. Can sauté, broil, barbecue, bake.

Shred: Cutting vegetables into fine long pieces such as shredding cabbage, fresh basil, lettuce, spinach, etc.

Sieve: A handheld device with equal sized grooves or holes, used for removing impurities and separating grains of different sizes. Not a colander. Sieves come in various-sized grooves for different uses or purposes.

Simmer: To cook food gently in liquid that bubbles steadily just below the boiling point. Food cooks evenly without separating.

Skim: Removing impurities or scum—fat from soups and stews form the surface layer of liquid that is allowed to stand—with a large spoon.

Sloppy Joe: We loved these in the sixties. Big hit back then. Any of Don's sandwich breads will work. This is simply a sandwich (burger buns are best) topped with mixed ground beef containing green peppers, spicy tomato sauce, onions, and garlic if you prefer. Yes, it's a mess to eat.

Slow Cooker: *See* Crock-Pot.

Smoke Point: We've already referred to smoke point in this Glossary. It means the level of heat where fat begins to smoke or emit smoke, and those acrid odors we really don't want wafting throughout our house. Generally you only have to be concerned when deep-fat frying. However, you can create smoke with a frying pan if you get it too hot with fat in the pan. Butter smokes at about 350°F while vegetable oils don't smoke until about 410°F to 450°F.

Snow Pea: Great for salads. Raw, these are edible and crunchy good. Pod and peas are eaten. Select crisp, brightly colored pods with very small seeds. Keep refrigerated in a sealed Ziploc bag. Also known as Chinese snow peas.

Soup: Any of a number of liquid concoctions that combine vegetables, meat (red and white), fish, and/or fowl. Soup can be made thick or thin, depending largely upon your own tastes. A thick soup often referred to as "gumbo" is usually a spicy soup made of okra and seafood. Thin soups are sometimes referred to as a consommé (kon-so-may), but are essentially a beef broth.

Make your soup smooth (a bisque for instance) or make it chunky like our chowder recipe. (*See* page 21, Leek Potato Soup.)

To make your soup presentable, always prepare or use a garnish— we recommend a garnish for each of our soups. You can use garnishes for looks or to enhance the flavor of the soup. Salt-free homemade croutons, low-fat sour cream, grated or sliced low sodium cheese all work well.

Soups may be served as a complete meal, and many of ours are designed just for that. Or, they may be served as a first course in a larger entrée setting. If you serve just the soup, then you might also want to serve one of our salads or sandwiches also found in this book.

Known for their thickness or thinness, they are referred to as: gumbo, bouillabaisse, consommé, vichyssoise, chowder, bisque, and so on. Served with crackers, croutons, or garnishes of dollops of sour cream or grated cheese. Served alone or with sandwich, muffin, corn bread, or salad.

Sour Cream: The rule of thumb in many products is, the lower the fat, the higher the sodium level. It's an exchange you may decide on for yourself. Our soups and salads and some sandwiches use sour cream now and then. We have selected a middle-of-road approach and generally recommend "light" sour cream for flavor and lower fat and sodium levels. Check the labels when you buy your sour cream and use your favorite, but adjust the sodium level for your daily count. A note to remember—the USDA figures on the FDA package labels and the figures listed with our recipes may differ slightly. The USDA usually "averages" their data. Manufacturers also have a 5-point leeway either side of the actual nutrient level. We use USDA figures for all ingredients exclusively.

Spinach: A cup of spinach has 23.7 mg sodium. Considered a good source for iron, vitamins A and C, and lutein, which is great for your vision and long-lasting eye health. Nutritional value is somewhat in question since it also contains oxalic acid. This oxalic acid gives spinach its slight bitter taste that many don't care for. We prefer the "baby spinach," found generally in those chillier sections of prepacked salad bags. This is a milder-tasting spinach and actually is great for salads with the added benefit of much better flavor.

Splenda: A sugar substitute used in cooking for diabetics and those who don't want sugar. Works just like sugar, is derived from sugar. Visit www.splenda.com to learn more about this unique product. Cooks just like sugar and tastes just like sugar. Used in some salad dressings, breads for sandwiches, and a few soups. No sodium—barely a calorie per serving.

Split Pea: Green or yellow, these are always "dried" before you get them. They are split down their seam. If not split, these are referred to as "field peas." Split peas require soaking before cooking. Makes a great soup.

Spoon, Round: Usually a stainless steel spoon (although you can now find many good spoons in plastic) with a rounded base. Designed for lifting off fat, gravy, or other wet preparations.

Stew: Many ask "What's the difference between soup and stew?" In some cases, they might be considered pretty much the same. Stew, however, is almost always made with meat (generally tough cuts) and vegetables and is always "stewed." Stews may also contain soup like broths (thicker than consommé) and the natural juices of the food being stewed (sometimes the juices that come in the no-salt-added cans of beans when used). *Stew,* the verb, literally means to cook food covered with liquid, simmered slowly such as in a Crock-Pot for long times. The slower, or longer, and the lower the heat, the tenderer the stew meat will become. Stewing is usually done in a tightly covered stockpot or Crock-Pot. This is to keep the liquid from evaporating. Not only does this method of cooking tenderize tough meat, it pulls the flavors in the ingredients out and blends together into a very fine, tasty meal.

Stir: When we call for sautéing or dry-roasting a preparation, the ingredients must be moved continuously in the fry pan or saucepan or on a griddle with a tool like a flat wooden or metal spoon.

Stir-Fry: To cook quickly in a hot wok or skillet seasoned with oil and/or ginger, garlic, and other vegetables and seasonings. Cooking is done while stirring constantly to cook evenly.

Stirring: Mixing foods with a tool like a wooden, metal, or plastic spoon with a circular motion and in contact with the pan. Stirring is required to prevent sticking or burning.

Stock: Also known as broth, stock is the liquid you get after cooking vegetables, beef, poultry, or fish with herbs and spices in water. Reduce the stock for a few hours and you end up with a very good sauce.

Strainer: Perforated- or mesh-bottom container used for straining liquids, semi-liquids, or cooked foods requiring straining. Some strainers are used for sifting flour and flour mixes. Cheesecloth is used by some as a strainer when making broth, stock, and jams or jellies.

Sugar: Not just the granulated white stuff. There are a variety of sugars that include:

- Granulated (White Sugar)
- Superfine Sugar (Castor in Great Britain and Australia)
- Confectioners' or Powdered
- Coarse or Decorating Sugar
- Colored Sugar
- Flavored Sugar
- Brown Sugar
- Barbados Sugar
- Turbinado Sugar
- Raw Sugar

There are also liquid sugars including maple syrup, molasses, rock sugar, sorghum, treacle, glucose, jaggery, and spun sugar. We also have a sugar substitute called Splenda. (*See* Splenda.)

In this book we use only brown sugar, white sugar, confectioners' sugar, and Splenda.

Sun-Dried Tomato: Tomatoes that have been dried in the sun or by other means. Chewy, highly flavored, and sweet, this dark red tomato, often packed in olive oil, is great for salads, sauces, soups, sandwiches, and other dishes.

Tabasco Sauce: There is only one Tabasco sauce. It's a name trademarked back in the 1800s. Consists of salt, vinegar, and fermented Tabasco peppers. Best known for Bloody Mary drinks, Tabasco is used in soups, stews, meats, salads, and tacos. A variety of this brand is now available at the market. The sauce is high in sodium, but the levels used are low, so we do use some.

Taco: A Mexican "sandwich" using a folded no-salt, low-sodium corn tortilla. Fill these with your favorite ground beef, pork, or chicken or turkey, or julienned beef. Add in chopped tomatoes, onions, lettuce, low-sodium Cheddar cheese, avocado, refried pinto beans, and your own homemade salsa. Top with a dollop of light sour cream and you've got yourself a full midday meal.

Tahini: Often too high in sodium, some is used in this book for one recipe. This is a paste made from ground sesame seeds. Usually used to flavor hummus or baba ghanoush, it also works for some salads.

Tarragon: Anise-like flavor. Used with chicken, fish, and veggies and in sauces and special spice/herb mixes. Grows well, is best fresh. Available in ground and dried forms. Don't use too much; it can dominate all other flavors.

Thyme: Mint family. Garden thyme is the most widely used variety of this herb. Available in fresh, dried, and powdered form, this is available year-round in all forms. Store in a cool, dark, and dry place. After 6 months, discard. Used for veggies, fish, poultry, and beef, and pork dishes, and in soups and stews. Mixes well with rosemary, sage, and basil.

Tomato: You know what a tomato is, but did you know there are literally scores of varieties? We use the standard red tomatoes you find in your stores, as well as Italian or Roma tomatoes, tomatillo tomatoes, beefsteak, cherry, and vine-ripened tomatoes. No-salt-added canned tomatoes are used extensively in our soups and stews. We also use canned no-salt-added tomato sauce and Contadina tomato paste. (Some brands are just coming to market with no-salt-added tomato paste.)

Tortilla: This flat corn or flour bread disk is Mexico's everyday bread. We use them for tacos and an occasional salad dish. If you can't find a no-salt (low-sodium) corn tortilla for our recipes, then make your own flour tortillas found in our baking book. Make them very thin, then prepare them just as you would the corn tortillas. However, almost all tortilla makers produce a no-salt corn tortilla with sodium ratings from 5 to 15 mg per tortilla.

Toss: This isn't baseball. Usually referred to in salad recipes. Reach into a bowl with two large soup spoons or tongs (or both hands), and gently "shuffle" by raising salad ingredients and dropping them back into the bowl, until all the ingredients are well mixed.

Turmeric: (Pronounced TER-murh-ik) is closely related to ginger. Used extensively in prepared mustards, turmeric is also used in soups, stews, and our spice mixes. See our suggested uses for seasoning section.

Vichyssoise: A creamy potato-leek soup that is served cold and topped with chives.

Vinaigrette: This may be the only salad dressing you can prepare yourself when eating out. Basically it's oil and vinegar in a 3 to 1 mix. Vinegar choices can be white, cider, red wine, balsamic. Add a dash of sugar or pepper and you have a quick vinaigrette. If you can get the waiter to bring you a lemon and some minced garlic, add that to the oil and vinegar to give it a bit more zip. Mix oil and vinegar in equal portions. If you're making it at home, you can add spices of your choice, herbs of your choice, onions, mustard, garlic, shallots, etc.

Vinegar: We use apple cider vinegar, red wine vinegar, and balsamic vinegar for our salad dressings and also in the sandwich breads (to extend shelf life). Other vinegars are available however throughout the world. They include distilled white vinegar, malt vinegar, fruit vinegars, herb vinegars, cane vinegar, and rice vinegar. The latter is often very high in sodium, although there is a low-sodium vinegar that will require sugar to make it palatable. Vinegar is also used in sauces, soups, sweet and sour, and marinades.

Waldorf Salad: Apples, celery, and mayonnaise originally from the Waldorf of Astoria Hotel in New York, circa 1890s. Walnuts have been added to modern recipes.

Whisk: To stir a liquid or batter vigorously with a wire whisk.

Wild Rice: Although this rice is popular for its nutty flavor and chewy texture it is not a rice. Instead, it's a long grained marsh grass that's native to the Great Lakes region. It was traditionally harvested by Native Americans. It's expensive and is usually combined with other rice varieties or grains. We use some in soups.

Yeast: We use bread machine yeast for all our bread recipes. Bread machine yeast is an active dry yeast designed to work in the environment of the bread machine, which does not use the "sponge" that handmade bread requires. Fleischmann's and Red Star recommend placing the yeast on dry flour if using a bread machine. This is to prevent the yeast from activating before the machine is ready to mix it in the warmed water and the mixture. If making by hand, we then use the standard procedures of creating a "sponge."

Yogurt: Yogurt is a dairy product that's made from milk that has fermented and coagulated from introduced or natural "friendly" bacteria. We use plain yogurt for our mayonnaise substitute (along with sour cream and dill). It comes in various flavors. Used in some salads in this book.

Zest: The outermost layer of orange or lemon skin can either be shaved off in strips or grated. Only the colored portion of the skin (not the white pith) is considered the zest. Bioflavinoids however are very good for you so we grate down through the white, which is where this healthy nutrient is found. The aromatic oils in citrus skin add considerable flavor to food and the acid works as a key ingredient in our bread enhancer.

CONVERSION TABLES

When purchasing bottles, cans, packages of ingredients, and other foods, converting the ounces or grams to what's listed on the packaging may be confusing. The FDA measures in gram weights, while manufacturers may list their canned or bottled goods in ounces (fluid or weight) or in grams. Our recipes have been converted to U.S. units. Here are charts and tables for you to convert most figures used on food products and in this book to the unit you prefer.

DRY CONVERSIONS

WEIGHT	U.K./U.S. UNITS	METRIC UNITS
1 oz.	⅟₁₆ lb.	28.34952 g
1 lb.	16 oz.	453.592 g
1 mg	0.000035274 oz.	0.001 g
1 cg	0.00035274 oz.	0.01 g
1 dg	0.0035274 oz.	0.1 g
1 g	0.035274 oz.	1.0 g
1 dag	0.35274 oz.	10 g
1 hg	3.5274 oz.	100 g
1 kg	35.274 oz.	1,000 g
1 kg	2.204625 lb.	1,000 g

MEASURE EQUIVALENTS

CUP	FLUID OUNCE	TABLESPOON	TEASPOON	MILLILITER
1 cup	8 oz.	16 Tbsp.	48 tsp.	237 ml
¾ cup	6 oz.	12 Tbsp.	36 tsp.	177 ml
⅔ cup	5 oz.	11 Tbsp.	33 tsp.	158 ml
½ cup	4 oz.	8 Tbsp.	24 tsp.	118 ml
⅓ cup	3 oz.	5 Tbsp.	15 tsp.	79 ml
¼ cup	2 oz.	4 Tbsp.	12 tsp.	59 ml
⅛ cup	1 oz.	2 Tbsp.	6 tsp.	30 ml
1/16 cup	½ oz.	1 Tbsp.	3 tsp.	15 ml

LIQUID CONVERSIONS

IMPERIAL	METRIC	U.S. UNITS
½ fl. oz.	15 ml	1 Tbsp.
1 fl. oz.	30 ml	⅛ cup
2 fl. oz.	60 ml	¼ cup
3 fl. oz.	90 ml	⅜ cup
4 fl. oz.	120 ml	½ cup
5 fl. oz. (¼ pint)	150 ml	⅔ cup
6 fl. oz.	180 ml	¾ cup
8 fl. oz.	240 ml	1 cup (½ pint)
10 fl. oz. (½ pint)	285 ml	300 ml
12 fl. oz.	340 ml	1½ cups

16 fl. oz.	455 ml	2 cups (1 pint)
20 fl. oz. (1 pint)	570 ml	2½ cups
1½ pints	900 ml	3¾ cups
1¾ pints	1 l	4 cups (1 qt.)
2 pints	1¼ l	1¼ qts.
2⅓ pints	1½ l	3 U.S. pints
3¼ pints	2 l	2 qts.

Solid Weight Conversions

½ oz.	15 g
1 oz.	30 g
2 oz.	55 g
3 oz.	85 g
4 oz. (¼ lb.)	115 g
5 oz.	140 g
6 oz.	170 g
8 oz. (½ lb.)	225 g
12 oz. (¾ lb.)	225 g
16 oz. (1 lb.)	455 g

Ingredients Used in This Book

Following is a table showing sodium levels and where you can buy ingredients used in this book. Numbers below are used in following pages for item locations.

Key to Ingredients	*WHERE TO BUY*
Most supermarkets and grocery stores	1
www.bobsredmill.com or supermarket	2
www.bocconicini.com or deli	3
heluvagood.com	4
Most grocery stores or meat markets	5
healthyheartmarket.com	6
spiceman.com	7
natural food stores or your garden	8
grocery store or your garden	9
Fish market or supermarket	10
Speciality meat markets or some grocery stores	11
Your local lake or river	12
Supermarkets or specialty Hispanic markets	13

INGREDIENTS

BREAD ITEMS	WHERE TO BUY
Sure-Jell/Fruit-Fresh (1 tsp. = 1.644 mg)	1
Vital Wheat Gluten (1 tbsp. = 2.25 mg)	1
White Best for Bread Machine Flour (1 cup = 2.5 mg) Brands include Stone-Buhr, Arrowhead Mills, King Arthur, Bob's Red Mill, and standard-brand flours. Stone-Buhr leads the list for best bread flour, but at this writing is available only in the West. Bob's Red Mill and King Arthur follow, a close second.	1
Whole-Wheat Flour (1 cup = 6 mg) Brands include Stone-Buhr, Arrowhead Mills, King Arthur, Bob's Red Mill, and standard-brand flours. Stone-Buhr leads the list for best bread flour, but at this writing is available only in the West.	1
Whole-Wheat Pastry Flour (1 cup = 6 mg)	1
Yeast, bread machine (2¼ tsp. = 3.5 mg)	1

DAIRY PRODUCTS	WHERE TO BUY
Alpine Lace Low-Sodium Swiss Cheese (1 oz.= 35 mg)	1
Butter, unsalted (1 Tbsp. = 1.562 mg)	1
Buttermilk, liquid, reduced fat, low sodium (1 cup = 130 mg)	1
Buttermilk Powder (1 Tbsp. = 33.6 mg)	2
Egg, white only, (1 large = 54.8 mg)	1

Egg, whole, raw (1 large = 63.6 mg)	1
Egg, yolk only (1 yolk = 7 mg)	1
Fresh Mozzarella, packed in pasteurized water (1 oz. = 4.48 mg)	3
Half and Half Cream (1 Tbsp. = 6.15 mg)	1
Heluva Good Low-Sodium Cheddar Cheese (1 oz. = 10 mg)	4
Milk, 2% (1 cup = 122 mg)	1
Nonfat Milk (1 cup = 126 mg)	1
Sour Cream (1 Tbsp. = 6 mg)	1
Sour Cream, light (1 Tbsp. = 9.145 mg)	1
Yogurt, plain, other (8 oz. = 159.4 mg)	1

GENERAL GROCERY ITEMS	*WHERE TO BUY*
Apple, raw, skin (1 large = no sodium)	5
Barley, pearl (1 Tbsp. = 1.125 mg)	5
Cauliflower, head (1 small = 74.8 mg)	5
Contadina Tomato Paste (1 Tbsp. = 10 mg)	1
Other brands, make sure no-salt-added (1 Tbsp. = 14.4 mg)	1
Corn, cob (1 large = 21.4 mg)	5
Cornstarch (1 cup = .72 mg)	5
Eden Organic Black Beans (1 cup = 30 mg)	6

GENERAL GROCERY ITEMS (CONT.)	WHERE TO BUY
Eden Organic Garbanzo Beans (1 cup = 20 mg)	6
Eden Organic Kidney Beans (1 cup = 30 mg)	6
Eden Organic Pinto Beans (1 cup = 30 mg)	6
Noodles, egg, enriched (2 oz. = 12 mg)	5
Olive Oil, sesame oil, other oils (1 Tbsp. = trace)	1
Peanut Butter, unsalted (1 Tbsp. = 2.72 mg)	5
Raisins, seedless, golden or black (1 cup, not packed = 17.4 mg)	5
Rice, white, long grain (1 Tbsp. = .58 mg)	5
Rice, wild (1 Tbsp. = .7 mg)	5
S&W (and other brands) No-Salt-Added Tomatoes (½ cup = 30 mg)	1
Tomato, red, ripe, whole, canned, no-salt-added (1 Tbsp. = 1.4 mg)	1
Vinegar, all (1 Tbsp. = .15 mg)	1
Vinegar, cider (1 Tbsp. = .15 mg)	1

MEATS/FISH	WHERE TO BUY
Ahi, aku, bonito, tuna (1 oz. = 10.4 mg) (fresh Albacore best)	10
Brisket, beef (1 lb. = 313 mg)	1
Chicken, half, edible part only (1 lb. = 253.3 mg)	5

Chicken, turkey, beef, pork
(averages 18 mg per oz.)
  Birds vary by light meat, dark meat, variety.
  Individual listings are with each recipe
  where used
	5

Clams, shell, fresh (1 medium = 8.12 mg)	10
Fresh Water Bass (3 oz. = 59.5 mg)	12
Fresh Water Trout, Rainbow (3 oz. = 26.4 mg)	12
Game, (Wild) venison (1 oz. = 14.5 mg)	11
Salmon, fresh, Pacific wild coho, raw (3 oz. = 39.1 mg)	10
Shrimp, shellfish, raw (4 large = 41.4 mg)	10

SPICES	WHERE TO BUY
Bay Leaf, crumbled (1 tsp. = .138 mg)	1
Caraway Seeds (1 tsp. = .357 mg)	1
Cardamom, ground (1 tsp. = .36 mg)	5
Cilantro, raw (1 tsp. = .864 mg)	5
Cinnamon, ground (1 tsp. = .598 mg)	1
Cloves, ground (1 tsp. = 5.103 mg)	1
Coriander Seed, ground (1 tsp. = .63 mg)	1
Cumin (1 tsp. = 3.528 mg)	1
Curry Powder (1 tsp. = 1.04 mg)	1
Dill Weed, dried (1 tsp. = 2.08 mg)	5

SPICES *(CONT.)*	WHERE TO BUY
Fennel Seed (1 tsp. = 1.76 mg)	1
Garlic Lover's Garlic (1 tsp. = trace)	7
Garlic Powder (1 tsp. = .728 mg)	1
Ginger, ground (1 tsp. = .576 mg)	1
Gingerroot, peeled (1 tsp. = .25 mg)	1
Grandma's Chili Powder (1 tsp. = trace)	1
Juice, apple cider (1 Tbsp. = .93mg)	5
Juice, apple Vit. A. calcium (1 Tbsp. = 2.167 mg)	5
Juice, lemon, fresh (1 Tbsp. = .15 mg)	1
Juice, orange, fresh (1 fl. oz. = .31 mg)	1
Lavender (1 tsp. = trace)	8
Marjoram, dried (1 tsp. = .462 mg)	1
Mint (1 leaf = .016 mg)	9
Mustard Powder (1 tsp. = trace)	1
Onion, dried (1 Tbsp. = 1.05 mg)	1
Onion Powder (1 tsp. = 1.134 mg)	1
Oregano, ground (1 tsp. = .255 mg)	1
Paprika (1 tsp. = .714 mg)	1
Pepper, black (1 tsp. = .924 mg)	1
Pepper, cayenne (1 tsp. = .54 mg)	1

Pepper, white (1 tsp. = .12 mg)	1
Poppy Seed (1 tsp. = .58 mg)	1
Rosemary, dried (1 tsp. = .6 mg)	1
Rosemary, fresh (1 tsp. = .182 mg)	1
Sage, dried (1 tsp. = .077 mg)	1
Savory, ground (1 tsp. = .336 mg)	1
Sesame Seed (1 tsp. = .33 mg)	1
Thyme, fresh (1 tsp. = .072 mg)	1
Thyme, ground (1 tsp. = .77 mg)	1
Turmeric, ground (1 tsp. = .836 mg)	5
Zest, lemon (1 tsp. = .12 mg)	1
Zest, orange (1 tsp. = .06 mg)	1

SUGAR/MOLASSES	WHERE TO BUY
Molasses, blackstrap (1 Tbsp. = 11 mg)	1
Molasses, grandma's (1 Tbsp. = 7 mg)	1
Molasses, sweet, no-salt-added (1 Tbsp. = 7.4 mg)	1
Splenda White Sugar Substitute (0 mg)	1
Sugar, brown (1 Tbsp., packed = 5.382 mg)	1
Sugar, white, granulated (1 tsp. = 0.42 mg)	1

VEGETABLES/FRUITS/SALAD/SOUP MIXINGS	WHERE TO BUY
Asparagus (1 large spear = .4 mg)	1
Avocado, California, peeled, raw (1 large = 20.8 mg)	1
Basil, fresh (5 large leaves = .1 mg)	1
Beet, red, raw (1 large beet = 64 mg)	1
Broccoli, raw (1 large floret = 2.97 mg)	1
Cabbage, Chinese (Napa), shredded (1 cup = 49.4 mg)	1
Cabbage, green, shredded (1 cup = 12.6 mg)	1
Carrots (1 large carrot = 25.2 mg)	1
Celery, stalk (1 large stalk = 55.7 mg)	1
Chili, hot (1 large pepper = 3.15 mg)	1
Chilies (Ortega), canned, diced (1 Tbsp. = 10 mg)	1
Garlic, fresh, raw (1 large clove = .51 mg)	1
Italian Parsley (4 large sprigs = 2.24 mg)	1
Leek, raw (1 large leek = 17.8 mg)	1
Mushroom, portobello (1 oz. = 1.701 mg)	1
Mushrooms (1 large mushroom = .92 mg)	1
Onion, green, raw (1 large green onion = 2.4 mg)	1
Onions (1 large onion = 4.5 mg)	1
Parsley, chopped (1 Tbsp. = 2.128 mg)	1
Parsnips, sliced (1 cup = 13.3 mg)	1

Potato, Russet, Other (1 oz. = 1.985 mg)	1
Potatoes, red, white, Yukon (1 oz. = 1.425 mg)	1
Red Bell, green bell, orange bell (1 large pepper = 3.28 mg)	1
Romaine lettuce, shredded (1 cup = 4.48 mg)	1
Salad Greens, mix, shredded (1 cup = 14 mg)	1
Serrano (pasilla) (1 large pepper = .61 mg)	13
Spinach, raw (leaf = 7.9 mg)	1
Squash, Acorn, peeled, raw (1 cup = 4.2 mg)	1
Squash, winter, peeled, raw (1 cup = 4.64 mg)	1
Tomato, cherry (one = 1.53 mg)	1
Tomato, fresh (large = 16.4 mg)	1
Zucchini, raw (large = 9.69 mg)	1

SPECIALTY	WHERE TO BUY
B&G Unsalted Bread and Butter Chips (5 chips = trace)	6
B&G Unsalted Crunchy Kosher Dills (½ large pickle = trace)	6
B&G Sweet Relish (1 Tbsp. = trace)	6
East Shore Mustard (1 tsp. = trace)	6
Ener-G Baking Soda (1 Tbsp. = trace)	6
Enrico's Low-Sodium Pasta Sauce (1 cup = 50 mg)	6

SPECIALTY (CONT.)	WHERE TO BUY
Featherweight Baking Powder (1 tsp. = 4.5 mg)	6
Hain Soynnaise (1 Tbsp. = trace)	6
Tahini (Sesame Butter) (1 Tbsp. = 17.25 mg)	1

INDEX

Books You May Want to Have

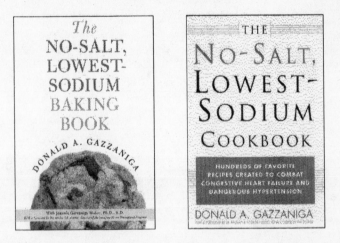

For great recipes to go along with the recipes in this book you'll want to have *The No-Salt, Lowest-Sodium Cookbook*, and *The No-Salt, Lowest-Sodium Baking Book*.

MegaHeart.com

To purchase, either visit your local bookstore or visit www.megaheart.com and click on the book images. Amazon.com will ship them to you immediately and contribute $1.00 a book to heart disease research.